B
U
P

Melania Franzese · Giordano Di Veglia

BUSINESS MODELS AND PROFITABILITY IN THE STRATEGIC BANKING PROCESS

Focus on Digitalization

Foreword by **Gimede Gigante**

Typesetting: Corpo4 Team, Milan
Cover: Cristina Bernasconi, Milan

Copyright © 2023 Bocconi University Press
EGEA S.p.A.

EGEA S.p.A.
Via Salasco, 5 - 20136 Milano
Tel. 02/5836.5751 – Fax 02/5836.5753
egea.edizioni@unibocconi.it – www.egeaeditore.it

All rights reserved, including but not limited to translation, total or partial adaptation, reproduction, and communication to the public by any means on any media (including microfilms, films, photocopies, electronic or digital media), as well as electronic information storage and retrieval systems. For more information or permission to use material from this text, see the website www.egeaeditore.it

Given the characteristics of Internet, the publisher is not responsible for any changes of address and contents of the websites mentioned.

First edition: September 2023

ISBN Domestic Edition	979-12-80623-18-8
ISBN Digital Domestic Edition	978-88-238-8701-5
ISBN International Edition	978-88-31322-93-5
ISBN Digital International Edition	978-88-31322-94-2

Questo volume è stampato su carta FSC® proveniente da foreste gestite in maniera responsabile secondo rigorosi standard ambientali, economici e sociali definiti dal Forest Stewardship Council®

Table of Contents

Foreword, by *Gimede Gigante* — VII

Foreword to the Italian edition, by *Ciro Vacca* — XI

Introduction — XV

1 The key role of value creation — 1
   1.1 The importance of earnings performance — 1
   1.2 Importance of value creation in BMA — 7
      1.2.1 The role of ROE in value creation — 7
      1.2.2 Shareholders remuneration — 10
      1.2.3 The role of the dividend growth rate in profitability analyses — 10
      1.2.4 Price-to-book ratio: The influence of ROE — 11

2 Characteristics of a business model — 15
   2.1 An outline of the approach to the banking literature — 15
   2.2 The definition of a business model — 22
   2.3 Corporate governance and BMA — 24

3 The supervision approach — 29
   3.1 The European regulatory framework — 29
   3.2 The European supervisory approach — 33
   3.3 The main changes impacting BM in the pre-pandemic context — 37
   3.4 Digital transfomation in the post-pandemic context — 41
   3.5 The other side of the digital transformation coin: Risks and the authorities' response — 47
   3.6 The approach to climate change: Outline — 51

4 Analysing the business model in seven steps — 55
   4.1 The ingredients for implementing a support tool — 55
   4.2 First step: Analysis of macroeconomic variables — 56
   4.3 Second step: An outline of environment and competitive positioning — 58

	4.4	Third step: Strategic decision making process	63
	4.5	Fourth step: Segment reporting and cost allocation	68
		4.5.1 Segment reporting for BM and profitability analysis	68
		4.5.2 Management control and information quality: Data Governance and Data Quality	68
		4.5.3 Management control and cost allocation policies	70
		4.5.4 From BMA to segment reporting	73
		4.5.5 From the analysis of segment reporting to the review of the strategic planning process	74
	4.6	Fifth step: Fund Transfer Pricing (FTP)	75
	4.7	Sixth step: Capital allocation	81
	4.8	Seventh step: Projection analysis	82
5	**Case study**		**87**
	5.1	The toolkit	87
	5.2	Business Case: Know your business	88
		5.2.1 Segmentation and sub-segmentation process	88
		5.2.2 Commercial segments and sub-segments: Performance analysis	95
		5.2.3 Commercial network: Efficiency analysis	101
	5.3	Business Case: Cost-cutting measures	105
		5.3.1 Rationalisation of the organisational model	105
		5.3.2 Optimisation of staff and their utilisation	108
		5.3.3 Business Case: Deep dive pricing scheme	110
		5.3.4 Segment Reporting: "An attempt"	112
	5.4	Digitalisation Case: Better bank or distributed bank?	114
6	**Conclusions**		**129**
	6.1	Red flags detected within the BMA	129
	6.2	Open issues	137

Acknowledgements 141

Bibliography 143

Web references 153

The opinions expressed by the authors are exclusively personal and do not in any way engage the responsibility of the institute they belong to. The sources used and quoted are in the public domain and the examples and case studies given are only hypothetical cases.

Foreword

by *Gimede Gigante**

The analysis of banking business models is of twofold importance in a dynamic and complex environment, such as the one the banking industry is currently facing. The approach offered by the authors in this book is an extremely valuable tool for banks to survive and successfully emerge in such circumstances. However, the macroeconomic context is continuously evolving and new risks have recently emerged, with particular links to the acceleration of dynamics related to digital transformation and environmental, social and governance (ESG) concerns, combined with concerns about the Ukrainian war.

Since the Covid pandemic, banks have undergone significant transformation with a rapid increase in their digital transformation programmes. Customers have shifted their preferences towards online banking services and nowadays the digital adoption among customers is at an all-time high. The Open Banking paradigm is reshaping the payment industry after the introduction of the PSD2 Directive, which has determined the opening of the payment system to external players, the so-called third-party providers. The latter can now operate on the existing banking infrastructure irrespective of the existence of specific agreements, multilateral or bilateral, with individual banks.

In addition, traditional credit institutions have to dynamically adapt to this changing environment in order to overcome the challenges presented by the bank democratisation trend. Fintechs in particular are now fuelling the competition among traditional banks, leveraging on a new business model which is fully digital and with no legacy. This aspect gives them an advantage over traditional banks as the latter are struggling to integrate new technological innovations into their existing structures. In fact, it has recently emerged that out of nearly 2000 directors in more than one hundred of the world's largest banks, only 10% of CEOs and boards of directors have professional technology experience[1].

Because of this lack of knowledge, the strategy of traditional banks, at the beginning, was to enter into partnerships with fintechs. However, nowadays all relevant credit institutions have developed a proper digitalisation strategy: the only solution

---

* Professor of Corporate Finance and Real Estate at SDA Bocconi and Director of ICE – Innovation and Corporate Entrepreneurship.

[1] Accenture, "Boosting the Boardroom's Technology Expertise – Focus on Banking" Report, 12 March 2021.

for them to remain competitive in the market is to change their business models and try to offer their customers a holistic service. The goal for the future has to be the extension of a bank's solutions in order to build an ecosystem together with a network of partners that will enable them to have a comprehensive view over their customers' journey. By doing this type of interaction, banks will ensure an effective value exchange with both customers and partners and, most importantly, will be able to preserve the right level of profitability.

Two main factors have to be considered in this change of business model:

a. Banks have to leverage on data exploration and extraction in order to fully take advantage of the information they hold, as many credit institutions still struggle to abandon their core banking focus and lack the instruments to analyse data and create value from it. The adoption of a technology-first approach, together with partnership with external service providers, is crucial to exploit the full potential of customers' data;
b. Banks have to exploit the endless possibilities offered by artificial intelligence (AI) that can help them to offer a best-in-class customer experience, for instance, by shortening the Know Your Customer and Anti-Money Laundering (AML) compliance requirements. At the same time, algorithms can be used to suggest the right investment decisions to customers in line with theirinanceial goals (the so-called robo-advisory service).

However, neither AI nor data extraction come without risk. In fact, issues may arise regarding data control and misuse once it is shared with third parties. Data management in general requires banks to implement well-defined policies to mitigate and eliminate risks that may compromise customer trust. In their current state, many banks do not have the right personnel to ensure that they are able to manage the risks arising with these new challenges.

An overall assessment of a bank's strategic positioning and its strengths and weaknesses is therefore crucial to determine how to adopt their business model to the changing environment.

In light of this, the approach proposed by the authors Giordano Di Veglia and Melania Franzese is extremely useful as it represents a "practical" tool that aims to help with reading business models in the new context of digital transformation. In addition, a point that is extremely appreciated about this book is the fact that it offers the right balance between academic analysis, on the one hand, and a managerial view with potential real-life cases, on the other. In fact, while Chapter 2 is dedicated to the listing of different approaches by the economic literature on the subject of business model analysis, in Chapter 5 the authors suggest some practical examples of business-as-usual case studies which are extremely detailed and useful.

The goal of the authors is to offer the reader a seven-step guide to which type of considerations should be made for the business model and profitability drivers of banks in the context of development of their business strategies. The approach proposed by this book is also useful for understanding why the sustainability of a bank's business model with respect to current risk factors is a priority for European supervisors, since they have to ensure that banks are able to define adequate risk assessment methodologies, thus guaranteeing a sound and prudent management of banks and a return on capital to their investors.

In addition to traditional risks, a new challenge for the regulatory and supervisory authorities has emerged with the Open Banking phenomenon. In fact, supervisors need to remodel their usual practices and adapt their traditional surveillance methodologies to the peculiar risks associated with the new environment, in particular concerning the regulation of new systems and infrastructures such as the so-called "platforms systems". At the same time, the regulatory authority has to encourage the market to offer their new services in order to pursue the ultimate objective of the PSD2 Directive, which is to increase the competition among the players in the payment ecosystem with the final benefit for the end customer.

In conclusion, the downfall of some traditional banks, such as Silicon Valley Bank and Credit Suisse, has cast a shadow on the resilience of the current banking system. The question is, then, how national and supranational authorities should respond to the current market turmoil and rising long-term systemic risk. Increasing a bank's shock absorption by imposing more stringent capital requirements is not a feasible solution in the long term as it will ultimately hurt the overall economy. An effective solution is represented by technology innovation, with the development of a more decentralised financial system, together with the promotion of digital banking among traditional credit institutions. However, such changes require banks to think fast and adapt their business models accordingly, as brilliantly suggested by the authors of this book. In fact, digitalisation still has some drawbacks which are often ignored, particularly concerning the speed with which users can leave an institution by withdrawing deposits. This aspect can represent a big threat for traditional banks, causing some of them to lose ground and eventually disappear from the market if they have not developed a sustainable business model in the meanwhile.

Foreword to the Italian edition*
by *Ciro Vacca***

The topic of business models has become progressively important over the years due to the complex economic, regulatory and market environment in which banks are called upon to operate.

Using a "seafaring" metaphor, it can be argued that, after a long period (from the 1990s up to the 2008 financial crisis) of calm sailing in good weather and low waves, banks have had to navigate increasingly rough seas with worsening weather conditions. This has finally led to the "perfect storm", as a consequence of a series of concurrent disruptive events:

a. The 2008 financial crisis, the 2010 economic crisis and the more recent one resulting from the Covid-19 pandemic;
b. The prolonged low interest rate environment and the substantial increase in the cost of risk (which is likely to increase as a result of the post-Covid-19 economic pandemic), which significantly weakened the income capacity of banks, limiting their ability to self-finance and attract new capital;
c. The processes of technological innovation and digitalisation, which have undergone an abrupt acceleration as a result of the lockdown. Therefore, bank customers have massively shifted to the online channel, with a consequent downsizing of the activities of physical distribution networks. Both these trends appear destined to consolidate;
d. The significant increase in the competitive tone of the entire value chain of the banking business and in particular segments (e.g. the payment system), linked to entry into the market of leading operators in the technology sector, able to offer products and services at competitive costs very quickly;
e. The high compliance costs deriving from the significant increase in banking regulation, at European and national level, following the 2008 financial crisis and the launch of the Single Supervision Mechanism;
f. The enforcement of the Bank Recovery and Resolution Directive (BRRD), which has made the management of banking crises much more complicated. This also

---

* A first edition of this book was published in Italy in 2020 by Aracne Editrice under the title "L'analisi del business model e della profittabilità nel processo strategico delle banche".

** Deputy Head of the Banking and Financial Supervision Department of the Bank of Italy from November 2019 to October 2021.

affected the cost of funding for banks, which is more expensive, as well as the obligation to equip themselves, in addition to capital, with capitalisation instruments which are being subject to bail-in and burden sharing measures.

Business model risk has therefore become a growing concern for supervisors to the point of being included, as of 2016, among the annual priorities of the European Central Bank (ECB). The ECB has launched specific initiatives in this regard, including a "Thematic review on profitability", in order to analyse the state of health of the largest European banks (the so-called significant banking groups with assets in excess of €30 billion) and to ascertain the presence of any organisational, procedural and management weaknesses. At the same time, the level of prudential control exercised as part of the Supervisory Review and Evaluation Process (SREP) was strengthened through an enhancement of the assessments carried out during the business model analysis (BMA).

In such a changed context, most of the major banks have launched analyses aimed at verifying the sustainability of their business model. Some of them have included in their new industrial plans initiatives intended to introduce significant technological and fintech innovations, which are progressively transforming the production-distribution-after-sales management chain while at the same time introducing a new business mix (products-customers-channels), often with an "Open Banking" approach. This transition process is, however, still shifting and evolving: many banks have only "added" spot initiatives, while others have developed a digital strategy with clear objectives and significant investments.

A few larger banks and most smaller banks have not yet decisively initiated a similar process, often remaining anchored to their "traditional" intermediary DNA and operating across the entire value chain. Banking biodiversity should be safeguarded but on condition that all intermediaries, including those pursuing mutualistic objectives, have a sustainable business model and a sound and prudent management that ensures conditions of operational and allocative efficiency.

The "perfect storm" makes "delaying" approaches inappropriate. All banks, regardless of their size and legal status, should undertake a timely but considered assessment of their strategic positioning, strengths and weaknesses that is crucial to decide the best business model to adopt and the best interventions to implement. This has led some operators to an in-depth revision of their business model and it cannot be excluded that, in some cases, the most appropriate solution may be that of an "orderly" exit from the market.

Against this backdrop, the efforts made by Giordano Di Veglia and Melania Franzese are therefore particularly appreciated. Indeed, they succeeded in dealing with the complex and delicate subject of the banking business model in an organic manner, with simplicity and pragmatism.

Moreover, the book does not limit itself to providing readers with theoretical statements on the various definitions of business models found in the economic and banking literature, but, particularly in Chapter 5, it contains a sort of "compass" made available to operators to help them identify those "changes of route" that can allow them to emerge from the "perfect storm" and hopefully return to sailing in calmer waters.

Finally, it should be underlined that, in addition to being a useful teaching tool, the book is also a guide for those who, as part of the governing bodies of banks, are called upon to make important strategic decisions on business models. A good knowledge of the subjects on which one is called to deliberate is a guarantee of conscious, appropriate and therefore successful choices.

Introduction

> "If you do not know to which port you are sailing
> then no wind is favourable"
> Seneca

In the previous Italian edition, the authors promoted the analysis of banks' business models using a seven-move code as a guidebook. In fact, the case studies presented showed that the business model biases, that to some extent undermined the concrete creation of value and therefore the resilience over time of the adopted business models, could be traced back to an unsatisfactory or superficial oversight of governance and organisational mechanisms in the reshaping of business models. These projects, although on paper were often flawless, showed shortcomings in the execution phase.

In light of this, a spotlight had been shone on strategic risk as a crucial factor in the analysis of the business model, an issue that European supervision had long placed among the priorities of supervisory action[1]. However, the context in which today's players operate is far beyond VUCA, so much so that it has recently been changed to VUCRA, adding a risk component to the already challenging acronym[2], in order to hinge the dynamics in a new context with structural and non-cyclical characteristics. The post-crisis management brought about by the pandemic, the powerful acceleration of the dynamics linked to digital transformation and to ESG factors and the consequences of the war in Ukraine have once again challenged the

---

[1] ECB has included business model risk as a priority since 2016. In the 2022–2024 and 2023–2025 supervisory cycles, following the increasing adoption by intermediaries of technologies to overcome the challenges posed by the pandemic and respond to changing customer preferences, business model risk has been anchored in Priority 2, aimed at encouraging institutions to address remaining shortcomings in the digital transformation and in relation to the steering capabilities of their governing bodies ("supervised institutions should keep a strong focus on addressing structural challenges and risks stemming from the digitalisation of their banking services with a view to ensuring the resilience and sustainability of their business models").

[2] The term VUCA, an acronym for volatility, uncertainty, complexity and ambiguity, was coined by the US Army at the end of the Cold War and is often used in times of business crisis. The VUCA model is described in Burt Nanus and Warren Bennis' work "Leader. Anatomy of leadership, the 4 keys to effective leadership", 1987.

banks' business models, forcing the supervisor to make a qualitative leap in analysing the new dynamics.

The new challenges

The English edition, in addition to updating the economic and financial trends, aims to backtest the findings of the previous Italian edition in order to capture the specifics of the new factors impacting the business models of the banking industry. In particular, making use of the previously proposed seven-character tool, the authors shine a light on the variables summarised below, with the aim of verifying whether the strong commitment tone from the top and a robust strategic process are still the success factors of a business model reshaping:

- digital transformation;
- ESG factors;
- changing interest rate scenarios;
- difficult geopolitical situation.

Even with these new variables, the interpretation of former ECB Chair Prof. Mario Draghi, who urged as early as 2018 to "adapt business models to the new technological requirements, address the issue of excess capacity and costs"[3], is still relevant.

On the change of scenario in the context of digital transformation, in a speech in February 2022 the Deputy General Manager of the Bank of Italy and member of the ECB Supervisory Board, Alessandra Perrazzelli, had stressed that "we are living through a complex historical period with extraordinary changes, characterised by great risks but also by numerous opportunities. The pandemic – which has so profoundly affected the lives of families and the activities of businesses over the past two years – has forced us to rethink and redefine behaviour, rules, and organisational models in both the private and public spheres. This process has been accompanied and facilitated by technology, which has enabled the adoption of innovative solutions that in some cases represent structural changes to established paradigms"[4].

According to a survey conducted by Banca d'Italia, fintech is spreading in the Italian financial industry mainly to support the innovation of lending processes and digital payments[5]. Spending on fintech technologies for the two-year period 2021–

---

[3] *Banche: Draghi priorità a bilanci, modelli di business e costi,* Askanews 26 March 2018.

[4] *Investimenti per lo sviluppo del fintech: start-up, decentralizzazione, asset tokenizzazione,* 28th Annual Assiom Forex Congress, 11 February 2022.

[5] Financial Stability Board (FSB, n.d.) defines fintech as technologically-enabled innovation in financial services that could result in new business models, applications, processes or products with an associated material effect on financial markets, financial institutions and the provision of financial services. Financial Stability Board, Financial Stability Implications from FinTech, Supervisory and Regulatory Issues that Merit Authorities; Attention, 27 June 2017.

2022 amounted to €530 million, up from the previous two-year period (€456 million)[6].

Some institutions are focusing on traditional optimisation measures, adopting a "follower" wait-and-see approach in the fintech field rather than taking on a "front runner" role. Still others are attracted by the enormous opportunities for brand expansion offered in the fields of decentralised finance (DeFi) and metaverse, seeking to satisfy an ever-increasing demand from specific customer segments interested in a system that is able to increasingly connect the real world with the many virtual realities that have been emerging in recent years from a banking and financial perspective.

According to market estimates, at the end of 2021 the Total Value Locked, that is the value of investments globally attributable to the DeFi ecosystem, amounted to approximately US$100 billion and had grown four times over the previous year[7]. With reference to the metaverse, the global estimates would be stratospheric. A study by Gartner predicts that by 2026, 25% of people will spend one hour per day in the metaverse for work, education, social, shopping and entertainment purposes[8].

Goldman Sachs, on the other hand, estimates that about 33% of the digital economy will spill over into the metaverse in the near future, creating a potential market worth $8 trillion[9]. With these multi-billion dollar prospects, the levels of "FOMO" for banking business models are higher than ever[10]. However, if the opportunities are more or less already clarified by market players, it is not as easy to foresee the real (or virtual) threats and the effects, in terms of strengths and weaknesses, on each business model, which will depend on the role the bank will choose to play in the current digital transformation process.

In addition, the supervisory expectations adopted by the ECB and other national supervisory authorities on climate and environmental risks are also triggered with regard to the integration of these risks into the business strategies, governance and control systems, risk management frameworks and disclosure of intermediaries[11].

---

[6] Banca d'Italia, *Indagine Fintech nel sistema finanziario italiano*, November 2021.

[7] Financial Stability Board 2021.

[8] www.gartner.com/en/newsroom/press-releases/2022-02-07-gartner-predicts-25-percent-of-people-will-spend-at-least-one-hour-per-day-in-the-metaverse-by-2026.

[9] www.news.bitcoin.com/goldman-sachs-metaverse-8-trillion-opportunity/.

[10] FOMO stands for "fear of missing out".

[11] ECB guide on climate-related and environmental risks and EBA report on management and supervision of ESG risks for credit institutions and investment firms. Particular reference is made to physical risk and transition risk. The former refers to the economic impact resulting from the expected increase in natural events whose manifestation may be extreme (floods, heat waves, droughts) or chronic (e.g. gradual rise in temperatures and sea levels, deterioration of ecosystem services and loss of biodiversity). The latter refers to the economic impact resulting from the adoption of regulations to reduce carbon emissions and encourage the development of renewable energy, from technological developments as well as from changing consumer preferences and market confidence.

The expectations are intended to provide general guidance and their implementation at the operational level is left to the individual intermediary, which will have to assess the relevance of the issues according to its business model.

In light of these challenges, business model and profitability analysis has been confirmed as crucial within the priorities of European supervision.

For the supervisory authorities, it has therefore become even more important for banks to be able to identify the most profitable innovations/assets/businesses and investigate their challenges and structural risks so that they can ensure an adequate return on capital over time and thus support their investments. It is therefore crucial for supervision to assess banks' ability to adopt adequate assessment methodologies for their business models.

It is emphasised again in this edition that BMA should be interpreted not so much as a means of arriving subsequently at a measurement and identification of the economic drivers assumed, but rather as a methodology to control (supervisors) and steer (bank management) the industrial process in the most efficient and profitable way possible.

However, the financial and economic literature does not provide perfectly tailored frameworks for such analysis. Academics have confirmed the focus on certain asset and liability characteristics and/or profitability drivers, clustering banks on the basis of their core banking activities and then aggregating them into the best-performing clusters from time to time.

As noted in the previous edition, identifying the business segments that contribute to the creation/destruction of value in the medium to long term, together with the opportunities to exploit fintech, are undoubtedly among the most challenging activities for bank management. Making decisions consistent with corporate sustainability is now an unavoidable step that banks must face, both in business as usual and even more so in the new environment.

Also in this new edition, the authors confirm the idea of not providing the reader with clusters and a posteriori performance analyses that only relate to one part of the BMA. In order to channel entrepreneurial initiatives to where more wealth is created, it is also necessary to reprocess that data in a granular way so that it can be interpreted *ex ante* by bank management.

In this respect, the lack of proper industrial accounting continues to be noted, also reflecting a certain obsolescence of the information systems, which hampers the possibility of making the best use of one's resources and/or grasping market trends.

The "practical" contribution proposed here has the ambition of providing readers with the tools to "read" business models in the strategic process of banks also in the new context of the digital transformation, highlighting how in the previous edition. This is done by proposing, on the one hand, a succinct compendium of analyses developed over time by market operators and economists and, on the other hand, a more managerial view from the inside, accompanied by examples and case studies focused mainly on the Italian banking sector and in some cases on European ones. It should also be noted that these examples are deliberately not articulated so as to represent a useful didactic instrument to understand, in the context of the assessment of the business model, the areas of operation and/or efficiency that could guarantee, given certain conditions, a sustainable return on equity (ROE).

* * *

The paper retains its six-chapter structure and in the first offers an up-to-date survey on the profitability of the banking system.

In the second, the approaches of the economic literature on the subject of BMA are broadly reiterated, highlighting the importance of the physiological return on invested capital, with some insights into the cost of capital.

The third chapter outlines the supervisors' approach to BMA, enriched by a series of reflections on new risks.

The framework proposed in Chapter 4 confirms the aim of guiding the reader step by step to an effective understanding of the analyses to be conducted on the business model and profitability drivers in the context of business strategy identification and development. In particular, it emphasises that these steps cannot be separated from the definition and implementation of an adequate risk-adjusted segment reporting.

In the fifth chapter, a number of business-as-usual case studies are presented to provide practical examples emerging from the analysis of segment reporting data, as well as new working hypotheses tailored to the new challenges.

As in the previous edition, the concluding section highlights some "red flags" as a proxy for the non-trivial difficulties that may arise when approaching business model assessment in the strategic process of banks, with some food for thought on new challenging scenarios.

Addressees of the publication

The idea for the first publication stemmed from the need felt during various presentations on the subject, mainly masters or seminars for analysts, to have a sort of handbook or "toolbox" to be utilised to unravel a complex range of topics related to BMA, which, taken individually, could themselves constitute autonomous elements of in-depth teaching.

In line with this objective, the book, although with some unavoidable references to economic literature that may recall a more didactic approach, had the ambition of having a decidedly more pragmatic slant. The idea behind it was that university and master's degree students in banking, as well as new graduates, could find practical suggestions and a point of synthesis to add to their theoretical background, along with the various topics addressed in the book, on some elements that characterise the assessment of the business model and profitability in the strategic process of banks.

The update of the volume does not aim to provide the reader with a new tool for analysing these variables, nor a new management dashboard; rather, it drops that seven-step strategic risk analysis access code also in addressing the new dynamics.

The seven steps remain the crucial junctures, "critical" areas of investigation to be carefully plumbed in order to arrive at a robust assessment of the quality of the strategic planning process and, in so doing, of the sustainability of the business model in the light mainly of the technological transformation and, to some extent, of business more inspired by ESG logics.

1 The key role of value creation

> "The entrepreneur always searches for change, responds to it, and exploits it as an opportunity"
> P. Drucker

1.1 The importance of earnings performance

Analysing earnings performance today in order to derive useful indications of prospective profitability is a very difficult exercise. Banks are required to "improve cost efficiency and reorient their business models towards resilience and value creation in the longer term"[1].

In this regard, in 2021 the results showed that the profitability and sustainability of banks' business models had continued to suffer from the pressures of an economic environment characterised by low interest rates and overcapacity, but speaking in Rome on 8 July 2022 at the Annual General Meeting of ABI members, Governor of Bank of Italy Ignazio Visco[2] stated "the impact on banks' profitability would be positive overall due to the expansion of the interest margin, the trend of which will depend on the maturity structure of individual banks assets and liabilities, with even significant differences between intermediaries. In the medium term, the amount of additional adjustments corresponding to the increase in impaired loans should be more than offset by the positive effect of rising interest rates on the interest margin".

And indeed, not only in the case of Italy, in Europe the 2022 Q2 balance sheets showed that the profitability of banks was substantially in line with pre-crisis levels, driven mostly by the increase in net interest income. However, some analysts consider the current interest margin to be overestimated as the pass-through to deposit rates is faster than expected and in the presence of an uncertain decrease in the cost of risk. The ECB's monetary policy has thus acted as a driver for profitability, increasing margins on money lent in the expectation that companies and households will then be able to honour their debts.

---

[1] This was stated by ECB President Christine Lagarde in the ECB Annual Report on supervisory activities 2021.
[2] Governor of Bank of Italy until October 2023.

In the writer's opinion, the profitability profile cannot be analysed without taking into account the complex transition of the banking system, which is full of challenges on the digital front, geopolitical uncertainties, increased competition from the non-banking sector, the likely forthcoming introduction of new prudential requirements and the need to adopt fintech models that also meet ESG requirements, which make the scenario much more competitive as they must respond quickly to the needs of all stakeholders.

In this context, according to a survey carried out in 2021 by the Bank of Italy, if on the one hand banks are aware of the need to adopt models that can be easily interpreted on the other hand they are not as attentive to the need to strengthen corporate governance controls. As it emerges from the Bank of Italy's Stability Report No. 2 of 2022, "Conditions in global financial markets have worsened since last spring. Against a backdrop of a progressive slowdown in economic activity and rapidly rising long-term interest rates, episodes of high volatility and deteriorating liquidity, including in government bond markets, have emerged in the main advanced economies. [...] The situation of banks is solid overall, but weakening macroeconomic conditions, inflationary pressures and some effects of rising interest rates could affect their balance sheets. In the third quarter, asset quality remained good and the loan deterioration rate remained at historically low levels. Profitability in the first half of the year improved, mainly due to an increase in the interest margin. [...] Looking ahead, higher debt burdens may affect the ability of households and businesses to repay their loans, potentially affecting credit quality. In addition, upward pressures on the cost of funding may emerge, also as a result of the need to replace funds acquired through the third round of targeted longer-term refinancing operations (TLTRO3) and to issue instruments to meet the minimum capital requirement and liabilities subject to bail-in (minimum requirement for own funds and eligible liabilities, MREL)."

These issues pertain more to the European banking system than to other systems. Even before the pandemic shock, the profitability of the European and Anglo-Saxon banking systems was suffering from lower margins than the American system. In 2021, while the profits of the US, UK and European global systematically important banks (G-SIBs) had exceeded pre-pandemic levels, US global banks that are systemically important were still performing almost twice as well as European and UK banks, and among the determinants analysts also pointed out less efficient BMs.

In September 2021, the Joint Committee Report on risks and vulnerabilities in EU financial systems highlighted among the risks affecting the prospective profitability of the banking system the high investments to close gaps in the technological transformation of business models.

The need to adapt and make business models efficient is therefore a preparatory variable for stabilisation of profitability margins, which is crucial for the entrepreneurial viability of banking enterprises in the short term and sustainability in the medium and long term.

In the previous edition it was emphasised that improving ROE and recovering profitability are the key challenges for banks. Nevertheless, these challenges are very demanding, even with rising interest rates. In 2016, an analysis conducted by KPMG on the main European banks showed that, to improve the return on regulatory capital by one percentage point, on average it would have been necessary to either increase the interest margin by 2.5 bps or reduce the ratio of non-performing loans (NPLs) to total loans by 2.5 percentage points, or decrease the cost/income ratio by 25% by cutting costs or diversifying revenues[3].

It should also be kept in mind that estimates of expected profitability also depend on the macroeconomic context: in the absence of structural measures to make business models more efficient, signs of recovery in the short term are immediately reabsorbed with depressing effects on ROE.

Lessons learned from the past may help to better understand this statement. Beginning in 2016, a survey carried out by the Bank of Italy on thirty-one listed European banks that were involved in the stress test carried out by the European Banking Authority (EBA) in cooperation with the ECB showed that the average cost of capital had fallen[4,5]. At the same time, the profitability expected by market analysts had increased[6]. In this regard, it should be noted that this data does not necessarily imply a consequential link, given that even though there is a reduction in the weighted average cost of capital (WACC)[7], the expected profitability (i.e. ROE) could remain stable or even fall following an increase in operating costs or provisioning levels.

The survey showed that the average cost of capital had fallen by 1.4 percentage

---

[3] KPMG International, *The profitability of EU Banks, Hard work or a lost cause?*, October 2016.

[4] The following listed banks were included as of 30 April 2017: for Italy, UniCredit SpA, Intesa Sanpaolo SpA, UBI Banca SpA; for Austria, Erste Group Bank AG, Raiffeisen-Landesbanken-Holding GmbH; for Belgium: KBC Group NV; for Germany: deutsche Bank AG, Commerzbank AG; for Denmark: Danske Bank AS, Jyske Bank AS; for Spain: Banco Santander SA, Banco Bilbao Vizcaya Argentaria SA, Banco de Sabadell SA, Criteria Caixa SAU; for France: Groupe BNP Paribas, Société Générale SA, Groupe Crédit Agricole; for the United Kingdom: Lloyds Banking Group Plc, HSBC Holdings Plc, The Royal Bank of Scotland Group Plc, Barclays Plc; for Hungary: OtP Bank Nyrt.; for Ireland: Allied Irish Banks Plc; for the Netherlands: ABN AMRO Groep NV, ING Groep NV; for Norway: DNB Bank Group; for Poland: Powszechna Kasa Oszczednoci Bank Polski SA; for Sweden: Swedbank Group, Nordea Group, Skandinaviska Enskilda Banken Group, Svenska Handels Group.

[5] Weighted average market capitalisation.

[6] The market capital asset pricing model (CAPM) was used in the survey. Using the CAPM it is possible to estimate the cost of capital from the risk-free rate (Rf) and the non-hedgeable risk premium required by shareholders; the latter, in turn, depends on the equity risk premium (ERP) and a measure of the systematic risk of each company's stock, according to the formula: $COE_{it} = Rf_{mt} + it*ERP_{mt}$ where i denotes the bank, t is the observation date, m denotes the stock's reference market and the beta coefficient (β) is a measure of stock-specific risk that expresses its expected variation in returns relative to market movements. A stock with a beta coefficient greater than unity presents a higher risk than that of the market portfolio and therefore a higher expected return demanded by investors, all other conditions being equal.

[7] The WACC is the weighted average cost of the resources through which the company finances itself, that is the weighted average of the costs of risk and debt capital, considering transactions such as injections or increases in share capital, bank debt, bonds, shareholder financing, etc.

points to 8.6[8]. About 30% of this reduction was due to a decline in the specific risk of securities (beta coefficients) and the remainder to a decrease in the equity risk premium linked to the domestic market[9].

The three-year ROE expected by market analysts for the banks in the sample had returned to values close to 9%, while the average for Italian banks was two points lower at around 7%. More generally, the share of European intermediaries for whom the expected profitability was lower than the cost of capital was around 50%, down from 62% in April.

Four years later, in 2020 a broader survey conducted by the ECB showed that out of ninety-five significant European banks representing about 90% of the assets of all significant banks, the cost of equity (COE) they calculated was 8.5% in Q4 of 2019 and about two-thirds of the sample had values between 8% and 12%[10]. Similar results were also shown by the survey conducted in the same time period by the EBA on sixty-five banks also operating in non-SSM EU contexts, such as the UK[11].

Based on its own analysis using the three-step approach combining multiple models of bank cost of equity[12], the ECB estimated an aggregate COE for the European sample of between 7.7% and 12.7%, slightly above the range of internal estimates of the cost of capital reported by banks to supervisors[13].

---

[8] The risk-free rate used for each country was the ten-year US government bond yield; the equity risk premiums were calculated as outlined by A. DAMODORAN, *Equity risk premiums (ERP): determinants, estimation and implications. The 2017 edition*; in particular, the equity risk premium for each country was calculated by adding the premium differential on sovereign credit default swaps (Cds) between the reference country and the US to the estimated risk premium for the US equity market. The beta coefficient is estimated using daily returns over a one-year moving window and is calculated relative to each bank's national market index; similar results are obtained using daily returns over a two-year time window or weekly returns over two- or five-year time windows (for methodology see BIS, 87th Annual Report, Basel, 2017).

[9] The decline was more pronounced for the three Italian banks included in the thirty-one sampled (3.4 percentage points); however, their cost of capital, averaging around 11%, remained higher than that of the other banks, due to the higher values of both beta ratios and the risk premium in the Italian stock market.

[10] About 12% of the significant banks reported COE values below 5% and four banks reported values above 12%.

[11] The SSM sample has a higher distribution of banks with COEs below 8% due to the different number and composition of the samples analysed.

[12] The first step (the estimation step) consists of estimating the cost of equity for each bank in the sample using a set of models that differ in terms of the amount of information used and the degree to which this information is forward-looking. The second step (the combination step) uses model combination techniques to average the results of the individual models across each bank. Finally, the third step (the aggregation step) generates results at various levels of cross-sectional aggregation using market capitalisation (for listed banks) or the book value of equity (for unlisted banks) of individual banks as weightings in the weighted averaging procedure. Fonte: ECB Occasional Paper Series No 254 / January 2021 "Measuring the cost of equity of euro area banks".

[13] As part of the self-assessment banks used various valuation criteria, in particular 41% of banks used some calibration of the CAPM, 9% (mostly listed banks) used other model-based approaches and the remaining part (mostly unlisted banks) used qualitative models or hybrids.

According to the study conducted by the ECB on the estimation of COE in the European banking sector[14] in the face of high heterogeneity across countries and business models, COE tends to be higher for banks that are riskier (higher impaired loan ratio), less efficient (higher cost/income ratio) with more unstable funding sources (higher relative dependence on interbank deposits), listed (compared to unlisted), large (higher complexity, diseconomies and presence of implicit state guarantees) and for those operating in countries that were among those most affected by the euro area sovereign debt crisis.

Applying these analyses to business models, the estimates place retail and small market lenders among the banks with COEs greater than 10%. Moreover, on the basis of analyses also conducted by the ECB, but on a sample of eight G-SIBs, six universal banks and twenty-three retail and consumer lenders and diversified lenders, G-SIBs would be placed at the top of the ranking, followed by universal and retail banks, due to their idiosyncratic management difficulties and the sensitivity of their assets and liabilities to market changes. It was emphasised that some business models are more dominant in certain countries and therefore reflect their macroeconomic dynamics[15].

It has been observed that in just over a decade (2008–2019), the COE of banks has consistently and significantly exceeded the ROE, causing the price/book ratios of the major banks to shrink to such an extent that the market value of banks' equities trades at a significant discount to the book value of their equity[16].

In the study conducted by the ECB, it also emerges that the COE is able to reflect the difficulties of intermediaries and the banking sector about a year in advance. According to these studies, the average COE of banks for which a distress event was identified increases monotonically from about four quarters before the stress date and peaks in the quarter following the identified distress event. On average, the estimated COE in the quarter of distress is about 30% higher than the level before the

---

[14] Occasional Paper Series No 254/January 2021, *Measuring the cost of equity of euro area banks*, Carlo Altavilla, Paul Bochmann, Jeroen De Ryck, Ana-Maria Dumitru, Maciej Grodzicki, Heinrich Kick, Cecilia Melo Fernandes, Jonas Mosthaf, Charles O'Donnell, Spyros Palligkinis.

[15] Among unlisted banks, on the other hand, while corporate/wholesale lenders (due to greater inefficiency and reliance on interbank funding) and diversified lenders had lower COEs than listed banks because they benefited from higher specialisation, during the period under review COEs were higher. No significant differences were found when analysing ownership dimension (all bank, cooperative bank, savings bank).

[16] Rostagno, M., Altavilla, C., Carboni, G., Lemke, W., Motto, R., Saint-Guilhem, A., and Yiangou, J. (2019), *A tale of two decades: the ECB's monetary policy at 20*, ECB Working Paper Series, No 2346.

Andersson, M., Kok, C., Mirza, H., Móré, C., and Mosthaf, J. (2018), *How can euro area banks reach sustainable profitability in the future?*, Special feature in Financial Stability Review, European Central Bank, November 2018, pp. 125-142

Altavilla C., Boucinha M., and Peydro J.-L. (2018), "*Monetary policy and bank profitability in a low interest rate environment*", Economic Policy, Vol. 33, No 96, pp. 531-586.

onset of the increase and tends to remain high for several quarters after the date of distress.

With specific reference to the pandemic crisis, the COE increased from the end of February 2020.

In ECB studies, the expected profitability of European banks in the following years was actually perceived to be increasing. In 2023, the ECB's annual report highlighted the recovery of profits, driven by the rising interest margin for the first time in several years[17], after having reached a low in 2020 at the peak of the pandemic.

At the aggregate level, although banks' annualised return on capital increased to the highest level observed in several years (7.6%, up 2.4% compared with pre-pandemic levels at the end of 2019), it still remains below the average cost of equity. The recovery of banks' profitability in 2021 was mainly driven by the cyclical reduction of impairment flows, which more than halved compared with the previous year, whereas in 2022 it was driven by the ECB's monetary policy.

In a similar trend, the profitability of less significant institutions also improved in 2021–2022, mainly due to lower write-downs and higher interest rates.

However, in an environment where high and rigid cost structures persisted, the ECB's annual report showed that the efficiency of the euro area banks remained relatively low, despite a drop of more than three percentage points in the cost/income ratio compared with 2021[18].

This important indicator showed that about 60% of the result of industrial activity (loans, finance, services) was absorbed by production costs (operating expenses), leaving only a small proportion of income to cover extraordinary expenses and to remunerate shareholders. Overall, banks managed to increase their net operating profits by 15%. Operating costs returned to pre-pandemic levels, reflecting the fact that the cost savings during the pandemic were only temporary.

How to analyse cost structures from a BMA perspective will be discussed in the following chapters.

It was also emphasised that mergers and acquisitions seemed to have gained momentum over the past two years, acting as a catalyst for the industry to increase efficiency and restore more sustainable levels of profitability. In particular, banks have been more actively engaged in targeted restructuring operations at the business line level. Some intermediaries expanded or diversified their wealth management, se-

---

[17] The increase in operating profit was mainly driven by the increase in interest margin (up 9.3% over the corresponding period), which benefited from an increase in margins supported by the rise in interest rates and a steepening of the slope of the yield curve, as well as an increase in lending volumes.

[18] Cost/income, as is well known, refers to the ratio of operating costs (such as administrative, personnel and property costs) to intermediation margin, which in the financial statements of credit institutions is the sum of interest margin, net commissions, dividends and similar income, net trading income, net hedging income, gains (or losses) and net income from financial assets and liabilities at fair value. It is one of the main indicators of the bank's management efficiency: the lower the value expressed by this indicator, the higher the bank's efficiency.

curities business, custody services and payment technology activities, while others downsized them to redirect resources into other areas[19].

1.2 Importance of value creation in BMA

1.2.1 The role of ROE in value creation

The brief overview in the previous section on the recent profitability performance of the banking industry introduced us to the issue of how banks create value; such analysis is crucial to verify the sustainability of the business model over time and the impacts of digital transformation.

However, before investigating how to create value we still deem it necessary to define what value creation is and for this it is useful to start with the concept of economic value added (EVA). Further indicators (payout ratio, dividend growth, etc.) described in the course of the chapter represent instead useful variables to evaluate the sustainability of the business model. As shown in **Figure 1.1** and stated in the previous chapter, in practice value creation is the result of a company's profitability that is able to exceed the cost of capital[20].

Some financial concepts related to profitability help us understand the importance of RoE in value creation, which, as shown in **Figure 1.1**, is given by:

Figure 1.1   **Is RoE greater than CoE?**

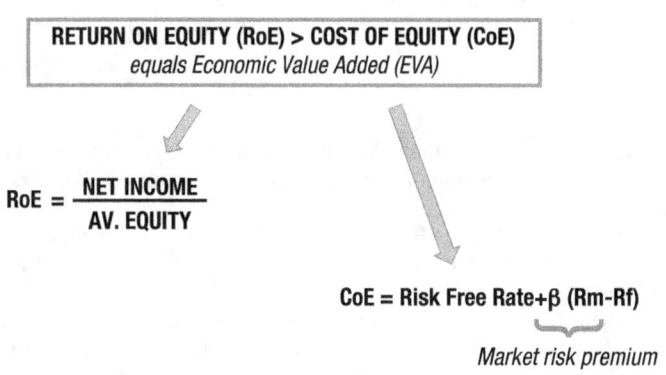

Source: Graphic elaboration of EVA by the authors.

---

[19] Financial Stability Review, BCE, November 2021.
[20] According to the cited November 2017 Stability Report of the Bank of Italy, "the cost of equity (CoE) is the minimum expected return on the risk capital invested in a firm. The difference between this indicator and the actual return on equity (RoE) is a measure of the adequacy of the company's profitability from the point of view of its shareholders".

$$RoE > CoE \text{ equals } EVA$$

where the CoE can be defined as[21]:

$$CoE = Risk\ Free\ Rate + \beta\ (Market\ Risk\ Premium)$$

and RoE is equal to:

$$\frac{Net\ Income}{Average\ Stockholder's\ Equity}$$

As is known, if the RoE equals the CoE, corporate profitability is able to cover the shareholders' cost of capital; if the RoE is lower than the CoE, there is value destruction; if the RoE is higher than the CoE, the bank generates excess economic benefits.

CoE has further implications in terms of financial stability and monetary policy as it can influence the size of countercyclical capital buffers and the ability to attract new investors, respectively.

Unlike the cost of debt, CoE is not directly measurable and is inevitably subject to estimation[22]. In this regard, the ECB proposes a multiple approach based on a three-step methodology (a three-step approach combining multiple models of bank CoE), which combines the CoEs derived from ten different analysis models for each bank (which can be grouped into two macro categories: multi-factor models and implied cost of equity models) by applying an equal weighting procedure in order to reduce possible idiosyncratic errors[23,24,25]. The last step, functional to a transversal analysis of the banking sector, involves the aggregation of the average COEs thus obtained on different dimensions, including that of business models.

While the methodology shows significant heterogeneity in the individual results

---

[21] Where β is "the sensitivity of an individual investment's price performance to the movement of the market" and market risk premium is *"Rm-rf* expected return on a well-diversified portfolio of stock's risk-free rate".

[22] In particular, the cost is related to the future flow of dividends and capital gains from which the shareholders may benefit and must therefore be inferred from other (observable) prices and quantities filtered through an econometric model.

[23] Standard one-factor CAPM, Fama French three-factor model, model with Fama French with orthogonalised factors, multi-factor model with credit variables, model with credit variables with orthogonalised factors.

[24] These models are based on some variants of the discounted cash flow model: free cash flow to equity model, residual income model by Gebhardt, Lee and Swaminathan (2001), residual income model by Claus and Thomas (2001), Ohlson and Juettner-Nauroth model (2005) and simplified Ohlson and Juettner-Nauroth model.

[25] For unlisted banks the methodology requires that the COE is estimated using bank fundamentals, specifically, (i) CET1 ratio as an indicator of leverage, (ii) interbank deposits to total assets as an indicator of dependence on unstable funding, (iii) the ratio of NPLs as an indicator of realised credit risk and (iv) the cost/income ratio to capture operating efficiency. The regression factors are the same as those used for listed banks.

1 The key role of value creation

of the ten models adopted[26], as each of them includes information that other models do not take into account, no systematic bias emerges as the goodness of each model may vary depending on the market conditions and the business models being evaluated. This implies that it is not possible to define a priori which valuation method is to be preferred for a given bank.

The analysis of the determinants of EVA are also important to increase the growth potential of the intermediary (HG high growth); it is indeed crucial to understand if the excess value comes from possible barriers to market entry, from the goodness of the products placed, from the innovation pursued or from the entry into new sectors or markets.

In the economic literature, the "follow the money" approach for the ROE breakdown, which is based on different methodologies, is now well established. In particular, the DuPont analysis decomposes the ROE profitability ratio into the three main sources of return on capital: operating efficiency ratio, asset turnover ratio and financial leverage[27].

In detail, ROE is the result of:

$$RoE = Net\ Profit\ Margin * Asset\ Turnover\ Ratio * Financial\ Leverage$$

whose sources in turn are the result of:

$$RoE = \frac{Net\ Profit}{Income} * \frac{Income}{Av.\ Assets} * \frac{Av.\ Assets}{Av.\ Equity}$$

In addition, the DuPont analysis also explains the relationship between RoE and return on asset (RoA, see below) as a measure of corporate efficiency, that is RoA*Leverage (Av. Assets/Av. Equity levels).

Therefore, a bank could improve its RoE by making its return on total assets (represented by net income/Av Assets) more efficient or by making its financial leverage management more effective (Av. Assets/Av. Equity).

Given that RoA is the result of:

$$\frac{Net\ Income}{Average\ Assets}$$

in turn, RoA by construction can be calculated as:

---

[26] Median estimates range from 7.1% for the CAPM to 12.1% for the Fama French three-factor model. Regarding percentiles, the Gebhardt, Lee and Swaminathan model produces the lowest estimate at the 10th percentile, while the Ohlson and Juettner-Nauroth model produces the highest estimate at the 90th percentile.

[27] As is known, the net profit margin measures operating efficiency and the erosion of income due to interest expense and taxes; the asset turnover ratio measures the efficiency of using assets to generate revenues; and the financial leverage measures the level of debt, that is the degree to which the company is dependent on external financial sources, so that the higher the value of leverage, the less balanced the financial structure will be judged to be.

$$RoA = (Operating\ RoA - Provisions)/Av.Asset*(1 - tax)$$

and the operating RoA is the result of:

$$NII + \frac{Fee\ Income}{\mu\ Assets} + \frac{Trading\ Income}{\mu\ Assets} + \frac{Other\ Income}{\mu\ Assets} - Cost\ of\ \mu\ Assets$$

This breakdown is useful for understanding that, by intervening on individual variables, benefits can be obtained in terms of ROE and therefore greater profitability.

In the box below, an example is given of how, using the above formulas, some determinants of changes in profitability reported in the banking industry in certain historical periods can be identified.

The role of leverage in pre-2008 crisis ROE growth

The top 100 largest European banks in the period 1990–1999 show that these banks achieved ROEs between 12% and 16% and between 22% and 26% in 2000–2007.
In this regard, it should be noted that, given that the leverage in 1990–1999 averaged about 1:16 and in 2000–2007 it was 1:28, it is easy to deduce using the above formulas that it was mainly debt that drove bank profitability in the pre-2008 crisis period.

1.2.2 Shareholders remuneration

Within the policies adopted by banks, another important constituent is commonly investigated by analysts: the dividend policy.

Although obvious, the attractiveness of an investment in the capital of a bank is directly related to the possibility of adequately remunerating the capital invested. We are talking about the payout ratio which is given by:

$$\frac{Dividend\ per\ Share}{Earning\ per\ Share} = \frac{DPS}{EPS}$$

In the literature, several approaches are proposed to analyse the bank's value, starting with the shareholders' remuneration, such as the Gordon model, the Modigliani and Miller model, the present value of expected dividends (PVED) or the present value of abnormal earnings (PVAE). These methodologies are mainly based on the dividend payout ratio (for more details please refer to the specific texts on the subject).

1.2.3 The role of the dividend growth rate in profitability analyses

Among the various financial indicators to be taken into account in the context of profitability analyses is the dividend growth rate, which can be calculated as:

$$g = b*RoE$$

1   The key role of value creation   11

where $b = 1\text{-}payout\ ratio$ represents the percentage of net income that the bank retains in its business to foster future growth (retention rate or plowback ratio).

The growth rate may increase in some periods due to particular competitive advantage factors (e.g. operations in emerging markets), but in general, a period of competitive advantage in the financial industry is usually shorter and more contained than in other industries. In fact, in the terminal value period, the growth factor g is by construction no greater than the nominal GDP growth of the countries in which it operates.

The box below provides some examples of how analysts use the dividend growth rate.

> **The dividend growth rate**
>
> Suppose that by policy a target bank defines 0.59 as parameter b and ROE as 8.5% in the base scenario and 10% in the best scenario. The dividend growth rate would increase from 5% (0.59*8.5%) to 5.9% (0.59*10%). In the case of ROE growth of a well-capitalised bank, analysts would expect an increase in the dividend payout (estimated in a range of 41–60%). By construction, the higher payout would reduce the dividend growth rate.

Another important element in the analysis of value creation is the assessment of banks' equity behaviour based on leverage trends (D/E ratio). The value of equity can grow at the same rate as returns on capital or decrease, depending on the dividend policies adopted and the expected ROE. In detail:

a. dividend payout ratio < 1-g/ROE
   – D/E decreases
   – Equity remains stable and grows
   – ROE decreases
b. dividend payout ratio > 1- g/ROE
   – D/E grows
   – Bank return equity
   – ROE grows

1.2.4 Price-to-book ratio: The influence of ROE

Among the indicators tested by the market, the best example is the price-to-book ratio (PBR), whose classic definition is:

$$\text{Price to book ratio} = \frac{\text{Market Value of Equity per Share}}{\text{Book Value of Equity per Share}}$$

However, some texts on the subject use a different representation; if we assume constant growth of RoE as iE as *cost of equity*, the PBR is given by:

$$\text{Price to book ratio} = \frac{(RoE - g)}{(iE - g)}$$

Once again, therefore, the central role of RoE in market scrutiny is highlighted.

When determining the share price, some analysts also take into account the PVED, which is made up of dividends and capital gains calculated year by year:

$$r_{t+1} = \frac{d_{t+1} + p_{t+1} - p_t}{p_t}$$

where p is the share price at time t and d is the dividend paid at time=1 (one year from now). Incorporating the expectations will give:

$$E(r) = E\frac{(d_{t+1} + p_{t+1}) - p_t}{p_t}$$

Therefore, in an efficient market where expectations of a share's returns are commensurate with the cost of capital (rE), the intrinsic share price will be given by:

$$p^* = E\frac{(d_t + p_{t+1})}{(1 + r_E)}$$

For the sake of completeness, further indicators examined by market analysts are mentioned, such as the PVAE, the present value of expected abnormal earnings, the present value of abnormal nopat and the present value of expected abnormal nopat (for further details of which, together with the previous analytical formulas, please refer to the specific texts on the subject)[28].

All the above formulas imply the cruciality of RoE in value creation and sustainability of strategic choices.

Having understood the importance of the ingredients that underpin value creation, market participants then assess certain indicators and strategic implications that directly or indirectly enter the algorithms described above.

For example, from the distribution of some indicators and in particular the price-to-earning ratio (given by the ratio between market value per share and earning ratio per share) and the aforementioned PBR[29], academics categorise banks using the taxonomy borrowed from the BCG matrix[30]:

As shown in the **Figure 1.2**, in the first cluster ("Dogs"), expectations are negative

---

[28] K. PALEPU, P.H. HEALY, V. BERNARD, E. PEEK, *Business Analysis and valuation using financial statements*, Cengage, fourth edition 2016.

[29] Chambers and Penman (1984), Penman (1987), Chai and Tung (2002) and Anilowski, Feng and Skinner (2007) have shown "that investors accrue positive returns during earnings management". Others including Aga and Kocaman (2008) showed "that the market reacts positively to good earnings announcements and negatively to bad earnings announcements". Particular mention is made of the 1984 analysis where the performance of the NYSE and AMEX was analysed by looking at their median for each year from 1968 to 1985. Checking the frequency of the distribution showed the following results: "a high PB and a high PE, a low PB and a high PE, a high PB and a low PE, a low PB and a low PE".

[30] The BCG matrix is a model developed by the Boston Consulting Group in the 1970s and is

1 The key role of value creation

Figure 1.2   **Clustering of banks based on PE and PB**

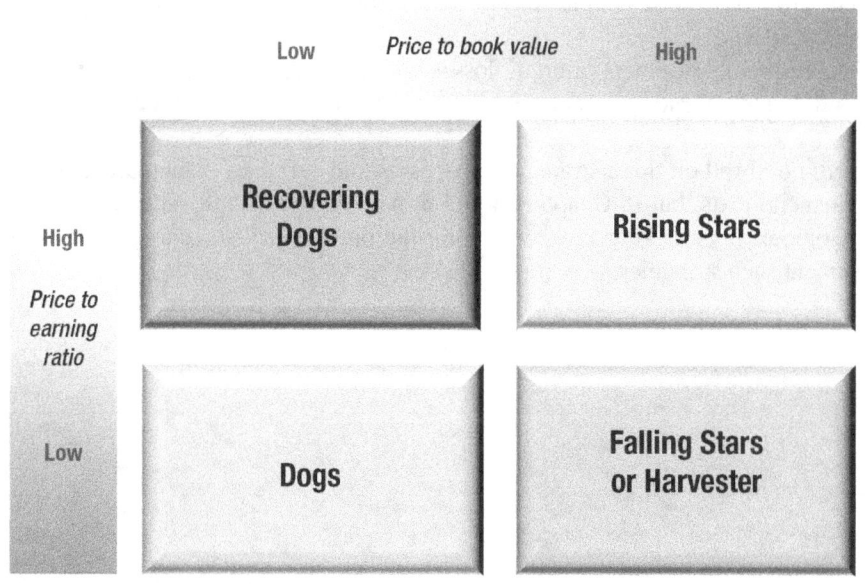

Source: Authors' elaboration of K. Palepu's clustering.

on both returns on capital and growth; in the second ("Falling Stars" or "Harvester") RoE is expected to exceed the return on capital only on existing investments, but forecasts on further investments do not confirm the positive trend; in the third ("Recovering dogs"), low profits are considered only temporary as adequate investments should lead to a return to profitability that is more than competitive; in the last cluster ("Rising Stars"), a positive current and prospective view is assumed (RoE>CoE and high growth).

Based on these considerations, the analysis of a bank's profitability cannot disregard assessments of the dimensions that impact ROE, among which are:

a. The increase/decrease in net interest income taking into account pricing policies, remuneration of deposits and commission contributions;
b. Intermediated volumes assessed on the basis of book values of outstanding assets and liabilities and underlying risk-weighted asset optimisation processes;
c. The cost-to-income ratio, taking into account the level of standardisation and automation of processes, the rate of investment in IT and optimisation of distribution channels and whether the company is a cost leader;

---

one of the tools used by company management to define strategies and allocate resources/budget to their projects.

d. The goodness of the capital ratio, the expected weight of low risk assets, the cost of equity and the steady earnings to influence β;
e. The growth potential and expansion of assets by customer base, geography, sector and products;
f. The future development of credit losses with regard to credit policies, growth potential, internal rating models and expected losses and concentration risks.

We will not dwell on these strategies, processes and variables, which are analysed in the financial texts, but in Chapters 4 and 5, with regard to cost rationalisation policies, some examples are given concerning the preliminary screenings necessary to implement such strategies.

2 Characteristics of a business model

> "Every once in a while, a new technology, an old problem,
> and a big idea turn into an innovation"
> D. Kamen

2.1 An outline of the approach to the banking literature

As mentioned in Chapter 1, ROE and value creation are the pillars on which BMA is based. Before entering into the analysis, it is necessary to clarify what is meant by a business model (BM) when applied to the financial industry in general and to banks in particular, since most of the literature on the subject has adopted a deductive approach.

Even before giving a holistic definition, in the writer's opinion, in the literature on the subject of BMs, based on the prevalent activity carried out, one finds clustering along different dimensions identified from time to time in order to emphasise the different levels of performance reported in the various clusters (Figure 2.1).

Figure 2.1 **Clustering first of all**

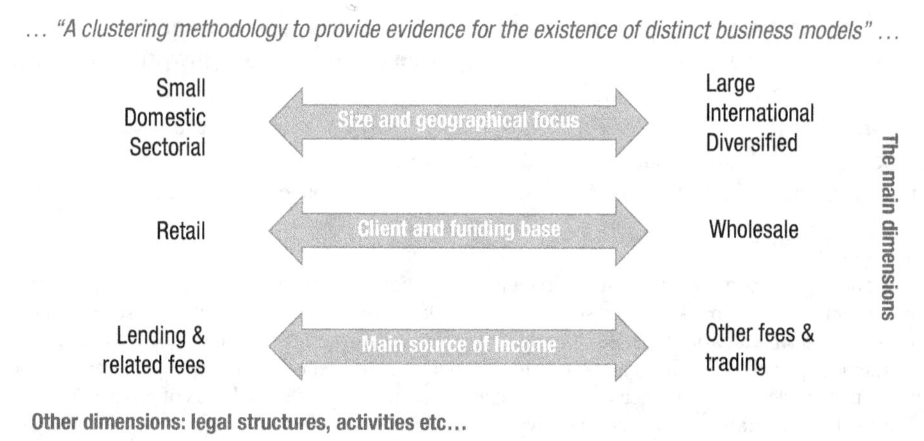

... *"A clustering methodology to provide evidence for the existence of distinct business models"* ...

Small Domestic Sectorial	← Size and geographical focus →	Large International Diversified
Retail	← Client and funding base →	Wholesale
Lending & related fees	← Main source of Income →	Other fees & trading

The main dimensions

Other dimensions: legal structures, activities etc...

Source: Authors' elaboration.

On the origins of the application of the concept of business models we find indications in some works by Hunt, Caves and Porter who, although highlighting some aspects related to BMA, do not give an accomplished definition applicable to the financial industry (see "A journey into the origins", below).

In 1988, Amel and Rhoades applied the concept of "strategic group" to the banking world[1]. The conclusions drawn from the analysis of the percentage differences between the clusters are in fact evidence of corporate business choices, but they too do not provide a complete definition of the BM concept.

A journey into the origins

- The term "strategic group" was coined to describe "a group of firms within an industry that are highly symmetric with respect to cost structure, the degree of vertical integration, and the degree of product differentiation, formal organisation, control systems, management rewards/punishments, and the personal views and preferences for various possible outcomes".
  M.S. HUNT, *Competition in the major home appliance industry*, 1960–1970. Unpublished PhD dissertation, Business Economics Committee, Harvard University, 1972.
- The entry barriers concept is extended to different groups of companies within the same industry.
  R.E. CAVES, M.E. PORTER, *From entry barriers to mobility barriers: conjunctural decisions and contrived deterrence to new competition* in Quarterly Journal of Economics 1977, Vol. 91, issue 2, pp. 241–262.
- "Finally, I will show that the empirically supported theory refutes the Demsetz/Mancke view that large firms earn higher profits largely because they are more efficient or lucky, and not because they possess market power".
  M. PORTER, *The Structure within industries and companies' performance* in The Review of Economics and Statistics 1979, Vol. 61, issue 2, pp. 214–227.
- For the first time, the strategic group concept is also applied to the banking sector.
  D.F. AMEL, S.A. RHOADES, *Strategic groups in banking* in The Review of Economics and Statistics, 1988, Vol. 70, issue 4, 685–689.

Over the last twenty years, the identification of the structural reasons for the performance of banking clusters has undoubtedly been one of the most investigated objects of study by academics and analysts.

Specifically in 2011, Ayadi, Arbak and De Groen note in the above-mentioned paper that retail banks outperformed investment and wholesale banks before, during and after the financial crisis[2,3]. On the basis of a database of 200 variables relating

---

[1] The paper reports observations of sixteen metropolitan banking markets, referring in particular to the composition of bank balance sheets in 1978, 1981 and 1984 for fifteen balance sheet variables using a clustering algorithm called "fastclus". The results showed the existence of six clusters and similar strategic choices within markets. This implied that differences in intra-industry performance were attributable to the existence of strategic clusters rather than different levels of efficiency.

[2] With large retail deposit base and diverse income sources.

[3] Typically, large institutions with low capital ratios and a strong dependence on short-term market funding.

> **Walking through the banking literature**
> - R. AYADI, E. ARBAK, W.P. DE GROEN, Business models in European banking: a pre-and post-crisis screening, CEPS Paperbacks, 2011.
> - M. MERCK MARTEL, A. VAN RIXTEL, E. GONZÁLEZ MOTA Business models of international banks in the wake of the 2007-2009 global financial crisis in Estabilidad Financiera, Banco de España 2012, n. 22.
> - R. ROENGPITYA, N. TARASHEV, K. TSATSARONIS Bank business models in BIS Quarterly Review, 2014.
> - M. FARNÈ, A. VOULDIS, Business models of the banks in the euro area, ECB Working Papers n. 2070, May 2017.
> - R. AYADI, D. CUCINELLI, W.P. DE GROEN Banking business models monitor 2019: Europe, CEPS, 2019.

to data referring to the four-year period 2006–2009, taken from the main twenty-six European banks clustered using statistical methods in three business areas (retail, investment and wholesale), the authors also conclude that business diversification activities per se were not characterised by particularly satisfactory results.

Further analyses based on different samples, such as those presented in the above-mentioned paper, "Business models of international banks in the wake of the 2007–2009 global financial crisis", actually confirm the conclusions of the CEPS work.

Also in the analyses published by the BIS quarterly review in December 2014, retail-funded commercial banks continued to be indicated as the most profitable banks, followed by capital markets-oriented banks. There were 222 banks observed in the years 2005–2013 and the paper also notes that changes in BM have a positive impact on the cost/income ratio.

In contrast, wholesale funded banks and securities holding banks were more efficient in terms of ROE and ROA[4], according to the May 2017 working paper published by the ECB[5]. This was based on statistical techniques applied to the FINREP[6], after clustering the intermediaries.

Finally, focused retail banks also show higher levels of financial performance and operational efficiency than diversified retail banks according to the study conducted on 3287 banks over the period 2005–2017 and published by CEPS in the paper "Banking business models monitor 2019: Europe".

---

[4] Banks with wholesale liabilities that make extensive use of derivatives, including trading derivatives, and have a number of shares of credit on their assets.

[5] Banks with liabilities characterised by deposits and assets by stocks and cash.

[6] The European economic area (EEA) and the EBA, with the aim of ensuring better financial transparency and promoting coordination between European banks and investment firms, introduced the Capital Requirements Directive IV (CRD IV), which came into force on 1 January 2014. This establishes, inter alia, a harmonised system of statistical (financial reporting, FINREP) and prudential (common reporting, COREP) supervisory reporting to which supervised banks should adhere.

In June 2017, the ECB introduced the theme that changes in the interest rate curve are able to explain the characteristics of banks' BMs on average[7].

In June 2018, the EBA published a paper that was the result of a requirement of the CRR[8] (preamble 95) concerning the analysis of the impacts on BMs deriving from excessive financial leverage from which it is inferred that this characteristic does not represent a differential factor along the different clusters of BMs ("Identification of EU Bank Business Models"). The analysis starts from a clustering of eleven groups substantially referring to four macro categories of BMs (universal, retail-oriented, corporate-oriented, specialised). For the purposes of assessing the exposure to the risk of excessive leverage, the volatility or inadequacy of the results, the stability of the deposits, the stability of the activities carried out and the degree of concentration of the assets were investigated (Figure 2.2).

The recovery of efficiency and profitability is also a widely discussed topic in the banking literature.

Among international works there is, for example, the analysis published by the International Monetary Fund in July 2017[9], that highlights the positive effects of bank consolidation processes for the recovery of efficiency and profitability in Italy[10].

In 2020, Ayadi, Bongini, Casu and Cucinelli show that in general banks that mi-

Figure 2.2 **Impacts of excessive financial leverage on BMs**

EBA Identification of EU Bank Business Model no. 2 – June 2018

i.   Cross-border universal banks
ii. Local universal banks
iii. Consumer credit banks (including automotive banks)
iv. Cooperative banks
v.   Saving banks
vi. Mortgage banks
vii. Private banks
viii. Corporate banks
ix. Custody banks
x.   Institutions not taking retail deposits
xi. Other specialised banks

Factors analysed
1) Volatility or inadequate results
2) Stability of the funds collected
3) Stability of the activity performed
4) Concentration level of assets

EBA Conclusions:
"Overall, the results do generally not give a strong indication for differences in the degree of exposure to the risk of excessive leverage (REL) across different types of credit institutions"

Source: Authors' elaboration on data published by the EBA.

---

[7] A. Lucas, J. Schaumburg, B. Scwaab, ECB working paper series No 2084, June 2017.
[8] Capital Requirements Regulation, Regulation (EU) 575/2013.
[9] A. Weber, *Bank consolidation, efficiency and profitability in Italy*, IMF July 2017.
[10] Similar were the considerations of Member of the Executive Committee of the ECB and Governor of Bank of Italy starting from 1st November, 2023, F. Panetta made during his speech at the Italy Day Conference in London in February 2018, "Experience teaches that aggregation operations, if based on a solid business plan, can generate significant gains".

grate to other BMs – mostly large banks with low profitability and high risk – benefit in terms of profitability, stability and efficiency. There were 3000 banks from thirty-two European countries observed in the years 2010–2017 and the results emphasise that not all migrations bring the same benefits, especially when migrating to diversified rather than specialised BMs.

On the cluster side, most of the studies focused on the strategies related to retail market, small-medium enterprises (SME), corporate banking, capital market, corporate finance, wealth management/private banking and asset management and their impact on profitability. In some cases, the studies provide a kind of recipe as a solution for the recovery of efficiency and profitability; in other cases, they explain the root causes for the decline in profitability of the banking industry.

Among the recipes, links to the market position have emerged through surveys that generally concern, as in all industries, some key elements such as business strategy analysis, accounting analysis, financial analysis and prospective analysis with a strong emphasis on equity evaluation. A series of elements have been analysed in order to provide indications for the recovery of profitability, such as: core customers today to target customers tomorrow, range of products offered and need for new products, domestic or international geographical area, competitive positioning today and positioning tomorrow, growth prospects against strategic initiatives, profitability targets in core business and new business and availability of capital and investments.

Other analyses focused on products and services offered in the large corporate, SME companies and retail segments or on the performance of the most important bank indicators[11].

The work carried out by academics and analysts would therefore seem to confirm an underlying inclination to understand whether and to what extent different BMs impact on banking performance in a backward-looking logic, rather than focusing on a clear definition of a BM from which to develop a pragmatic proposal for a framework to analyse it.

With reference to the digitalisation process and open innovation in particular, few works have been conducted on the topic reflecting the (historically) poor application of open service and product/service innovation recorded in the banking industry. These works, however, have pointed to a substantial convergence of opinions for over a decade in concluding that the definition of effective, rapid and productive innovation strategies is, for banks and intermediaries, the key to survival in a rapidly evolving industry (Oliveira, Von Hippel, 2011; Chesbrough, 2011; Bell, Loane, 2010; Fasnacht, 2009; Akamavi, 2005).

---

[11] By way of example, the analyses include: ROE/ROA, EPS/share, Div/Share, Dividend yield, NII, non-interest income/total income, cost income ratio, NPL ratio, coverage ratio of NPLs, Tier 1 ratio (core equity ratio), total equity/RWA, total equity/assets, loan to deposit ratio, liquidity ratios & liquidity structure (liquidity coverage ratio (LCR); net stable financing ratio (NSFR); liability term structure, funding classes, maturity structure and currencies), asset and liability growth, loan concentration by sector, country/regions, names, products, rating classes, maturity, collateral, fixed and variable interest rate.

One of the most widespread issues that academics have wondered about is the nature of the barriers that have slowed down, and in some cases hindered, the full implementation of open innovation strategies by banks (Martovoy, Dos Santos, 2012; Martovoy, Mention, Torkkeli, 2012; Chaston, 2011; Bátiz-Lazo, Woldesenbet, 2006).

Among them, issues related to:

- uncertainties about the organisational set-up and cultural inertia resulting from possible cooperation, preferring, especially for large operators, the internal development of the necessary skills and capabilities in new product and services development processes;
- business execution inconsistent with the strategic design;
- poor involvement of customers and other stakeholders in the innovation process as it is considered complex and time consuming.

Other scholars, however, have focused on analysing the impacts that the implementation of strategic digital initiatives has on BMs and banking performance. The results of the studies have shown that BMs are inevitably and significantly impacted, since digitalisation is a process that entails significant changes in terms of the combination of resources, structure and processes, corporate culture and stakeholder relations (Niemand, Rigtering, Kallmuenzer, 2020; Vial, 2019; Clohessy, Acton, Morgan, 2017).

From a performance point of view, net of significant cyber incidents[12], it too is positively affected as, by leveraging its digital capital[13], the intermediary is able to achieve efficiency, new business/market and high value-added service goals (Zhou, Kautonen, Dai, Zhang, 2021; Branzoli, Supino, 2020; Sibanda, Ndiweni, Boulkeroua, Echchabi, Ndlovu, 2020; Forcadell, Aracil, Úbeda, 2020; Chesini, Giaretta, 2019; Ciciretti et al., 2009; Beccalli, 2007; Casolaro, Gobbi, 2007; DeYoung, Lang, Nolle, 2007; Hernando, Nieto, 2007), which in turn enhances its reputation (Bernini, Ferretti, Angelini, 2022) and consequently its funding capacity and its ability to attract and retain highly skilled resources (Fombrun, Gardberg, Barnett, 2000; Turban, Greening, 1997).

Naturally, the emergence of new business opportunities has led to an increase in competitive pressure (Barba Navaretti, Calzolari, Pozzolo, 2017; Buchak, Matvos, Piskorski, Seru 2017; Philippon, 2016) to which banks have mostly reacted by entering into partnerships with fintechs, thus postponing the strategic decision to upgrade their ICT infrastructures (Brandl, Hornuf, 2017). Analysing instead the impacts that digitalisation has on the organisational structure, based on some studies conducted on large EU banking groups (Arnaboldi, Clayes, 2010), it would seem

---

[12] ECB, ECB Banking Supervision: Risk Assessment for 2020.
[13] Digital capital is represented by a new category of intangible assets (e.g. AI, open standard application programming interfaces, internet of things, big data, distributed ledger technology, blockchain, social networks, digital skills, etc.) that combines with the more traditional one (brands, reputation, know-how, etc.) Vial, G. (2019).

that the creation or acquisition of dedicated "internet banks" would result in a lower level of synergies when compared with the cross-selling potential offered by the online and traditional banking mix, albeit in the presence of lower cost savings. If, on the other hand, we focus on the impacts on the physical branch system, some studies believe that it can act as a "complement" (Xue, Hitt, Chen, 2011; Campbell, Frei, 2009; Ciciretti, Hasan, Zazzara; 2009) or as a "substitute" (Galardo, Garrì, Mistrulli, Revelli, 2021; Carmignani, Manile, Orame, Pagnini 2020; Bonaccorsi di Patti, Gobbi, Mistrulli, 2003) for brick-and-mortar transactions. According to other studies, digitalisation also produces significant effects on the bank-customer distance, exacerbating the trend, and on the centre-periphery distance within the geographical network by strengthening the parent company's control system over local branches.

In February 2018, the Basel Committee in its paper "Sound Practices Implications of fintech developments for banks and bank supervisors" provides initial indications for the development of new BMs for intermediaries and a regulation of the financial sector that adequately presides over its risks[14], without being an obstacle to technological innovation. "The emergence of the fintech phenomenon is only the latest of the waves of innovation that banks are facing", whose characteristic features lie in its potential to redefine the relationship with the customer, to lower the barriers to entry to the financial services market and to elevate the role of data as a "key commodity"[15]. The paper also proposes, among other things, five different scenarios (not to be considered mutually exclusive) to simulate banks' short to medium-term approach to the new fintech environment:

1. The better bank. That is, traditional banks digitise all their processes, use new technologies to evolve their business model and make the most of the extensive market and customer knowledge they already possess.
2. The new bank. New all-technology banks that will replace banks that have failed to embrace and implement the challenge.
3. The distributed bank. In this scenario, the relationship with the customer is shared between banks and fintechs. Joint ventures, partnerships and strategic alliance agreements are signed, but the services offered to customers are modular, so the bank sells the services offered by fintechs like any service offered by a third party.

---

[14] "Fintech presents a wide variety of risks that cut across various sectors and often blend both tactical and strategic risk elements. A number of these risks feature more or less prominently in all five scenarios: strategic risk (...), high operational risk (...), AML/CFT (...), data privacy (...), outsourcing risk (...), cyber risk (...), liquidity risk and volatility of banking funding sources (...)". BASEL COMMITTEE, Sound Practices Implications of fintech developments for banks and bank supervisors, February 2018.

[15] Furthermore, among the relevant opportunities offered by fintech to be considered, the Basel Committee mentions financial inclusion, better and more tailored banking services, lower transaction costs and faster banking services, improved and more efficient banking processes and potential positive impact on financial stability due to increased competition, Regtech.

4. The relegated bank. In this scenario, considered unlikely at first, traditional banks will become providers of commodity-services (i.e. no longer perceived by the customer as value-added services), while value-added services and the relationship with the customer will be managed by the new technological intermediaries, fintech or bigtech, which in this scenario will have the predominant control of customer data, which is the most valuable asset.
5. The disintermediated bank. This is the scenario considered to be the most extreme and remote: banks will by now have become irrelevant and customers will interact directly with fintech companies without intermediation or connection with the traditional bank.

Hence the Basel Committee's call for banking supervisors to re-evaluate their current supervisory models and resources to ensure effective and continuous monitoring of the banking system.

2.2 The definition of a business model

We have so far spoken of BMs without, however, giving it a concrete definition.
In the writer's opinion, it is in the industrial sector rather than the banking sector that scholars have attempted to frame and define the concept of the BM. Indeed, the notion of a BM refers in the first instance to a theoretical and conceptual rather than financial aspect (Teece, 2010). There is no universally accepted definition among scholars and numerous attempts at classification have been proposed over the years.

The high level of interdisciplinarity that characterises the concept of the BM makes it difficult to establish a theoretical foundation in business studies (Teece, 2010). The same term is often used by authors to refer to different aspects of the same phenomenon.

According to the results of some research (Ghaziani and Ventresca, 2005 and Zott, Amit and Massa 2011) interest in the BM exploded in particular in the fifteen years after 1995[16].

The main rationale for this trend has been identified by scholars by the fact that in the late 1990s there was an increased academic interest in capturing the evolution of hi-tech BMs in light of the advent of the Internet and the growth of emerging markets[17].

---

[16] In particular, Ghaziani and Ventresca quantified the use of the term "business model" in management articles published from 1975 to 2000 (during the twenty-five years considered, the term had been cited for 90.4% of the last five years and only the remaining 9.6% in the previous years) while Massa, Zott and Amit in academic and journalistic publications between 1975 and 2009.

[17] For example, TIMMERS P., *Business Model for Electronic Markets*, 1998; FRIEDMAN J.P., LANGLINAIS T.C., *Best Intention: a Business Model for the eEconomy*, 1999; WEILL P., VITALE M., *Place to Space: Migrating to E-business Models*, 2001; AMIT R., ZOTT C., *Value Creation in E-business*, 2001.

While countless contributions have been written on the subject of the BM, there have been just as many definitions and hypotheses for classifying the concept. In particular, the BM is:

a. An architecture for the product, services and information flows provided (Timmers, 1998);
b. The core logic of an enterprise in order for it to function (Friedman, Langlinais, 2000);
c. A dynamic concept, constantly evolving (Linder, Cantrell, 2000);
d. An architectural configuration aimed at identifying opportunities (Amit, Zott, 2001);
e. Focused on how to combine all elements of a system into a functioning whole (Magretta, 2002);
f. An abstract representation of certain aspects of a company's strategy (Seddon, Lewis, 2003);
g. A business triangle, a conceptual tool containing a set of objects, notions and their relationships to the business objective; it concerns the creation and transmission of value to its consumers (Osterwalder, Pigneur, Tucci, 2005);
h. A representation of the core logic underlying a business and the strategic choices made to create and reappropriate value in a given value network (Shafer, Smith, Linder, 2005);
i. A set of choices and consequences (rigid or flexible) arising from those same choices (Casadesus-Masanell, Ricart, 2007);
j. How the logic of the business articulates in deliberating the value proposition for its customers and sustaining it through a profitable cost and revenue structure. There is no such thing as an absolute good BM; each company should design and implement its own in order to operate at its best (Teece, 2010);
k. The rationale by which an organisation creates, distributes and captures value (BM Canvas, Osterwalder, Pigneur, 2012);
l. A system of interconnected and interdependent activities that determines the way a company does business with its customers, partners and suppliers (Amit, Zott, 2012).

In light of the multiplicity of views adopted by scholars, the "key words" used to define the BM in industrial realities can thus be roughly summarised as follows:

a. "Architecture" or "pattern" (Timmers, 1998; Dubosson-Torbay, Osterwalder, Pigneur, 2002; Brousseau, Penard, 2006);
b. "Statement" or "description" (Stewart, Zhao, 2000; Weill, Vitale, 2001);
c. "Structural template" or "representation" (Amit, Zott, 2001; Morris, Schindehutte, Allen, 2005; Shafer, Smith, Linder, 2005);
d. "Method" or "conceptual tool" (Afuah, Tucci, 2001; Osterwalder, 2004; George, Bock, 2009);
e. "Framework" or "set" (Afuah, 2004; Seelos, Mair, 2007).

Figure 2.3   A possible definition of a BM applied to banks

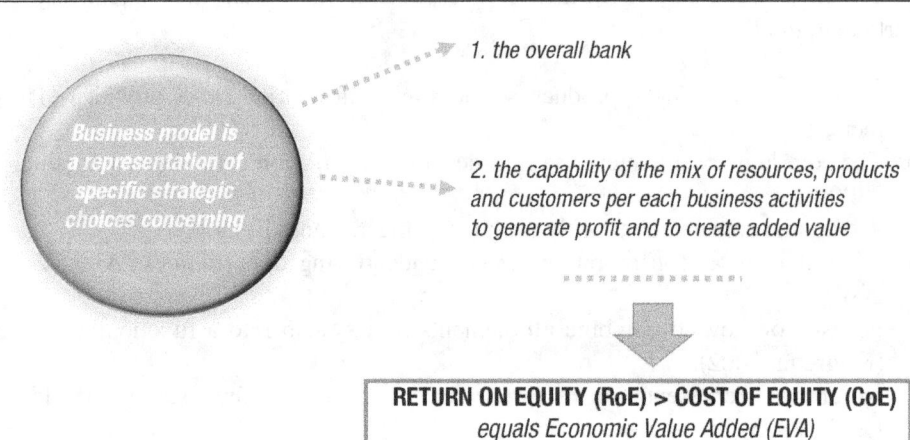

Source: Authors' elaboration.

If we want to continue the development of the existing literature, laconically represented here without any claim to exhaustiveness, towards a less abstract and forward-looking concept of BM aimed at summarising a holistic definition of the BM in the strategic process of banks, we could state that a business model is a representation of the set of specific strategic choices concerning:

- both the bank as a whole,
- and the way in which the combination of resources, products and customer segments contributes to creating value in the different business areas (**Figure 2.3**).

This definition – which summarises the different views of consultants, operators, supervisors and academics – gives an initial explanation of the stickiness of this analysis in the Italian and European banking industry, which historically suffers from a delay in the transition from a traditional planning and management control model to a more evolved strategic model, aimed at harmonising the information to support business decisions and carrying out analyses and assessments from a perspective viewpoint.

2.3   Corporate governance and BMA

It has been said that the BM is a representation of the set of specific strategic choices concerning the bank as a whole.

At this point, it is necessary to clarify that the corporate governance process, represented by the circular flow proposed by the authors in **Figure 2.4**, can be found in

2 Characteristics of a business model

Figure 2.4 Overview of interdependencies in bank governance

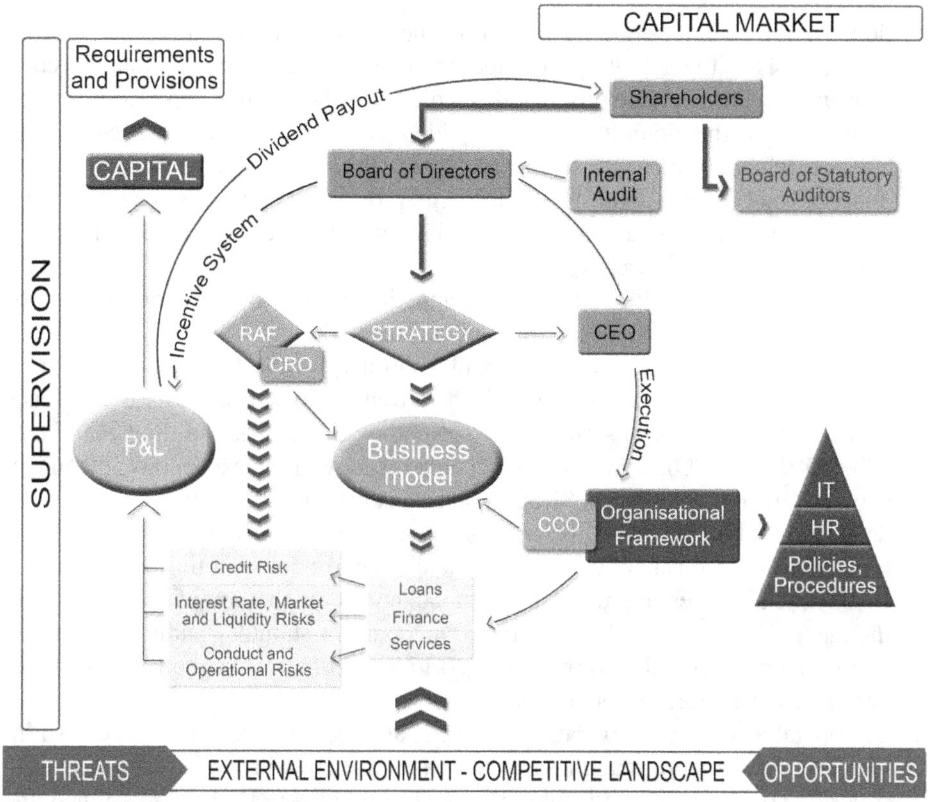

Source: Authors' elaboration.

all banking intermediaries that differ precisely in the BM implemented and that we can in fact consider it the "heart" of a bank's strategic choices.

Therefore:

a. The shareholders appoint the board of directors (BoD) that best represents them in achieving the investment objective, which can be summarised in the creation of value;
b. In turn, the directors define a strategy aimed at maximising investment by shareholders (RoE>CoE) and appoint a management body (e.g. CEO) to implement the strategies;
c. The board of executive members implements the organisation to be used (ideally broken down into its three essential variables of IT, HR and operating rules and procedures) to translate strategies into concrete operations;
d. The operations put in place should be consistent with the strategic choices of the

BM (e.g. commercial bank, investment bank, etc.) and therefore with the amount of loans disbursed, the financial assets held and the services provided, bearing in mind the challenges and opportunities of the external environment and competition. This is where digital transformation and the risks arising from it come in[18];

e. On the basis of the activity performed, the bank will assume risks that are commensurate with the loans disbursed (credit risk), the securities portfolio owned (market risk), the liquidity needs (liquidity risk), the maturity transformation choices (interest rate risk) and the degree to which the balance sheet is "tilted" (asset or liability sensitive). In addition, the provision of services opens the door to operational, conduct and reputational risks, which undermine all banking operations and impact customer risk;

f. Such risks shall be in line with the risk appetite outlined by the directors and the acceptable tolerance level (Risk Appetite Framework);

g. The operations carried out by the bank, outlined by the CEO, should then be assessed *ex ante* and *ex post* by both the CRO[19], who will assess the adherence to the risk-return profile strategically defined by the board, and the Compliance Chief Officer (CCO), who will verify compliance with the exogenous and endogenous regulatory framework. These controls constitute the bank's second line of defence, in addition to the line controls, guaranteed mainly by IT, and the third level controls performed by the internal audit department reporting directly to the BoD, which verifies mainly *ex post* the adherence of the company processes to the theoretically expected procedures. The board of statutory auditors appointed by the shareholders, also to protect minorities, will then have the function of supervising these three levels of control;

h. The operations and the coverage of the risks assumed will contribute to determining the company's profit and loss account, the result of which will in turn be used, if positive (income), both to strengthen the capital to cover the risks assumed, the extent of which is generally decided by regulators and then concretely declined by supervisors, and to implement the incentive and remuneration policies decided by the BoD. Ideally, the circular flow chart ends with the remuneration of shareholders who, on the basis of the approved dividend policies, will see their expectations of a physiological return on invested capital met.

---

[18] ECB Supervisory priorities 2023–2025: "while strong internal governance and effective strategic steering by management bodies are key for the development and execution of successful digital transformation strategies, banks also need to tackle vulnerabilities and risks stemming from a greater operational reliance on IT systems, third-party services and innovative technologies. At the same time banks are operative in a highly volatile and uncertain environment. Taking decisive steps towards achieving strong strategic steering, sound governance and proper risk data aggregation and reporting capabilities can help banks to support the sustainability of their business models against the challenge ahead".

[19] For the sake of exposition, a typical example of the traditional system has been proposed whereby the CCO and CRO are placed on the same level. In reality, this alignment may not always be true since the CRO is, as is often the case, also a member of the Board.

2 Characteristics of a business model

The process of corporate governance described as the basis of the strategic choices that determine the BM will therefore be subject to interventions of efficiency, reshaping and transformation, when the company's results are not able to create value to the extent desired by the expectations of all the company's stakeholders.

In addition, it has been said that the BM is also the way in which the combination of resources, products and customer segments contributes to creating value in the different areas of activity.

Figure 2.5 provides a concise representation of the strategic process, taking into account the mix of resources, products and customers.

This mix, which characterises the BM of banks, cannot be separated from the need to fully develop or "rethink" the three main dimensions from which to carry out a complete BMA (Figure 2.6), as well as from a robust management control system. In the writer's opinion, a correct analysis of profitability should therefore be preceded by an adequate understanding of the company's choices in terms of:

a. *Cost allocation.* Cost allocation should follow precise rules governing the level of cost attribution, standard cost and client allocation.
b. *Fund transfer prices (FTP).* In particular, FTP should also include, in the product company perimeter, ECB funding, the impact of negative rates, NPLs and group imputed fees.

Figure 2.5 **The mix of resources, products and customer segments in value creation**

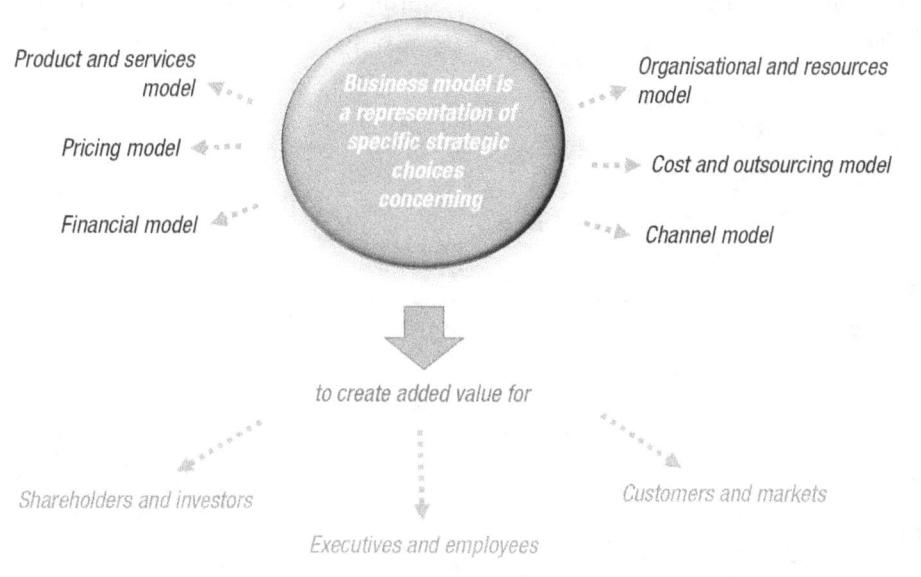

Source: Authors' elaboration.

Figure 2.6 **Profitability analysis: starting with the fundamentals**

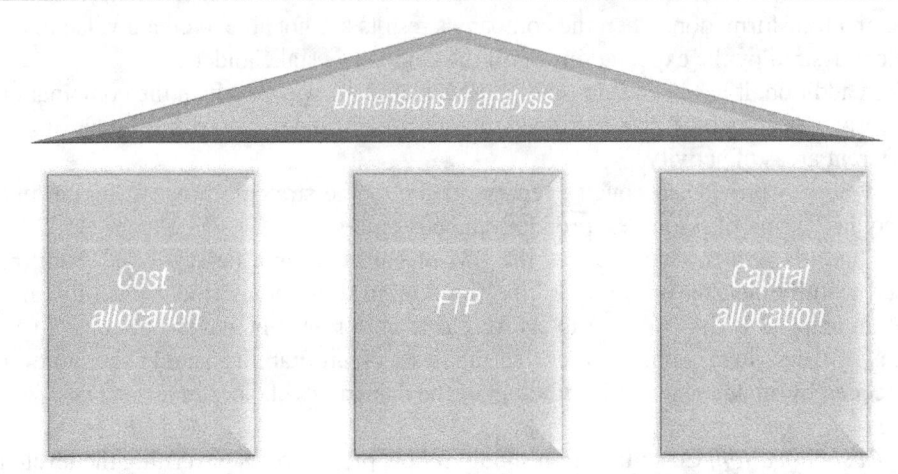

Source: Authors' elaboration.

c. *Capital allocation*. Capital allocation should not only be based on risk-weighted asset (RWA) assessments but also on thorough consideration of internal models, capital requirements of the SREP and the strategic use of Excess Capital, if any.

The three dimensions of the analysis, which are also of central importance in the digital transformation process and embedded in a broader assessment framework (a tool characterised by seven moves), will be further explored in the following chapters.

3 The supervision approach

> "There is nothing permanent except change"
> Heraclitus

3.1 The European regulatory framework

The supervisory approach to BMs should take into account the delicate balance between entrepreneurial freedom and the system of requirements defined by prudential supervision. **Figure 3.1** shows that the lessons learned since the 2008 crisis have tilted the balance more in favour of prudential requirements.

In this delicate balance, Directive (EU) 2019/878 of the European Parliament and of the Council of 20 May 2019, known as "CRD V"[1], refers to "the institution's busi-

Figure 3.1 **Constraints on entrepreneurial freedom**

Starting from 2008 global financial crisis...

Supervisory Requirement

Entrepreneur Freedom

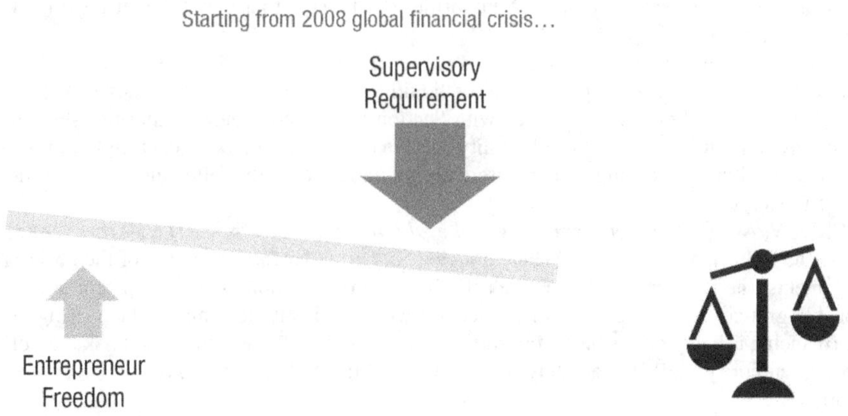

Source: Authors' elaboration.

---

[1] CRD V, transposed on 28 December 2020 by member states, amends Directive 2013/36/EU of the European Parliament and of the Council of 26 June 2013 on the access to the activity of credit institutions and the prudential supervision of credit institutions and investment firms (CRD

ness model"[2] without defining what is to be understood by BM from the perspective of European legislation, as was the case in the previous Directive (EU) 2013/36.

In particular, the term "BM" is used to:

1. Affirm the principle of proportionality, both in the organisational solutions of the supervised institutions and in the supervisory action on them[3];
2. Assess the adequacy of the financial leverage ratio of institutions[4];
3. Impose specific liquidity requirements[5];
4. Assess the institution's exposure to money laundering risk[6].

Regulation (EU) 2019/876 of the European Parliament and of the Council of 20 May 2019 (CRR II) with regard to the business model[7], in addition to confirming paragraphs 46 and 95 of the preamble of the previous regulation (EU) No 2013/575

IV), with regards to exempt institutions, financial holding companies, mixed financial holding companies, remuneration, supervisory measures and powers and capital conservation measures.

[2] CRD IV, Art. 98 (1)(i) *Technical criteria for the supervisory review and evaluation*, not amended by CRD V: "In addition to credit, market and operational risks, the review and evaluation performed by competent authorities pursuant to Article 97 shall include at least [...] the business model of the institution".

[3] CRD IV, Art. 74 (2) *Internal governance and recovery and resolution plans* amended by CRD V, Art. 1 (19)(2) as follows: "The arrangements, processes and mechanisms referred to in paragraph 1 of this Article shall be comprehensive and proportionate to the nature, scale and complexity of the risks inherent in the business model and the institution's activities".

[4] CRD IV, Art. 98 (6) *Technical criteria for the supervisory review and evaluation*, not amended by CRD V: "In determining the adequacy of the leverage ratio of institutions and of the arrangements, strategies, processes and mechanisms implemented by institutions to manage the risk of excessive leverage, competent authorities shall take into account the business model of those institutions".

[5] CRD IV, Art 105 (a) *Specific liquidity requirements* not amended by CRD V: "For the purposes of determining the appropriate level of liquidity requirements on the basis of the review and evaluation carried out in accordance with Section III, the competent authorities shall assess whether any imposition of a specific liquidity requirement is necessary to capture liquidity risks to which an institution is or might be exposed, taking into account the following: (a) the particular business model of the institution".

[6] CRD IV, Art. 97 *Supervisory review and evaluation* amended by CRD V, Art. 1 (28)(d) addending the following paragraph: "Where a review, in particular the evaluation of the governance arrangements, the business model, or the activities of an institution, gives competent authorities reasonable grounds to suspect that, in connection with that institution, money laundering or terrorist financing is being or has been committed or attempted, or there is increased risk thereof, the competent authority shall immediately notify EBA and the authority or body that supervises the institution".

[7] CRR II, transposed on 28 June 2021 by member states, amends Regulation (EU) No. 575/2013 on prudential requirements for credit institutions and investment firms (CRR), as regards leverage ratio, net stable funding ratio, own funds and eligible liability requirements, counterparty risk, market risk, exposures to central counterparties, exposures to collective investment bodies, large exposures, reporting and disclosure requirements and Regulation (EU) No. 648/2012 of the European Parliament and of the Council of 4 July 2012 on OTC derivatives, central counterparties and trade repositories.

3 The supervision approach

Figure 3.2   BM in the CRR II and CRD V

Art. 98 CRD V *Technical criteria for the supervisory review and evaluation*
1. In addition to credit, market and operational risks, the review and evaluation performed by competent authorities pursuant to Article 97 shall include at least: (....)
(i) the **business model** of the institution;

More in general in the CRR II and CRD V the business model is mentioned with reference to:

Proportionality (Art. 74 CRD V, point 2, and CRR II Preamble no. 46)	*The arrangements, processes and mechanisms referred to in paragraph 1 shall be comprehensive and proportionate to the **nature, scale and complexity** of the risks inherent in the business model and the institution's activities*
Supervisory review and evaluation (Art. 97 CRD V, point 6)	*Where a review (...) of the business model gives competent authorities reasonable grounds to suspect that, in connection with that institution, money laundering or terrorist financing is being or has been committed or attempted, or there is increased risk thereof, the competent authority shall immediately notify EBA and the authority or body that supervises the institution*
Leverage ratio (Art. 98 CRD V, point 6, and CRR II Preamble no. 95)	*When reviewing the impact of the leverage ratio on different business models, particular attention should be paid to business models. (...) EBA should in cooperation with competent authorities develop a classification of business models and risks*
Specific liquidity requirements (Art. 105 CRD IV)	*The competent authorities shall assess whether any imposition of a specific liquidity requirement is necessary to capture liquidity risks to which an institution is or might be exposed, taking into account the following:* *(a) the particular business model of the institution*

Source: Authors' elaboration.

(CRR) on proportionality and financial leverage[8,9], also introduces the implementation by the EBA of an electronic tool called the "compliance tool"[10]. This is aimed at

---

[8] CRR Preamble (46) not amended by CRR II: "Member States should ensure that the requirements [...] apply in a manner proportionate to the nature, scale and complexity of the risks associated with an institution's business model and activities".

[9] CRR Preamble (95) not amended by CRR II: "When reviewing the impact of the leverage ratio on different business models, particular attention should be paid to business models which are considered to entail low risk [...]. EBA [...] should in cooperation with competent authorities develop a classification of business models and risks [...] should be an assessment of the appropriate levels of the leverage ratio that safeguard the resilience of the respective business models and whether the levels of the leverage ratio should be set as thresholds or ranges [...] After adoption of the leverage ratio requirements, EBA should publish an appropriate statistical review, including averages and standard deviations, of the leverage ratio in relation to the identified categories of institutions".

[10] Established in 2011 by Regulation (EU) No. 1093/2010 of the European Parliament and of the Council of 24 November 2010.

guiding institutions through the relevant provisions, rules, guidelines and models in relation to their size and BM. The regulatory points that take up the BM concept are summarised in Figure 3.2[11].

Directive (EU) 2019/879 (BRRD II)[12] of the European Parliament and of the Council of 20 May 2019 reaffirms the principle of proportionality of resolution measures on the basis of the "BM" established by the previous Directive (EU) 2014/59 (BRRD[13]) under the harmonised regime for bank crisis management[14]. As is known, this regime is designed to ensure that failure can be managed in a timely manner to safeguard the continuity of the essential functions of institutions.

Furthermore, the BRRD II, in the early intervention measures, reiterates the possibility of "requiring changes in the business strategy of the institution"[15].

Finally, on the subject of (minimum requirement for own funds and eligible liabilities)[16], the BRRD II renews the "size, business model, financing model and risk profile of the institution" as one of the criteria on the basis of which the Resolution Authority should determine the minimum requirement of own funds and eligible liabilities of each institution subject to resolution[17].

---

[11] CRR II Preamble (68): "In order to facilitate institutions' compliance with the rules set out in this Regulation and in Directive 2013/36/EU, as well as with regulatory technical standards, implementing technical standards, guidelines and templates adopted to implement those rules, EBA should develop an IT tool aimed at guiding institutions through the relevant provisions, standards, guidelines and templates in relation to their size and business model". Moreover, according to the CRR II Art. 1 (144) in Part Ten, the following title is inserted, Title IIA "Implementation of rules" and the following Art. 519 (c) "Compliance tool". In particular, the paragraph (2)(a) of this article "The tool referred to in paragraph 1 shall at least enable each institution to: a) rapidly identify the relevant provisions to comply with in relation to the institution's size and business model".

[12] BRRD II, which entered into force on 27 June 2019, amends the BRRD with respect to the loss absorbency and recapitalisation capacity of credit institutions and investment firms.

[13] Directive 2014/59/EU of the European Parliament and of the Council of 15 May 2014, establishes a framework for the recovery and resolution of credit institutions and investment firms and amends Council Directive 82/891/EEC, and Directives 2001/24/EC, 2002/47/EC, 2004/25/EC, 2005/56/EC, 2007/36/EC, 2011/35/EU, 2012/30/EU and 2013/36/EU and Regulations (EU) No 1093/2010 and (EU) No 648/2012, of the European Parliament and of the Council.

[14] BRRD II Art. 18 (2) *Powers to address or remove impediments to resolvability: group treatment*: "The report shall consider the impact on the group's business model and recommend any proportionate and targeted measures that, in the view of the group-level resolution authority, are necessary or appropriate to remove those impediments". Moreover, BRRD II Preamble (12) requires "For specific top-tier banks, resolution authorities should, [...] limit the level of the minimum subordination requirement to a certain threshold, taking also into account the possible risk of disproportionately impacting the business model of those institutions".

[15] BRRD, Art. 27 (1)(f) *Early intervention measures*: "Where an institution infringes or, due, inter alia, to a rapidly deteriorating financial condition, including deteriorating liquidity situation, increasing level of leverage, non-performing loans or concentration of exposures, [...] Member States shall ensure that competent authorities have at their disposal [...] require changes to the institution's business strategy".

[16] The MREL is a requirement introduced by the BRRD, whose objective is to ensure the proper functioning of the bail-in mechanism by increasing the bank's loss-absorbing capacity.

[17] BRRD II, Art. 45b (9)(e) *Eligible liabilities for resolution entities*: "When taking those de-

Figure 3.3   **BM in the BRRD II**

Art. 27 BRRD II *Early intervention measures*

1. Where an institution infringes or, due, inter alia, to a rapidly deteriorating financial condition, including deteriorating liquidity situation, increasing level of leverage, non-performing loans or concentration of exposures, (…) is likely in the near future to infringe the requirements of Regulation (….) competent authorities have at their disposal (…) at least the following measures (…):

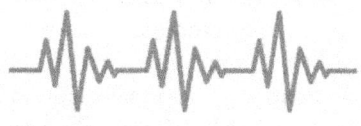

f) require **changes to the institution's business strategy**

Art. 45c BRRD II *Determination of the minimum requirement for own funds and eligible liabilities*

1. The requirement referred to in Article 45(1) shall be determined by the resolution authority, after consulting the competent authority, on the basis of the following criteria (…):

d) the size, **the business model, the funding model** and the risk profile of the entity.

Source: Authors' elaboration.

3.2   The European supervisory approach

The supervision of banks in the area of BMA has been integrated into the broader annual review and prudential evaluation process (i.e. SREP)[18]: *"same business, same risk, same supervision. Necessity to ensure consistent application of high supervisory standards for all banks under SSM"*[19].

In order to ensure high and consistent supervisory standards under the single su-

---

cisions, the resolution authority shall also take into account […] the resolution entity's business model, funding model, and risk profile, as well as its stability and ability to contribute to the economy". BRRD II, Art. 45c (1)(d) *Determination of the minimum requirement for own funds and eligible liabilities*: "The requirement referred to in Article 45(1) shall be determined by the resolution authority […] on the basis of the following criteria […] the size, the business model, the funding model and the risk profile of the entity".

[18] The concept of SREP was first introduced in June 2004 with the Basel II Accords defined by the Basel Committee on Banking Supervision. Updated rules were implemented in 2006 across the EU and have since been adhered to by national supervisors. The general criteria and methodologies used by the Bank of Italy, in line with European regulations, in the prudential review and assessment process, are described in Circular 269 of 7 May 2008 "Guidance for supervisory activities".

[19] www.ecb.europa.eu.

pervisory mechanism (SSM), since 2014 all national central banks adhere to the joint supervisory standards and the supervisory review programme[20], which contains the strategic and operational planning objectives of supervisory activity[21]. Within this framework, the BM and determinants of profitability have been included as supervisory priorities to promote a harmonised approach, thereby enhancing the efficiency of the supervisory process.

But why is it important for the ECB to analyse the BM of banks[22]? And why is it associated with digital transformation today? There are certainly several reasons for this. First and foremost, euro area banks are characterised by a high degree of diversity in their BMs. It is therefore necessary for supervisors to understand this diversity and its implications for a proper risk-based and proportional approach (**Figure 3.4**).

Second, the BMA becomes crucial in safeguarding the stability of the European banking system as well as the public interest.

The ECB's approach to analysing BMs focuses on key vulnerabilities and the sustainability of strategic plans over time. In this sense, the BMA is the first pillar of the SREP (**Figure 3.5**).

Figure 3.4 **Why do supervisors analyse BMs?**

| Business model analysis is a supervisory priority up to 2025 and an integral part of the annual Supervisory Review and Evaluation Process (SREP) | | New threat/challenge for MBA: Fintech, ESG factors, post COVID-19 |

Source: Authors' elaboration.

---

[20] The legal basis for the operational arrangements relating to the prudential tasks of the SSM is essentially Council Regulation (EU) No 2013/1024 of 15 October 2013, establishing the SSM composed of the ECB and the national competent authorities (NCAs or National Central Authorities) of participating member states (SSM Regulation) and Regulation (EU) No. 2014/468 of the ECB of 16 April 2014 establishing the framework for cooperation within the SSM between the ECB and the NCAs and with the designated national authorities (SSM Framework Regulation ECB/2014/17). The ECB directly supervises all institutions classified as significant on the basis of the criteria included in the two above-mentioned regulations (around 120 groups representing approximately 1200 supervised entities) with the assistance of the NCAs. NCAs continue to conduct direct supervision of less significant institutions (approximately 3700 entities) under the supervision of the ECB. The ECB may also assume direct supervision of less significant institutions when necessary to ensure the consistent application of high supervisory standards. The main purposes of the SSM are: (i) to safeguard the safety and soundness of the European banking system; (ii) to enhance financial integration and stability; and (iii) to ensure consistent supervision.

[21] Strategic planning involves setting supervisory priorities for the next twelve to eighteen months but also significant activities envisaged over a three-year period.

[22] Some of the considerations expressed come from the "Panel II: sustainable business model for bank's today" held at the ECB on 7 November 2017 and available on the ECB_SSM YouTube channel.

3 The supervision approach

Figure 3.5 **The link between BMA and additional own fund requirements (Art. 104 CRD V supervisory powers)**

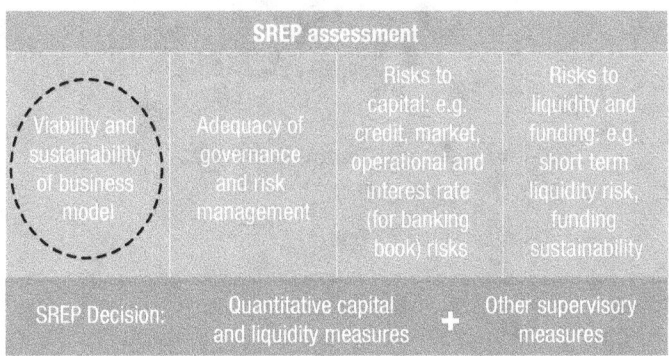

Source: Authors' elaboration on SSM Supervisory Manual - published version.

The focus on BMA is therefore one of the most significant innovations in the "SSM approach to SREP", whose procedures and methodologies are described in the "EBA Guideline on common procedures and methodologies for the supervisory review and evaluation process".

The BMA therefore takes on the crucial role of being the starting point of the SREP in order to holistically understand the sources of the main risks and those of capital generation that are components of the minimum capital requirements.

In full compliance with entrepreneurial freedom, the competent authorities conduct regular analyses of the BM in order to assess the operational and strategic risks, as well as the viability of the BM, based on its ability to generate acceptable profits over the next twelve months and the sustainability of the institution's strategy, based on its ability to generate acceptable profits over a time horizon of at least three years, according to its strategic plans and financial forecasts. Investors tend to be concerned with whether returns are acceptable when compared with the cost of equity. From a supervisory perspective, it is more important that the returns follow on from an appropriate funding and capital structure and a suitable risk appetite through a full business and economic cycle.

Such analyses are preparatory to the assessment of the level of BM risk exposure in the European banking system. The BM risk can result from both internal factors (e.g. reliance on an unrealistic strategy, excessive risk concentrations, poor funding and capital structures or insufficient execution capabilities) and external factors (e.g. a challenging economic environment).

In other words, the BM supervisor is called upon to assess the entrepreneurial viability of the institution and its sustainability over time by understanding its risks, leveraging three intrinsically linked dimensions: strategies, backward-looking and forward-looking analysis of profitability drivers (**Figure 3.6**).

Figure 3.6   **Dimensions of analysis**

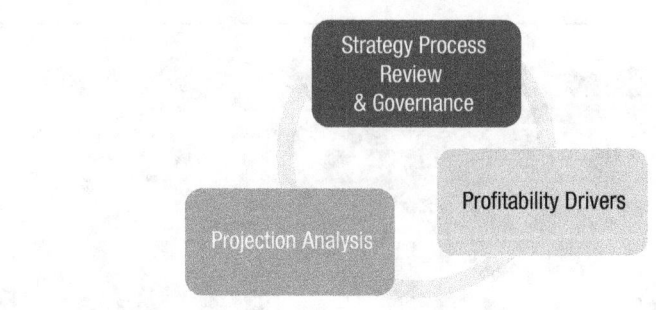

Source: Authors' elaboration

In this context, the Internal Capital Adequacy Assessment Process (ICAAP) and the Internal Liquidity Adequacy Assessment Process (ILAAP), governed by the "EBA Guideline on ICAAP and ILAAP information", are also of crucial importance, requiring a multi-year forward-looking approach on BMs and strategy, a strong integration between BM and Risk Appetite Framework (RAF, see par. 4.4.) and a cost-benefit allocation of liquidity[23].

More generally, correctly measuring cost absorption and revenue generation means improving the monitoring of overall performance and providing substantial support for business decisions, thus representing an effective driver for the production of competitive advantage.

And here we return to the synallagma BM and digital transformation. The supervisors' objective of intercepting the entrepreneurial vitality and sustainability of banks and the banking system remains firm, but digital transformation requires a rethinking of analysis methods.

In this vein, a speech in April 2022 by the Deputy Governor of the Bank of Italy, Dr Piero Cipollone, addressing the opportunities and risks of digital platforms compared with traditional ones, pointed out that "supervision or supervisory schemes based on the old paradigms, which postulate responsibilities clearly ascribable to specific entities and subjects, risk failing to grasp in their entirety the elements of interconnection and interdependence between the subjects themselves, interconnections and interdependences that are the founding features of the new ecosystems.

It is therefore necessary to start developing models based on a 'scheme' logic, so

---

[23] The RAF is a management tool through which the bank clarifies and monitors its risk-return profile over time, declaring the maximum degree of risk it intends to assume. The RAF should indicate: i) the types of risk the bank intends to take on; ii) for each type, it sets risk targets, tolerance thresholds (if any) and operating limits under both normal and stress conditions; iii) the circumstances, including the outcome of stress scenarios, under which the assumption of certain categories of risk should be avoided or limited in relation to the targets and limits set. The BoD approves the primary indicators and related thresholds (risk capacity, tolerance and appetite).

as to consider not only the 'operators/intermediaries' dimension, but also the technological factor as the key to understanding the relationships between subjects, infrastructures, tools, services and smart contracts".

3.3 The main changes impacting BM in the pre-pandemic context

In the pre-Covid-19 context, a proper reshaping of the BM had to take into account the continuing macroeconomic environment of low/negative rates, increased competition (e.g. fintech) and stricter regulation (e.g. MREL, calendar provisioning).

The BM found in the Italian banking system, with due specificity, was focused on the traditional type of intermediation for the purpose of greater diversification of business and distribution channels. In some medium-sized companies, the strategic model had changed, or was changing, from the so-called "federal" model to one with a higher level of integration.

After the interventions on distressed banks, the European banking system presented itself with adequate fundamentals (capital and liquidity) but with profitability to recover and a major critical issue represented by the stock of doubtful loans[24].

In recent years, Italian banks have been disposing of NPLs, bringing their incidence to levels lower than pre-crisis 2007–2008; as of 30 June 2022, gross NPLs accounted for 1.2% of loans (0.5% net of adjustments).

In this context, the changeover to the new international accounting standard IFRS 9 required intermediaries to make a considerable adapting effort to face the impacts deriving from the fully phased[25]. It was necessary to define credit policies and processes to govern the disbursement and monitoring of credit that were also consistent with the choices of the "hold to collect" BM, which envisaged holding until maturity. Banks also had to assess the impact of rating attribution and credit monitoring methodologies on the definition of credit policies.

---

[24] In his speech at the 24th ASSIOM - FOREX Congress on 10 February 2018, Governor of the Bank of Italy I. Visco highlights that "a profound revision of banks' operating models, in Italy as in the whole of Europe, remains inevitable. Important elements that could curb profitability should not be underestimated. The dynamics of adjustments may be affected both by regulatory interventions and by possible major provisions related to disposal operations. Competition in the asset management market is set to increase, as is the scale required to operate profitably. Banks' costs, which are still burdened by high personnel expenses, will be affected by the necessary investments in new digital technologies, which have so far been limited. In addition, the introduction of new European rules – on loss-absorbing liabilities in the event of a crisis and on the provision of investment and payment services – will tend to increase the cost of wholesale funding, competition for some services, compliance charges and those associated with the need to ensure full customer protection".

[25] Examples are the efforts related to the adaptation of the information and management systems, the adaptation of the information set, the creation of moments of connection between the different internal accounting and risk management structures in order to optimise the risk measurement and control systems.

Regulatory changes have often required banks to make additional compliance efforts that have inevitably impacted their BMs. MIFID II[26], for example, introduced important changes in the European financial market in order to reduce the level of conflict of interest between banks and investors, thus strengthening the level of investor protection and the transparency and competitiveness of operators. Here, too, corporate choices have had an impact on business. For example, having to represent an "overall cost", the distributor had to decide which product to focus on (managed vs. administered; active instruments with a high management content vs. passive instruments). The emphasis on the factory cost element led to a choice for intermediaries to internalise or externalise factory costs/revenues. Banks have had to implement systems capable of calculating the *ex post* cost for individual clients of collective investment instruments. In the same asset management schemes, the focus during the period was on the first-level costs of the management mandate, on the trading of individual instruments and on performance fees.

The previous edition highlighted five common strategic processes adopted by banks since 2015 aimed at recovering profitability and noted that the corrective actions identified to improve profitability had led in several cases to the simplification of the organisational model,[27] the reshaping of the territorial presence, the creation of "asset enhancement" units and special purpose vehicles for NPLs, the deleveraging of assets, the downsizing of personnel costs, a generalised spending review and the relaunching of indirect deposits and specialised segments.

The real strategic challenge today is digital transformation: in 2016, a study carried out by McKinsey highlighted that the digitalisation process has direct effects on the banking system's profits, not only because of the entry of new competitors into the system but because it forces the bank itself to redesign its BM[28]. Digital is therefore no longer an option for the financial industry but a necessity for business sustainability in the medium to long term.

It has been observed by various market participants that the impacts of fintech on the BM follow a kind of fil rouge due to the evolution of the business relationship with customers. Until the early 1990s, bank-customer relationships were based on the intermediation between counter operators and customers. Subsequently, the development of multichannelling allowed manual access by operators through a technological interface developed ad hoc by intermediaries. Since 2010, the emergence of the first fintechs has rapidly changed this pattern: the rapid digital transformation and the increasing use of technologies such as AI and Big Data have enabled banks

---

[26] As of 3 January 2018, the new MiFID II Directive (2014/65/EU) entered into force across the EU, with impacts on the advisory service (art. 24), suitability assessment (art. 25 and art. 54 of the delegated regulation), product governance (art. 16 and 24) and client disclosure (art. 24 and art. 50 of the delegated regulation).

[27] Capital strengthening and capital management, revision of the distribution model, selective resumption of lending, revision of credit processes/policies, structure efficiency and cost containment.

[28] https://www.mckinsey.com

to improve the quality of their services. Indeed, international studies showed that the amount of data exchanged internationally in 2018 was at least forty-five times higher than in 2005, while the cost of storing data was ten times lower than in 2010.

The first steps of digital transformation

Before the pandemic, the most significant developments in fintech were in the payments system and they had quickly spread to other sectors, primarily credit[29], but also securities trading, risk management and compliance (Regtech).

A Bank of Italy survey published in 2018 showed that domestic intermediaries were engaged in a significant number of initiatives; however, the value of investments was modest, falling below that of other major EU countries.

According to an analysis conducted in 2018 by ABI Lab[30], more than half of Italian banks were engaged in the development of innovative projects in the payments sector, followed by security issues (more than 35% of banks) and investment and lending platforms (more than 20%).

According to the Bank of Italy's February 2019 report[31], "banking operators (incumbents), aware of the need to adapt to the changed market environment, are responding with different strategies and intensity. There is a tendency on the part of these players to develop 'platform services', which involve the integrated management of banking processes and services open to several operators in a multichannel perspective. This is a phenomenon already experienced in other sectors, first and foremost the telecommunications sector: in this market – also due to the liberalisation of the so-called 'last mile' – there has been a progressive and uninterrupted development of infrastructure services which have completely changed the previous competitive paradigms".

The paper pointed out that, in some cases, acquisitions or alliances between banking intermediaries and fintech firms had resulted in the integration of physical and virtual channels. In other cases, pure digital banks with no branch network and extremely low cost structures were created. In terms of technologies tested, more than a third were active in big data analytics, blockchain, distributed ledger technology (DLT) and AI; a quarter favoured cloud computing initiatives and the digitisation of traditional services. According to Politecnico di Milano's FinTech & Digital Finance

---

[29] Speech by C. Barbagallo, Head of the Banking and Financial Supervision Department of the Bank of Italy until 1 July 2019, to the Association of Lecturers in the Economics of Financial Market Intermediaries and Corporate Finance – Winter Conference "FinTech: Role of the Supervisory Authority in a Changing Market", 8 February 2019: "In the Global Monitoring Report on Non-Bank Financial Intermediation 2018, Financial Stability Board of 4 February 2019 gives an account of the development in recent years of FinTech lending, which has grown rapidly around the world although its size varies considerably across economies. The differences reflect economic developments and the structure of financial markets: the higher a country's income and the less competitive its banking system, the greater the FinTech credit activity".

[30] www.abilab.it

[31] See intervention in footnote 29.

Observatory[32], during 2017, 16% of Italians had used at least one fintech service and 56% of bank customers accessed their institution's services from PCs, tablets and smartphones.

As Fabio Panetta observed in 2018, "I do not expect fintechs to replace banks. The value chain of banks includes bundled services such as deposits, payments and loans. Fintechs generally perform one or more of these activities in an unbundled manner. However, bundling offers powerful economies of scope. If fintechs wish to expand their activities to take advantage of these economies of scope, then they will probably have to transform into banks"[33].

In 2018, the former Deputy Governor of the Bank of Italy Salvatore Rossi observed that "the transfer of information that this implies highlights a fundamental difference compared to other productive sectors, such as manufacturing: a car engine factory can have a component made by a supplier, even a technologically very sophisticated one, without revealing almost anything about the complete design of the engine. A bank, whose business is based on the processing of information, is today forced in the payments market to open its black box of data".

However, the Bank of Italy Governor's final considerations in 2019 highlighted that the spread of the digital economy in Italy was slower than in the main European countries. Several factors contributed to this delay, including the fragmentation of the production system and the low degree of digitalisation of public services.

In discussing the evolution of the market, Banca d'Italia illustrated in 2019 that "the term Fintech refers to numerous business segments (including digital payments and currencies, crowdfunding, peer-to-peer lending) as well as heterogeneous techniques and tools (among others, robot advisers, big data, AI). These are very heterogeneous realities, but with one trait in common, represented by the high use of technology, streamlined procedures, a minimal or non-existent network of branches, and a small but highly specialised workforce. These actors have exploited the 'unbundling' of banking services by focusing on specific segments (payments, loans, investments) to capture market share, thanks also to the possibility of practising very aggressive pricing policies"[34].

In a speech at the University of Genoa in January 2020, Deputy Governor of the Bank of Italy, A. Perrazzelli, also highlighted the need for a reconfiguration of the bank-customer relationship model, the need for immediacy, simplicity and accessibility that should guide the choices of purchase and use of banking services and techniques based on AI for AML purposes and for the credit assessment of more opaque subjects (start-ups or small businesses)[35].

---

[32] www.som.polimi.it

[33] The former Deputy Governor of the Bank of Italy defined fintech as any application of digital technologies to finance. In the world of credit, crowd-funding, peer-to-peer lending, automated scoring; in the world of payment services, instant payments; in the world of financial advisory services, robo-advisers.

[34] See intervention in footnote 29.

[35] *Lectio magistralis* "Fintech, risks and opportunities for young future bank managers" held

3.4 Digital transfomation in the post-pandemic context

In the post-pandemic context, as the NPL alarm has subsided, particularly in the Italian market[36], business plans show the lowest common denominator that is substantiated by the need to adopt BMs based on different entrepreneurial schemes marked by digital transformation. Empirical analysis in the field, however, has shown that despite declarations of principle, every initiative in a world as articulated as that of banking companies collides with a system of significant complexity.

Banking groups have stated that they are increasingly focused on sustainable income generation, seeking to overcome structural challenges such as low cost efficiency, limited revenue diversification and, in some jurisdictions, high stocks of legacy assets. However, balancing risk management and performance strategies is always a recipe that requires boards to make an informed choice between the incremental approach and starting from scratch (Figure 3.7).

As a matter of fact, in the current post-pandemic environment, banks' BMs are evolving along three different lines:

1. Bank as fintech (the bank embraces new technologies and competes directly as fintech).
2. Platform bank (the bank integrates its own or third-party fintechs while maintaining its privileged access to the customer).
3. Bank as provider of fintechs (the bank becomes a service provider for the fintechs which control the relationship with the customer).

Figure 3.7 **The manager's dilemma**

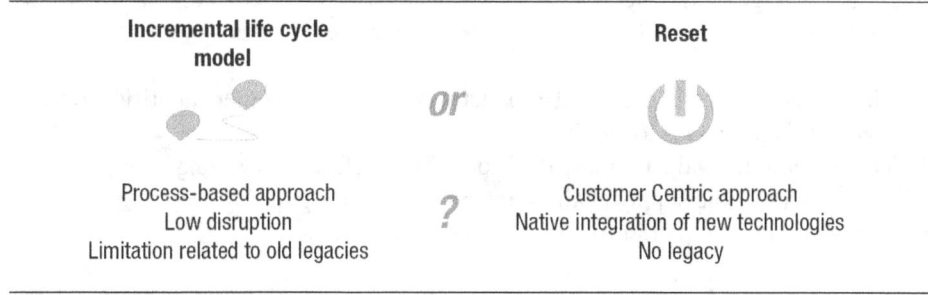

Source: Authors' elaboration.

---

by the VDG of the Bank of Italy A. Perrazzelli at the Aula Magna of the University of Genoa, 24 January 2020.

[36] The Bank of Italy's "Notes on Financial Stability and Supervision" in the note "Recovery Rates of Non-performing Loans in 2021" shows that in 2021, NPLs amounting to approximately €17 billion were closed (eliminated from the balance sheets). According to a Banca IFIS report dedicated to the NPLs market, the average NPE ratio of Italian institutions stands at 3.5% and estimates of NPL flows in the 2023/2024 period would stand at €56 billion, lower than in previous years.

Looking at bank balance sheets, it emerges that digitalisation is already impacting on the performance of commercial banks where a cost reduction path can be observed due to a higher degree of automation and a certain shift of revenues towards operators that are more efficiently and effectively able to meet customers' needs.

What analysts observe is the increased integration of digital and physical (phygital) channels along two major lines. On the one hand, the optimisation of the back end, to allow flexibility in the composition of the product and service offering. On the other hand, the restructuring of a front end, which offers basic products, such as a payment account, within the customer's shopping experience (e.g. for obtaining a good or service) and instead offers value-added financial services (e.g. advisory services) within the financial value chain.

At the centre remains the customer around whom banks are developing customer experience analysis techniques in order to better understand their needs. Research by EY highlights the need for banks to review their processes and act as start-ups with a customer focus and faster product and service launches[37].

> **Focus: digitisation projects**
>
> Among the various digitisation projects pursued by European banking institutions, the EBA has identified two main trends: (i) digital transformation and (ii) "digital disruption". The former involves an overhaul of internal processes and aims to digitise and optimise processes as much as possible. "Digital disruption" represents a radical change of the traditional banking market in its current form, and moves towards the creation of a new market enabled by the use of innovative technologies, including new ways of interaction aimed at improving the customer experience[38].

Analysts converge on the fact that new digital technologies (cloud computing, AI, big data analytics, internet of things) offer three main major benefits (**Figure 3.8**):

1. The increase in efficiency and productivity (e.g. in customer identification and verification processes for AML);
2. The increase in evaluation and decision-making effectiveness (e.g. mapping relationships along the supply chain to intercept tension signals);
3. The widening of the offer to new products and services.

Looking at the evolutionary processes within banking organisations, it has also been observed that while in the past innovation in banks took place only through input from internal processes, in today's banking enterprises "innovation" is not only mutated by endogenous drives but also by external drives and the emergence of new market trends (**Figure 3.9**).

---

[37] EY, Report on Covid-19 Banking challenges and the New Normal, May 2020.
[38] EBA, *Report on the Impact of FinTech on incumbent Credit Institutions' Business Models*, 3 July 2018.

3 The supervision approach

Figure 3.8 **The benefits of digital transformation on the BM**

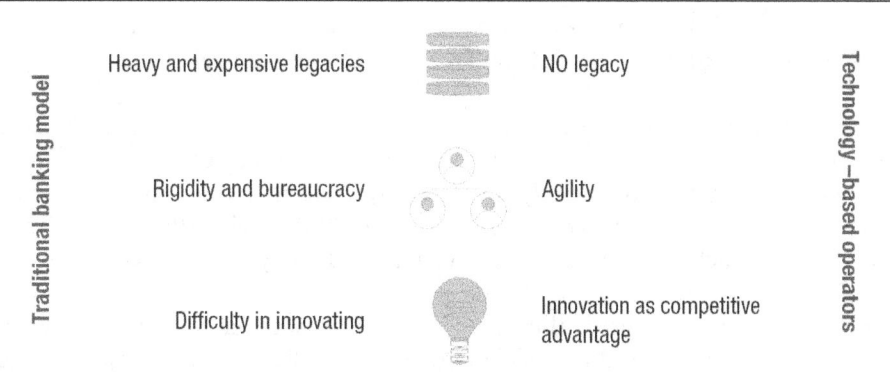

Source: Authors' elaboration.

Figure 3.9 **The evolutionary process of innovation**

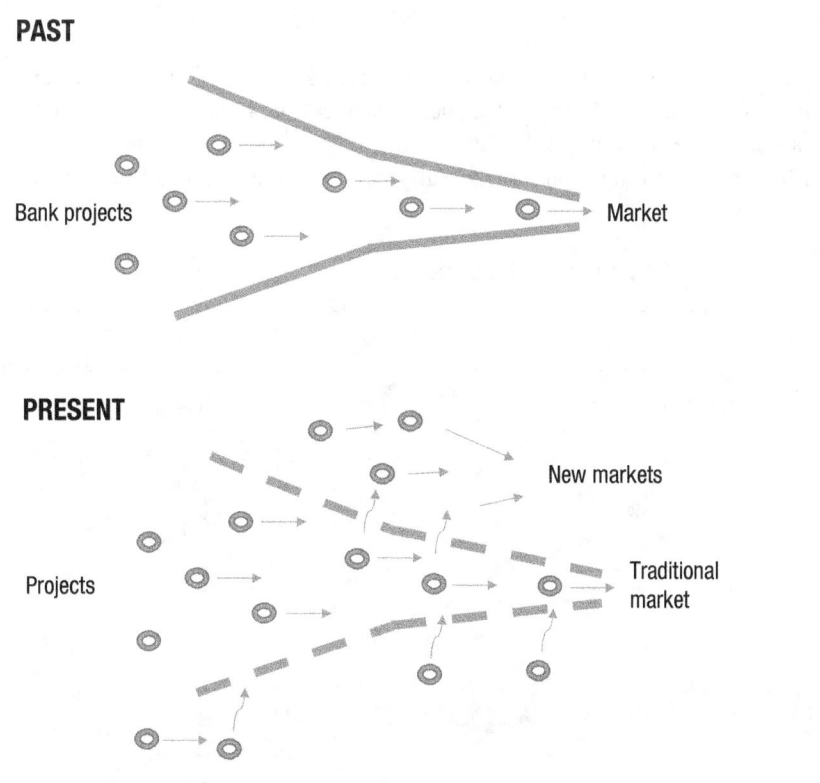

Source: Authors' elaboration.

Returning to the thread of the previous paragraph, customer relationship modes have changed: the time spent by consumers on mobile devices is definitively higher than that spent on desktops. Regulatory developments have also contributed to this, in particular the European PSD2 directive, which has allowed new operators to enter the market.

In the payments sector, for competition reasons it requires banks to let so-called payment initiation service providers (PISP), new companies that initiate payment for an e-commerce transaction directly from the buyer's bank account rather than via a credit card, access their customers' accounts. The PISP provides the user with software through which the user can initiate a payment directly from his own account to that of another user (Figure 3.10).

In addition to the PISPs within the scope of the so-called third-party payment providers, account information service providers (AISPs) and card issuer service providers (CISPs) intervene as players. AISPs provide an online information service with regard to one or more payment accounts held by the payment service user with another payment service provider or with several payment service providers. CISPs are payment service providers that issue card-based payment instruments. They are entitled to immediate confirmation from the account issuer that the amount required for the execution of a card-based payment transaction is available in the payer's account. There must, of course, be the explicit consent of the payer to respond to such a request.

It should be remembered that in 2018 the then Head of the Department of Supervision of the Bank of Italy, Dr Carmelo Barbagallo, already observed that: "the basic idea is that the most valuable element of the production chain is constituted by 'data': the ability to read them horizontally becomes the true added value of the digital

Figure 3.10 **The path of cashless payments**

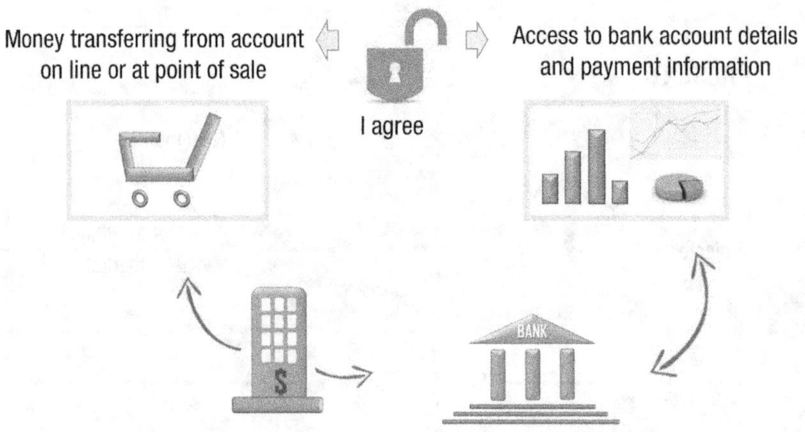

Source: Authors' elaboration.

economy; the 'payment account system' itself rises to the role of 'essential infrastructure' *sui generis*, with significant impacts on the system of relationships that binds the operators. It is of paramount importance that banks quickly decide what role they intend to assume in the digital financial services sector in order to effectively address a revolution that is already underway in foreign markets and that is destined to profoundly change the domestic one as well."

In 2020 in the midst of the pandemic the VDG of the Bank of Italy Alessandra Perrazzelli said "a demand for innovative financial services is also emerging from companies, which are increasingly directing their demand for services (payment, financing) towards solutions that are able to combine convenience, speed and transparency. Traditional intermediaries are trying to adapt the range of services offered to the new expectations of companies by collaborating or competing with new players entering the market. In the US, a technology giant has launched in partnership with a bank a short-term lending platform for businesses that makes speed of credit risk assessment and disbursement its strong point.

In Italy, the offer of online loans is still limited; only one in twenty banks provides such a service".

However, it should be kept in mind that fintech companies start from a different point than traditional banks as they do not have, for the time being and in any case to a lesser extent, organisational, process, distribution and regulatory costs[39].

VDG Alessandra Perrazzelli made the point that "the digital revolution, by disrupting the schemes traditionally used by intermediaries to offer financial services, is changing the market structure and forcing operators to substantially rethink their models and strategies. Fully digital banks are emerging, able to serve large market shares with much lower costs than traditional intermediaries. Fintech operators expand their offerings from payment services to asset management services. Multinationals in the technology sector (BigTech) have been offering financial services on their own platforms instantaneously worldwide to billions of people for several years now.

The activities of the BigTech companies exploit new synergies between traditional financial services (such as payment, credit and insurance services) and those of a commercial nature, through a process of unbundling and re-bundling that radically changes competitive scenarios. Technological innovation is also having major effects on the configuration of distribution channels. Between 2017 and 2021, the number of active branches in the country decreased by about 21%, with 5700 branches closed[40].

The availability of digital channels means that the reduction in the number of physical points of contact with the customer no longer, unlike in the past, leads to

---

[39] Back in 2018, ECB board member Fabio Panetta pointed out that "competition from fintech firms is beginning to erode the margins of the traditional banking sector. It is estimated that over the next ten years, as fintech firms expand into all market segments, they could erode 60% of the profits that banks generate from retail services."

[40] Bank of Italy Statistics Series - Payment System, September 2022 TSP Table AG010.

losses in market share, at least as far as deposit accounts are concerned. Instead, the gains in terms of operating costs are potentially very high."

With a view to development and adaptability to change, it has been observed that the new BM seems to reward time to market so that the bank, understood as an organisation, can adapt in all respects to changes that may occur in the market.

The survey on IT in the Italian banking sector conducted by the Interbanking Convention for Automation (CIPA) in 2021 on a sample of twenty-one national banking groups – representing 93.4% of the Italian banking industry – showed a steady increase in total cost of ownership (TCO) since 2007 (up 18%, of which 9% compared to 2020)[41]. In particular, the areas most impacted by investments were in this order:

- Adaptive and corrective as well as evolutionary maintenance of applications, peripheral systems (ATM, POS etc.);
- IT security;
- Data centres (mainframes and server farms).

With reference to the technologies used, the survey showed that in payment, banking and financial services, as well as in credit, the main technologies used were Open APIs and AI, followed by DLT-Blochain and RPA (**Figure 3.11**).

Figure 3.11 **Banking system evolution: from twentieth to twenty-first century**

20th century	21st century
Hierarchical, closed and slow	**Cooperative, open and fast**
Card as product	Data as product
Physical (premises and people)	Digital (software and experience)
Proprietary technology	No proprietary technology
Regulation as barrier	Regulation as facilitator
High capital intensity	Low capital intensity

Source: Authors' elaboration.

---

[41] The total cost of ownership represents the total cost of owning technology in a company. It is an approach developed by Gartner in 1987, used to calculate all life-cycle costs of IT equipment, for its purchase, installation, operation, maintenance and disposal (source: Wikipedia).

3 The supervision approach   47

3.5 The other side of the digital transformation coin: Risks and the authorities' response

As repeatedly emphasised by the supervisory authorities, innovation is not risk-free: the financial industry will therefore have to carefully take into account the emerging risks associated with digitalisation in the process of rethinking BMs, bearing in mind the fact that certain activities are not yet regulated. As the Head of the Banking Supervision Department G. Siani observed[42], "the new business paradigm introduced with DLT is based on three strongly interconnected but distinct dimensions. The first is technological, with the introduction of a distributed market infrastructure, enabling the transfer of value or rights, without a centralised trust authority. The second is in the way of digitally representing value, with the introduction of tokens that can be unbacked, such as Bitcoin, or digitally represent financial instruments or other assets (backed crypto assets). The third novelty is the market entry of new entities, which can also operate in a decentralised manner through special governance mechanisms. These three plans (technology, tokens, new actors) are also the basis of the so-called decentralised finance or DeFi. They can be analysed individually in a coherent and effective manner and thus favour the maintenance of traditional analysis perspectives by intermediary and/or product type. However, only an integrated assessment of them, which makes use of specialised skills and resources in different areas, can make it possible to monitor their risks."

The cyber risk

Banking institutions are continually attacked by hacker groups that break into bank systems and manage to steal thousands of email addresses. In general, intrusions into current accounts are rare because the systems that handle financial transactions are usually more robust. But data breaches confirm how actors in the financial world are a target for cyber criminals. In this context, over the years more or less all credit institutions have had to deal with cyber-intrusions and certain regulatory measures, such as strong customer authentication, that is the double verification that has become mandatory for movements on current accounts, are no coincidence. The entire financial system is always under fire and data from the October 2022 Clusit report confirms that cyber attacks on the finance/insurance sector in the first six months of 2022 increased by 76.7% compared with the same period last year[43].

Of the financial services organisations, 83% said they have cyber insurance coverage against ransomware but the most constant danger remains phishing, the classic decoy email that passes off hackers as the bank. It is the most popular gateway for "attackers".

This is the background to the EU Parliament's response with the launch of the

---

[42] Luiss University of Rome, 3 May 2022, *The regulation of new technologies based on DLT*.
[43] Italian Association for IT Security (www.clusit.it).

Dora Regulation, the Digital Operational Resilience Act, with the aim of securing fintech banks, insurance companies and crypto operators, which will have two years to adapt. In the digital finance package, in addition to Dora, the regulation of crypto asset markets (Mica, which, after an informal agreement, still remains pending in negotiations between EU institutions) and a proposal on DLT have been issued. The obligations of the new regulation will come into force within twenty-four months of publication so operators will have until December 2024 to prepare to meet the new requirements. The industry will actually have less than two years as draft regulatory technical standards (Rts) will have to be submitted within twelve months.

What must be emphasised is that, with the launch of Dora, there will be a common response by the entire European continent to equip itself for what is the real challenge of the future: cyber resilience, that is the ability to stop or react in a timely manner to cyber attacks that can also come from third states (sovereign attacks) and that can affect not only individual services, but also infrastructures. Dora promises therefore, according to operators, to be a real revolution, which will no longer allow the issue of digital resilience to be relegated to some corporate function, but will become a direct responsibility of top management.

The regulation lays down stricter cybersecurity requirements with regard to risk management, reporting obligations and information sharing. The requirements cover, among other things, incident response, supply chain security, encryption and vulnerability disclosure. Dora will impose a paradigm shift in the approach to digital and related risks, affecting the BM: the top management of all operators concerned will have to worry not only about financial sustainability, but also about "resilience", that is the ability to continue operating in the event of incidents or disruptive events caused by the digital domain. The advent of Dora will immediately require a commitment from companies and will open up new markets, because it will be necessary to provide companies with adequate solutions that meet the stringent requirements of Dora. Regulators themselves will have to start thinking in completely new terms and develop the digital skills needed to regulate the new reality.

On the Italian side, in relation to the growing sophistication and pervasiveness of the cyber threat to the financial sector, the Bank of Italy, the Italian National Commission for Companies and the Stock Exchange (Consob) and the Institute for the Supervision of Insurance (IVASS) have jointly adopted the TIBER-IT National Guide[44], as a reference methodology for individual financial entities to conduct advanced cybersecurity testing on a voluntary basis. Financial entities perform such tests, guided by cyber threat analysis, in a manner commensurate with their business and operational models and related risk scenarios. The aim is to strengthen the proactive defence capability of individual financial entities, enabling them to improve the cyber resilience of the financial system as a whole and, by doing so, its overall stability.

---

[44] The Guide basically constitutes the transposition of the Threat Intelligence-Based Ethical Red teaming framework (known as TIBER-EU), issued by the ECB, a reference model for conducting advanced cybersecurity tests harmonised at European level.

> **Legal rereference on cybersecurity**
> - Regulation (EU) 2022/2554 of the European Parliament and of the Council on digital operational resilience for the financial sector (DORA), 2022.
> - Directive (EU) 2022/2555 of the European Parliament and of the Council on measures for a high common level of cybersecurity across the Union (NIS2), 2022.
> - Directive (EU) 2022/2557 of the European Parliament and of the Council on the resilience of critical entities (CER), 2022.
> - FSB Achieving Greater Convergence in Cyber Incident Reporting, 2023.
> - EIOPA Supervisory Statement on Management of non-affirmative cyber exposures, EIOPA-BoS-22-414, 2022.
> - EIOPA Supervisory Statement on Exclusions in insurance products related to risks arising from systemic events, EIOPA-22/419, 2022.
> - G7 Fundamental elements for third-party cyber risk management in the financial sector, 2022.
> - G7 Fundamental elements of ransomware resilience for the financial sector, 2022.
> - Standard ISO/IEC 27001:2022 Information security, cybersecurity and privacy protection - Information security management systems – Requirements, 2022.

Crypto assets

With regard to the risks arising from crypto assets, a distinction must be made between the technology and the activities that use it: with regard to the latter, in October 2022 the Governor of the Bank of Italy recalled "the need to make a clear distinction between crypto assets issued against real or financial assets and those, on the contrary, with no intrinsic value".

In June 2022, the Bank of Italy sent a communication to all supervised entities, monitored operators within the payment system and technology service providers emphasising the need for adequate safeguards to mitigate the risks associated with the use of DLT ("Communication of the Bank of Italy on decentralised technologies in finance and crypto assets", June 2022). According to the Governor, "further clarity will be provided with the final approval of the European Union regulation on crypto-assets (Markets in Crypto-Assets regulation, MiCAR). Common rules for the issuance and public offering of these instruments and requirements for the provision of related services will promote user protection, integrity and stability of the financial system, while at the same time creating the conditions for the opportunities offered by technology to be seized in Europe as well. The regulation on a pilot regime for market infrastructures based on distributed ledgers (the so-called DLT pilot regime), published last June, will also allow the testing of new ways of issuing and circulating financial instruments under the supervision of Consob and Bank of Italy."

In the meantime, global cryptofinance has already highlighted its criticalities with the collapse in November 2022 of FTX, the fourth largest trading platform for cryptocurrencies such as Bitcoin or Ethereum, and the collapse of Silvergate Bank in March 2023, a Californian bank specialising in cryptocurrencies. But the stories of FTX and Silvergate add to the fact that in 2021/2022, traders estimated that the market value had collapsed and that the sector had started to be overwhelmed by a cascading crash since the spring of 2022[45]. Additionally, in 2014 the Japanese platform MtGox went bankrupt and the defrauded users have not yet received their refunds.

Buy Now Pay Later

One of the businesses that certain institutions adopt, indeed more so in the financial industry operating in digital markets rather than in traditional banks, is that of the buy now pay later (BNPL), which in its conventional form consists of a short-term loan of a limited amount, with which the consumer splits the payment of a purchase into a variable number of interest-free instalments. A Bank of Italy paper of November 2022 reveals the weakness of the existing regulatory framework[46], both in terms of contractual discipline and with reference to its authorisation regime, and in particular discusses the need to protect consumers from the unwitting accumulation of an excessive amount of debt. And it is precisely this concern from supervisors that should be taken into account by intermediaries, namely that this activity may, in the long run, encourage loans that cannot be repaid. BNPL is not a regulated sector and so far there are no protection clauses for consumers, who may find themselves encouraged, especially younger consumers (Gen Z and Gen X), to a kind of "moral hazard", that is to spend without worrying about their accumulated commitment.

Focus: Competition in BNPL payment services

With the pandemic, the BNPL market has experienced significant growth related to the need to install and defer even essential expenses, as well as the possibility of indulging in goods not immediately within one's reach in the knowledge that one does not need to have the necessary budget right away. This is an increasingly popular payment method for purchases referred to by operators as leisure, such as travel and consumer electronics. Some e-commerce players, such as Amazon and Apple, have proprietary services, but the bulk of the market is handled by specialised fintechs that act as intermediaries, so to speak, between the merchant and the consumer. BNPL services offer a convenient and fast payment service for small sizes: according to the Compass Observatory[47], the average value of purchases made with BNPL is approximately €100; not to mention that it is usually sufficient to register on a site that uses a particular BNPL solution in order to be able to access the same service on any other linked site, whether e-commerce or marketplace.

---

[45] Beginning with the failure of the Terra-Luna stablecoin and followed by the defaults of the Three Arrows Capital Singapore-based cryptocurrency hedge fund and cryptocurrency lender Celsius, one of the world's largest cryptocurrency deposit accounts.
[46] Economics and finance issues (occasional paper) Buy Now Pay Later, market characteristics and development prospects - November 2022 by Lorenzo Gobbi Bank of Italy Milan Branch.
[47] www.compass.it

3   The supervision approach   51

3.6   The approach to climate change: Outline

As is well known, the risks arising from climate change, loss of biodiversity, degradation of social conditions and the quality of business management – the so-called ESG risks that affect the actual and potential growth of the economy – should not be overlooked in BMA.

Globally, investors' attention to ESG factors has increased: based on the World Economic Forum's 2022 survey[48], environmental and sustainability profiles are among the most relevant risk categories, in terms of both probability and severity of potential impacts. The Global Sustainable Investment Alliance reported that, in 2020, sustainable financial investments, which constituted about 36% of global assets under management, had reached US$ 35.3 trillion, more than double the value in 2016[49]. It is therefore necessary to understand concretely what this is all about and then drop it into the analysis of the BM.

In May 2022, the Bank of Italy pointed out that taking ESG factors into account in investment decisions means directing capital as well as personal savings towards companies and projects that are considered sustainable, for example, those that respect the environment, are attentive to the inclusion and welfare of workers and favour the presence of women in management bodies. This is referred to as sustainable finance.

Environmental factors concern the need to favour production processes that are less energy-intensive and have a lower impact on the environment; social sustainability factors refer to labour relations, inclusion, community welfare and respect for human rights; finally, corporate governance factors concern compliance with diversity policies in the composition of companies' BoDs, the presence of independent directors or the way executives are remunerated, all of which play a central role in ensuring that social and environmental aspects are taken into account in the decisions of companies and organisations.

There are specialised agencies that draw up scores, the so-called ESG ratings, which express a summary judgement on the level of sustainability of issuers (companies, states, supranational organisations), financial securities and collective investment instruments (UCITS and ETFs) that define themselves as "sustainable" or "ESG" precisely on the basis of the scores obtained. However, it is important to clarify that internationally agreed standards for assessing sustainability are currently lacking.

European regulation is working precisely to establish uniform criteria for constructing ratings so that we know unambiguously which asset or instrument is actually "sustainable". The main role in combating climate change and ESG risks lies with governments. However, these risks are also important for central banks and supervisory authorities, as they can affect their ability to achieve their institutional

---

[48] www.weforum.org/
[49] www.gsi-alliance.org

objectives relating to the stability of prices, the financial system and individual intermediaries.

The ECB published the results of its thematic review on climate risks, which show that banks are still far from adequately managing environmental risks. Frankfurt is now setting a roadmap for banks to meet supervisory expectations. The ECB also published a compendium of good practices observed in some banks, demonstrating that rapid progress can be made. The review found that although 85% of banks have adopted at least basic practices, more sophisticated methodologies and granular information on climate risks are still lacking. Banks significantly underestimate the extent of these risks and almost all banks (96%) have shortcomings in identifying them. The ECB has set deadlines to be reached by the end of 2024. In the first phase, the ECB expects banks to classify climate risks and conduct a comprehensive assessment of the impact on their activities by March 2023. In the second phase, by the end of 2023, the ECB expects banks to include climate risks in their risk management. A wait-and-see approach prevails in most banks. Finally, by the end of 2024, banks will have to meet all remaining expectations outlined in 2020[50], including integration into the ICAAP and stress tests. The deadlines will be monitored and, if necessary, measures will be taken. The authorities are already including the banks' climate results in the SREP. The ECB has imposed binding quality requirements on more than thirty banks in the annual SREP.

In addition, for a small number of banks, the outcome of the 2022 climate risk supervisory exercises had an impact on SREP scores. These affect the Pillar 2 capital requirements. Only later will the ECB be able to define specific capital requirements for climate risk.

Finally, in December 2022[51], the ECB published a set of best practices for climate risk stress tests, the exercise of which has become a key tool for supervisors in assessing the impact of climate-related risks on the banking system.

The report highlights which practices are considered preferable to ensure alignment with the ECB's expectations – with particular reference to Expectation 11 of the Guidance that focuses on the need to adequately incorporate climate and environmental risks into banks' stress test frameworks – and offers suggestions and examples to help banks overcome the challenges and meet expectations by the end of 2024[52]. On this point, the ECB emphasises that this collection of best practices does not prescribe a "one-size-fits-all" approach to climate risk stress tests but, rather, each bank must find its own way, depending on the specific circumstances and needs of its business model.

---

[50] ECB Guide on climate-related and environmental risks supervisory expectations relating to risk management and disclosure, November 2020.

[51] ECB report on good practices for climate stress testing, December 2022.

[52] In terms of climate risk stress testing frameworks, data requirements for climate stress testing and integration of climate-related risks to stress test credit risk models.

3   The supervision approach   53

Focus: International regulatory and supervisory initiatives

In 2015, the FSB established the Task Force on Climate- related Financial Disclosure (TCFD) with the aim of studying climate change-related financial risks and encouraging financial firms' awareness and transparency on climate-related financial risks. In 2017, the TCFD published a set of recommendations (updated in 2021) that have become an international benchmark for improving the consistency, quality and comparability of information disclosed by public and private institutions. By the end of 2021, eight jurisdictions (including the European Union) had reporting rules in line with the TCFD recommendations, covering the following main areas: governance mechanisms, strategy, risk management, metrics and targets. In more recent years, the Network for Greening the Financial System has developed recommendations, guidelines and climate scenarios, with the aim of supporting central banks, supervisors and market participants in integrating climate and environmental factors into their risk management activities and procedures, and in particular to make use of standardised scenario-based analysis. From a strictly prudential perspective, the Basel Committee on Banking Supervision is investigating whether and to what extent the current regulatory framework is adequate to sufficiently capture climate change-related financial risks (with regard to Pillar 1, 2 and 3); among the initiatives already taken, in November 2021 the Committee published a guidance document for consultation addressed to banks and supervisors on the effective management of climate risks.

At the European level, the European Commission published an "Action Plan for Sustainable Finance" in 2018, in which measures were proposed to strengthen the role of the financial sector in achieving a socially and environmentally sustainable economy. Among the various proposals of the Action Plan, the entry into force of the EU Taxonomy Regulation1 in July 2020 and the Sustainable Finance Disclosure Regulation (SFDR)2 in March 2021 is notable. The European Commission also adopted a package of measures aimed at fostering capital flows to sustainable assets across the EU, including amendments to the delegated acts of MiFID II, UCITS and AIFMD that integrate sustainability factors and risks into the provisions applicable to investment service providers and fund managers, in particular in governance and risk management systems. In order to facilitate the application of the sustainable investment taxonomy, the Commission has prepared a taxonomy compass, which provides a visual representation of the contents of the taxonomy itself, with which operators can assess the activities included therein, the objectives to which they contribute and the criteria they must fulfil for climate change mitigation and adaptation management. In June 2021, the "EBA Guidelines on Lending and Loan Monitoring" also came into force, which recommend that intermediaries incorporate ESG factors and associated risks into their credit risk management policies, adopting a holistic approach. In parallel, the EBA published the "Report on ESG risk management and supervision", which introduces a common definition of ESG risks, discusses their transmission channels and identifies methodologies for their management and inclusion in banks' regulatory and supervisory frameworks. In the area of supervision, of particular note is the publication in November 2020 by the ECB of a specific guide on climate and environmental risks, which sets out expectations on how climate and environmental risk should be integrated into the strategy and business model, governance processes and risk management framework of SSM-significant banks, along with the type of information to be published as part of public disclosure.

4 Analysing the business model in seven steps

> "Changes are inevitable and not always controllable.
> What can be controlled is how you manage,
> react to and work through the change process"
> K. A. Morgan

4.1 The ingredients for implementing a support tool

When carrying out a BMA, it is necessary to analyse a series of key elements that contribute to entrepreneurial viability and sustainability in the medium and long term. The proposed methodology enriches the traditional backward-looking and forward-looking analysis with further specific insights aimed at identifying the operating segments that contribute to the creation/destruction of value in the medium/long term (Figure 4.1).

Figure 4.1　**Backward- and forward-looking profitability analysis**

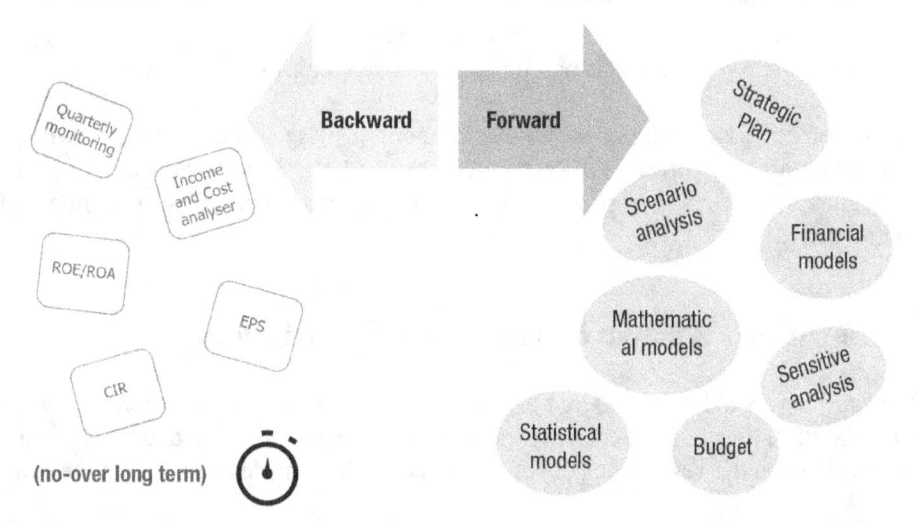

Source: Authors' elaboration.

Figure 4.2   **Seven dimensions of analysis**

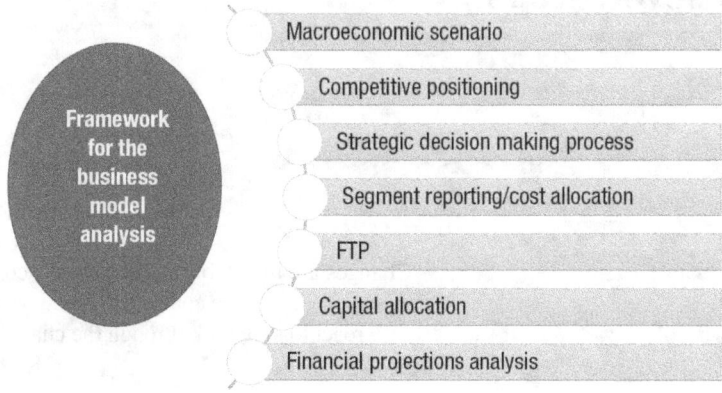

Source: Authors' elaboration based on CRD V and EBA Guidelines.

The proposed framework is developed through seven dimensions of analysis, namely:

1. Current and prospective macroeconomic, political and social variables;
2. Competitive positioning and reference market (products, geography, etc.);
3. Medium and long-term strategic process that should hinge on clear corporate governance mechanisms;
4. Current and prospective profitability drivers;
5. Revenue allocation mechanisms that take into account the interdependencies between different business areas;
6. Governance of capital allocation and incentives;
7. Prospective SWOT analysis based on alternative scenarios.

The systematic assessment of these seven dimensions (Figure 4.2), which, as will be seen below, are also reflected in certain forecasts of CRD V and even more so in the EBA guideline, offers a more methodical and integrated approach to planning and control activities.

4.2   First step: Analysis of macroeconomic variables

The first step should be considered preparatory to the definition and coherence analysis of the BM[1]. In fact, it is necessary for banks to define medium- and long-term business horizons and assess the impact of macroeconomic variable estimates on the BM.

---

[1] See CRD IV, Article 88(a) and EBA Guidelines GL13/2014, title 4 chapter 4.1, point 58(i).

4 Analysing the business model in seven steps

Figure 4.3 **Analysis of macroeconomic variables**

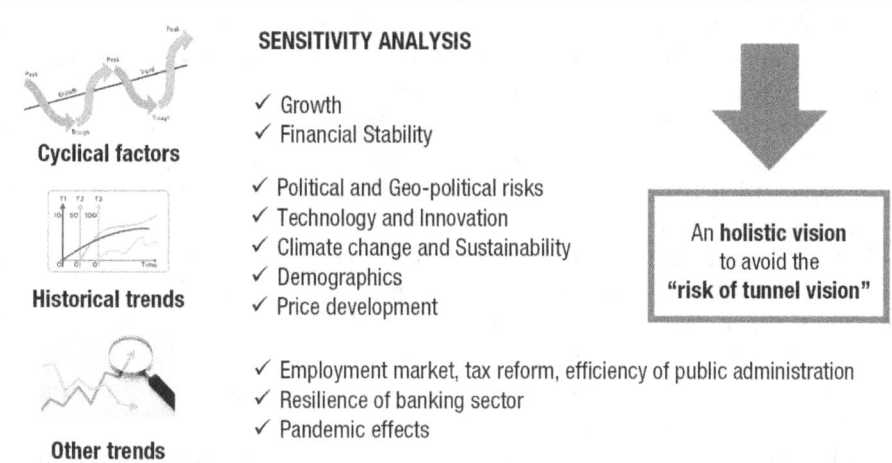

Source: Authors' elaboration.

There are at least seven macroeconomic variables that could affect the credit sector and in particular the core business of a commercial bank[2]:

a. Growth;
b. Financial stability;
c. Political and geopolitical risks;
d. Technology and innovation;
e. Climate change and sustainability;
f. Demography;
g. Price trends.

The first two trends on the list relate to cyclical factors, the third to risks and shocks and the last four to historical trends.

The list is clearly not exhaustive and there are many issues that need to be factored into macroeconomic forecasts. In addition to those mentioned above, there are other "traditional" sub-factors, such as labour market reforms, tax reforms, competitiveness in domestic markets, pension and health reforms, banking sector resilience and public administration efficiency. Alongside these, there are emerging factors that reflect possible crises (e.g. pandemics) or opportunities in a given business cycle[3] (**Figure 4.3**).

---

[2] See Moody's Investor Service, *Turn outlook into insights*, Milan 9.2.2018.
[3] For example, GDP growth in the EU or China, Brexit, the US presidential election, commodity prices or the volatility of oil prices, interest rates, quantitative easing, etc. Finally, all forecasts should consider post-pandemic scenarios.

Moreover, sensitivity analyses should also be carried out with reference to the bank's main strategic initiatives (launched or to be launched) and to the type of its core customers. For example, GDP growth should also be analysed taking into account the outlook of the various economic sectors to which the bank's assets are most exposed (e.g. real estate, manufacturing, telecommunications, consumer products).

Having a clear process with which to investigate the effects of macroeconomic variables on business allows one to address "cum grano salis" any vulnerabilities in the banking balance sheet generated by current and prospective macroeconomic, political and social variables.

The lack of a holistic view of the macroeconomic environment and its drivers that impact on one's business could increase the "risk of tunnel vision" of business initiatives[4], where the assumptions underlying the strategic processes are not fully consistent with the bank's complete business framework.

There are many sources of information to draw on, some of which are illustrated in **Figure 4.4**.

With reference to industry-related risk factors (**Figure 4.5**), they are traditionally separated into legal, technical and socio-demographic.

Priority number one for the ECB's 2023–2025 supervisory cycle emphasises the need for "strengthening resilience to immediate macro-financial and geopolitical shocks".

4.3 Second step: An outline of environment and competitive positioning

In supporting major strategic and/or commercial projects related to business initiatives[5], banks should conduct a thorough and adequate assessment of their competitive positioning with respect to other players, market risks and opportunities[6], and customer and investor expectations[7]. This assessment, which should be systematic in nature, should hinge on reliable analyses and assumptions that are consistent with the strategic plan, business plan and RAF and be the subject of regular reporting to the board.

The economic literature offers countless contributions, such as the well-known Pestel analysis, Porter's five forces, cost-benefit analysis accompanied by sensitivity analysis and SWOT analysis.

It would be functional if they were always carried out "vis-à-vis" with competi-

---

[4] In the medical field, the term tunnel vision is used to indicate "the loss of peripheral vision with the retention of central vision, resulting in a circular tunnel as a restricted field of vision".

[5] Such as launching new commercial products or entering new markets.

[6] Including potential contagion risks.

[7] Possible changes in customer preferences, for example, in terms of climate related and environmental, digitalisation, distribution channel, service, product pricing, new products, must be taken into account.

4 Analysing the business model in seven steps   59

Figure 4.4 **Analysis of macroeconomic variables: possible sources**

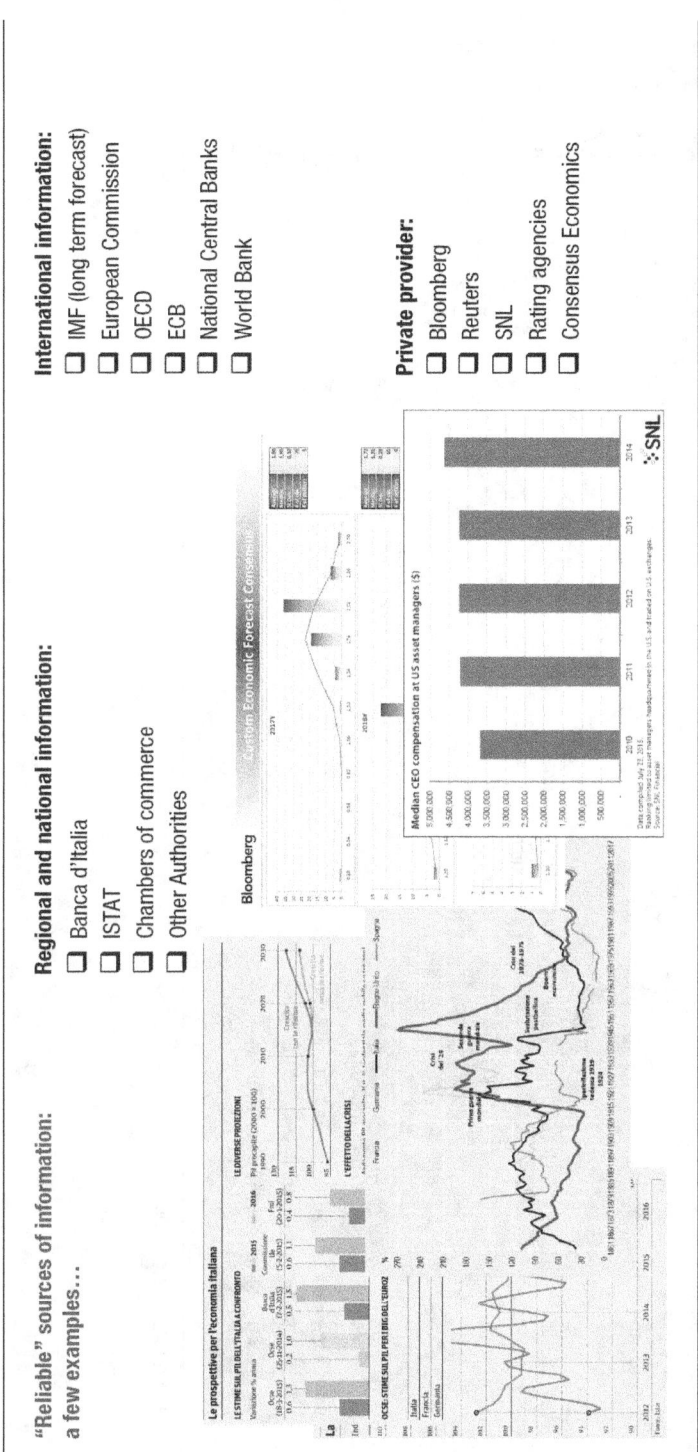

Source: Authors' elaboration.

Figure 4.5 Industry-related risk factors

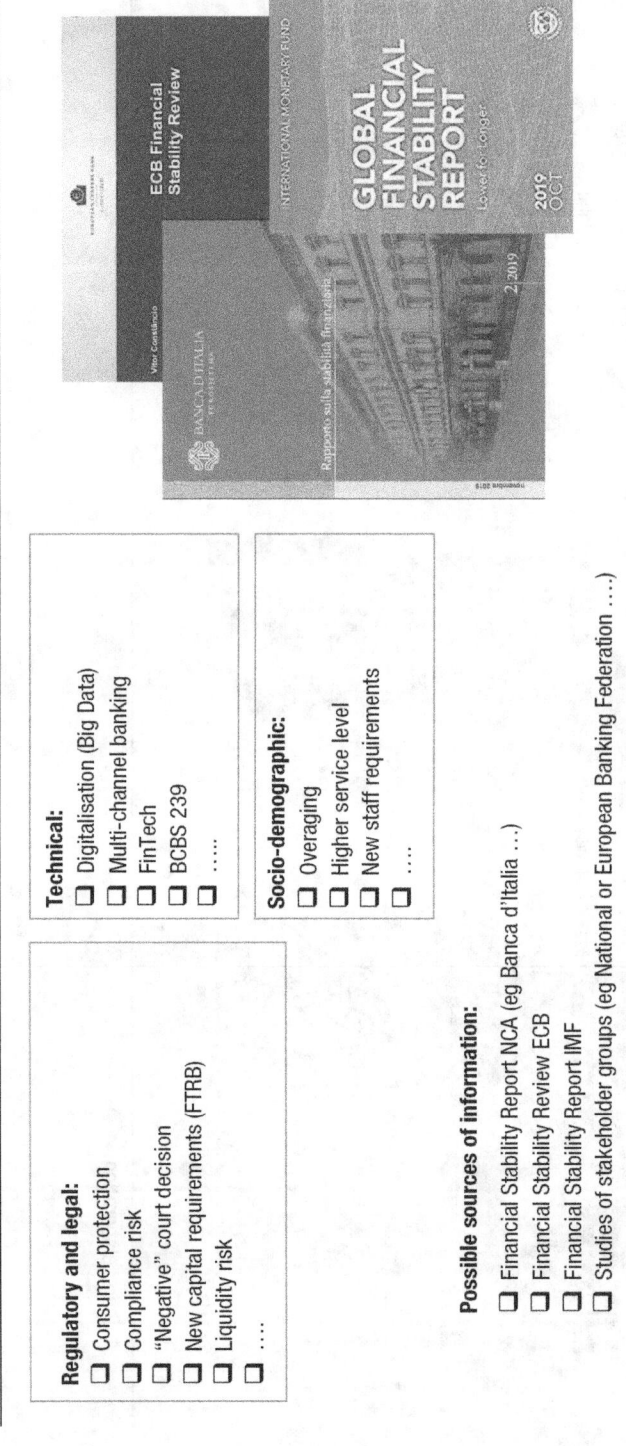

Regulatory and legal:
☐ Consumer protection
☐ Compliance risk
☐ "Negative" court decision
☐ New capital requirements (FTRB)
☐ Liquidity risk
☐ ….

Technical:
☐ Digitalisation (Big Data)
☐ Multi-channel banking
☐ FinTech
☐ BCBS 239
☐ ….

Socio-demographic:
☐ Overaging
☐ Higher service level
☐ New staff requirements
☐ ….

Possible sources of information:
☐ Financial Stability Report NCA (eg Banca d'Italia …)
☐ Financial Stability Review ECB
☐ Financial Stability Report IMF
☐ Studies of stakeholder groups (eg National or European Banking Federation ….)

Source: Authors' elaboration.

tors in order to reduce potential risks of "self-referentiality", regardless of the analysis adopted.

Compared with traditional marketing analyses, in banking particular rigour is required in the selection of peers and external benchmarks[8], which are more or less challenging for the bank. These peers should not only be consistent with the bank's BM and risk appetite, but once the peer group has been identified it should also be used on a permanent basis in the various areas of analysis in order to avoid potential arbitrage by top management when reporting to the board. In other words, one should avoid using different peers according to the areas investigated (remuneration, commercial, finance, etc.) so they do not distort the competitive comparison.

In general, the peer group is made up of around eight to ten competitors which can be selected not only on the basis of their BM but also taking into account numerous variables, such as nationality, size, attitude to innovation, particular risk exposures (e.g. NPLs) or ratios (e.g. CIR), geographical exposure, funding and ownership structure.

Institutions should also select a set of key performance factors in order to monitor the environment and check, from time to time, whether the assumptions underlying the strategic or financial plans show potential vulnerabilities to the competitive environment.

In Figure 4.6, examples are given of how to analyse the levels of performance achieved compared with competitors, once the peer group has been identified: market shares, type of portfolio, method of credit financing, etc.

The revolution introduced by the European directive on payment services (PSD2) and the opening of application programming interfaces (APIs) inevitably places banks in a more competitive environment and forces them to reflect on the logic of Open Banking and the business implications in terms of new and potential service models for the customer[9].

Hence in the digital field, banks, pending their own strategic decision on how to overcome the concept of traditional banking, find themselves having to interpret their competitive positioning in relation to one of the possible BMs related to different approaches to the use of APIs, which differ in terms of different levels of integration of the value chain and intensity of investment[10] (Figure 4.7).

---

[8] See EBA Guidelines GL13/2014, title 4, chapter 4.2, point 62 (b); chapter 4.4, point 64; chapter 4.7, point 75 (c).

[9] European Directive 2015/2366, which entered into force in Italy on 13 January 2018, was created as a result of the continuous evolution of the use of electronic payments, including through mobile devices, and promotes, among other things, the development of mobile payments through Open Banking.

[10] The digital bank is characterised by the adoption of "end to end" solutions in the digitalisation of services and processes; the "outsourcer bank" model involves the selective in-house production of products, services and processes considered core and the outsourcing of non-core ones; banks as service platforms finally exploit open infrastructures to intermediate between customers and technology partners.

Figure 4.6   **Industry-related risk factors**

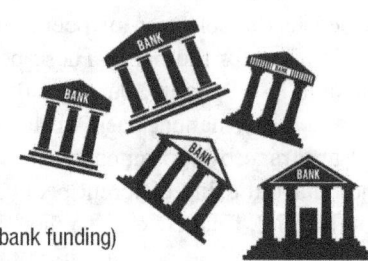

Customized peer group by:
- ✓ Country
- ✓ Business model
- ✓ Dimension:
  - Size
  - Cyclical relevance (e.g. NPEs)
  - Key ratios (e.g. CIR, CET1 *ratio*)
  - Geographical exposure
  - Funding (e.g. high reliance on interbank funding)
  - Ownership

Peer analysis:
Few examples…

- ✓ **Market share:** per deposits, per loans
- ✓ **Sources of Interest Income:** debt securities, loans to non financial corporations, loans to households
- ✓ **Balance Sheet Composition:** loans and advances, debt securities, other
- ✓ **Administrative expenses:** per employees
- ✓ **Loans:** per branches, per employees
- ✓ **Mortgage Interest Rate Type:** tracker, variable, fixed
- ✓ **Movement in Gross Loan Book: demographic:** performing, non performing

Source: Authors' elaboration.

Figure 4.7   **Business models related to individual API usage approaches**

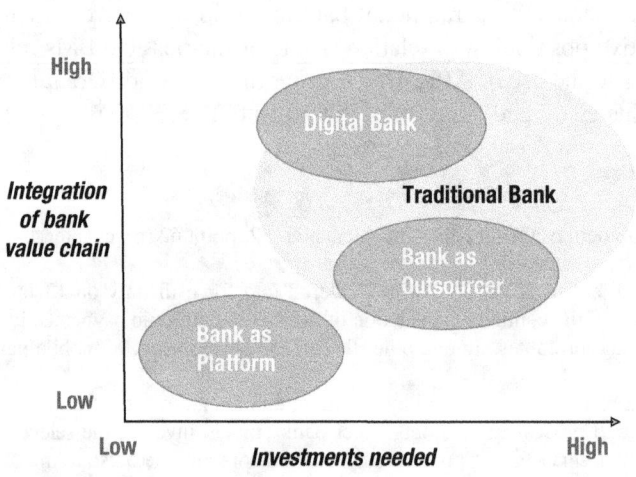

Source: Authors' elaboration.

Clearly, models with greater control of the system through, for example, proprietary platforms, will inevitably have less ability to respond to change.

The question bank management must therefore ask itself is, when is the right time to invest structurally in digital transformation? And it is at this stage that the analysis of competitive positioning is relevant: it is necessary to be aware of how important the online relationship is for the bank, to choose its marketing strategy in case it wants to preside over the market in foreign countries and consequently to strengthen the international brand and push it through the web.

4.4 Third step: Strategic decision making process

First of all, it is necessary to clarify what is meant by adequate corporate governance mechanisms in the BMA[11].

Article 88.1 of CRD IV/CRD V helps us to define its meaning and scope. The body with strategic oversight functions shall have full responsibility for the institution and approve and supervise the implementation of the strategic objectives and related risks, verify the implementation and effectiveness of the strategic choices and, if any, overcome weaknesses in the strategic process.

Focus: Art. 88(1) Governance arrangements

"The management body defines, oversees and is accountable for the implementation of the governance arrangements that ensure effective and prudent management of an institution, including the segregation of duties in the organisation and the prevention of conflicts of interest. Those arrangements shall comply with the following principles:
a) the management body must have the overall responsibility for the institution and approve and oversee the implementation of the institution's strategic objectives, risk strategy and internal governance;
[...] the management body monitors and periodically assesses the effectiveness of the institution's governance arrangements and takes appropriate steps to address any deficiencies."

It is therefore necessary for the board to define broad guidelines in terms of diversification, size, growth, internationalisation, governance, risk taking, capital levels and allocation.

Once the specific business strategies underlying the BM have been defined, it is important to ensure that the board and generally all banking staff have the appropriate know-how and skills to support that particular BM.

Given that value creation implies risk taking, it is crucial to adopt a robust risk objective system (i.e. RAF, **Figure 4.8**) that includes the policies[12], processes, meth-

---

[11] See CRD IV art. 66 (1)(a) and EBA Guidelines GL13/2014, title 6, chapter 6.6.3, point 222.
[12] It goes without saying that for the financial industry, the RAF, conversely, represents a constraint on value creation.

Figure 4.8   Risk Appetite Framework

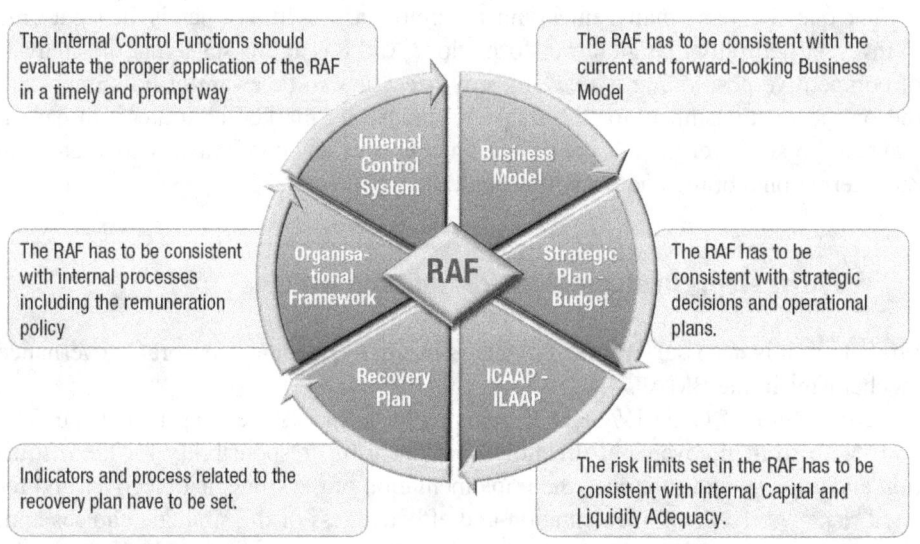

Source: Authors' elaboration on EBA Guidelines.

odologies, and controls by which the bank's risk appetite is defined, communicated, managed and monitored, consistent with the maximum amount of risk that can be taken:

a. Current and prospective BM;
b. Strategic plan and budget;
c. Available capital and liquidity (ICAAP and ILAAP);
d. Recovery plans[13];
e. Organisational structure and remuneration systems;
f. Internal system controls;
g. Corporate risk culture.

---

[13] Recovery plans represent an additional risk management tool to support overall corporate governance. As part of the regulations introduced by the BRRD on the management of bank crises, banks are required to prepare, review at least annually and if necessary update an individual recovery plan containing measures to address a significant deterioration in the bank's capital and financial position. The framework for recovery plans is also set by the provisions of the Consolidated Law on Banking (TUB) Title IV, Chapter 01-I, and by the EU delegated regulation 2016/1075 of 23 March 2016, which provides key guidance on the content of the plans and the assessment criteria. The EBA has also issued technical guidance concerning quantitative and qualitative indicators (EBA/GL/2015/02), scenarios to be used in stress tests (EBA/GL/2014/06) and provisions on simplified requirements (EBA/GL/2015/16).

However, to enable the effective definition and implementation of the RAF, it is necessary to establish a robust system of alert thresholds in terms of capacity, tolerance and target threshold, towards which management must ensure compliance even in situations of value creation (Figure 4.9):

a. *Risk capacity*, the maximum level of risk that a bank is technically able to take on, given available capital and liquidity as well as supervisory requirements;
b. *Risk tolerance*, the potential deviation from the target that one is willing to assume, with the exception of the ongoing business;
c. *Soglia target*, the objective, or risk appetite, that is set specifically for each indicator, consistent with the budget, to optimise the risk-return profile.

In the definition of the corporate strategy it is crucial that the board is supported by a strategic intelligence unit, that is, by a steering committee made up of transversal managerial figures with advisory functions. The regular functioning of this unit becomes even more vital in banking groups where the network banks and/or product companies are delegated with competences in terms of commercial and operational strategies, in order to guarantee a "high" vision of the opportunities and challenges of the BM adopted.

The lack of such a strategic unit may not guarantee the board a holistic view of the strategies put in place and the preparation of appropriate initiatives. More generally, this is part of the board's necessity to challenge bank managers and fully perform its strategic oversight function.

Figure 4.9   **The traffic light procedure**

Source: Authors' elaboration on EBA Guidelines.

The strategic intelligence unit (Figure 4.10), as part of its support to the board, is normally assigned the following advisory responsibilities with reference to:

a. Commercial and business strategies relating to transversal issues and, for groups operating in different countries, of an international nature (e.g. multichannel, fintech, etc.);
b. Monitoring group performance (monthly/quarterly economic trends);
c. Initiatives and/or issues of strategic importance or significant impact on the management, organisational and operational aspects of the subsidiaries;
d. Analysis of macroeconomic scenarios with reference to the business context;
e. Assessment of the competitive environment and positioning of the group in relation to competitors;
f. Alignment on key aspects relating to capital, risks and liquidity;
g. Facilitator of information exchanges between the boards of the group companies;
h. Coordination of the actions of group companies, ensuring consistency of operational management with the guidelines formulated by the parent company;
i. Key management issues and internal control system;
j. Customer satisfaction;

Figure 4.10   **Strategic intelligence unit**

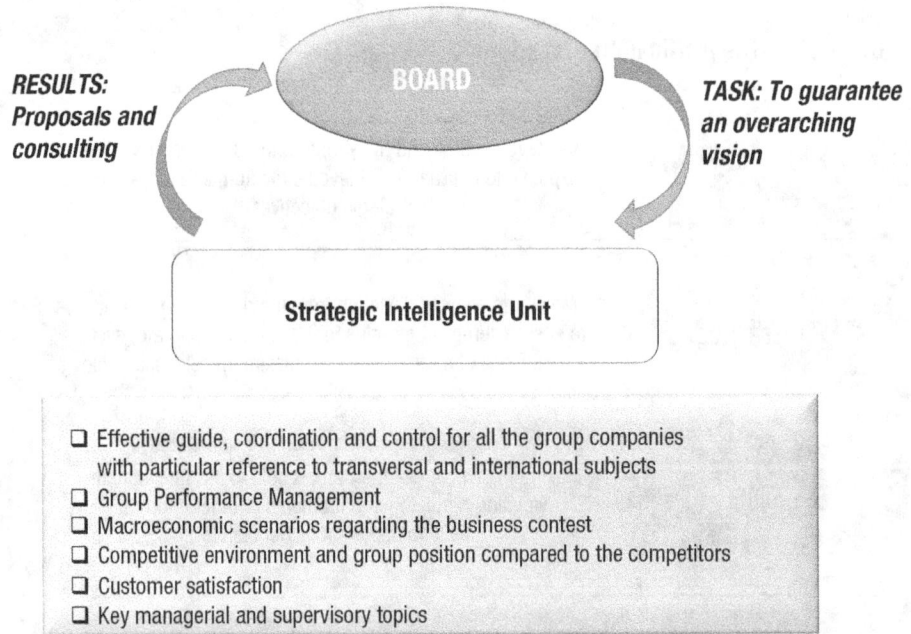

Source: Authors' elaboration.

k. Regulatory developments with a strong transversal/international character;
l. Translation in organisational terms of the bank's corporate strategies that reflect the company's history, distinctive competencies and competitive context.

Ancillary to these responsibilities, in the era of digital transformation the strategic intelligence unit must start from the assumption that information systems increasingly pervade bank processes, from the programming and planning of production flows to the collection of corporate data through the integration of tools and software into the corporate information "network", from intelligence on operational results to the construction of predictive analyses, from customer chain interaction to the control of economic and financial resources, from document management to substitute archiving.

This triggers managerial choices that affect the value extraction of different activities (e.g. product differentiation, customer segmentation, process and cost efficiency and financial risks).

The combination of core businesses and business strategies forms the mix of assets, liabilities and sources of income underlying the bank's BM.

However, this business mix cannot be separated from a holistic view. Within this consolidated logic, elements of weakness that should be overcome are the fragmentation of reports and management control reporting[14].

Operational efficiency should also be represented not only at the level of the individual legal entity but also and especially at group level by using appropriate segment reporting.

Along these lines, it is useful that the estimated variables underlying the business mix are backtested by the risk management functions and also integrated into the framework available to the CRO.

Within the European supervision priority 2023–2025, "deficiencies in management bodies' functioning and steering capabilities" were identified as a vulnerability[15]. Specifically, it was emphasised that "sound internal governance arrangements and effective strategic steering are crucial in ensuring the sustainability of banks' business models, both during the crises and in normal time, and in successfully adapting to ongoing trends, such as digitalisation and the green transition. The collective suitability, including adequate collective knowledge, skill and experience, and the diversity of banks' management bodies strengthen their risk oversight role and are essential to their effective functioning."

---

[14] The fragmentary nature of the management control activity is one of the issues addressed by EBA guideline 13/2014 (title 4 chap. 4.9. point 79); EBA GL 44/2011, III, II A.5.4, 5d and A 6.1. Also noted in BCBS 328/2015, principle 5.

[15] Strategic objective: Banks should effectively address material deficiencies in the functioning, oversight and composition of their management body by developing and swiftly implementing sound remedial action plans.

4.5 Fourth step: Segment reporting and cost allocation

4.5.1 Segment reporting for BM and profitability analysis

In business as usual, corporate functions are engaged in drawing up types of segment reporting, with essentially two kinds of purpose:

a. Information towards external stakeholders (e.g. supervisory authorities within the framework of the information supervision obligations to which they are subject or investors within the framework of bank financial statements prepared on the basis of international accounting standards);
b. Internal monitoring and management reporting to banking management.

On the other hand, its implementation as a tool to support the strategic planning process, in order to assess how each business sector contributes to the creation or destruction of value within its BM, is rather marginal.

Constructing risk-adjusted segment reporting, that is one that also takes into account the capital allocated to cover the risks that need to be accurately quantified, requires time and a deep understanding of the data. It is necessary to break down and recompose the entire banking business: the combination of resources, products and customer segments contribute, like the pieces of a huge puzzle, to creating value in the different business areas.

It is necessary to move away from the concept of legal entities, brands and operating segments (IFRS 8 and SFAS 131) and look at the whole group as one huge corporate entity with its own value chains to be identified and measured. Then, for each category, the bank should identify sub-categories to allocate direct and indirect costs.

Therefore, in order for segment reporting to adequately support the strategic analysis of the BM and the identification and measurement of profitability drivers and commercial objectives, it is necessary that prior to its construction, the bank adequately reflects on its BM, on the correct definition of commercial segments, distribution channels and categories of products and customers and how to allocate the overall group activity among them.

Then, for each category, the bank should identify sub-categories to allocate direct and indirect costs, including those related to funding and credit risk. For example, business units could be divided into core, non-core and other central units where they exist (e.g. legacy books, ALM, internal service providers, corporate centre, etc.) while the customer portfolio could be subdivided according to the main categories to which they belong, such as – in the case of a retail banks – mass market, SME, large corporate, etc. (**Figure 4.11**).

4.5.2 Management control and information quality: Data Governance and Data Quality

The implementation of segment reporting in a bank has significant impacts on processes, procedures and IT infrastructure as it requires an advanced management con-

4 Analysing the business model in seven steps

Figure 4.11 Decomposing and recomposing

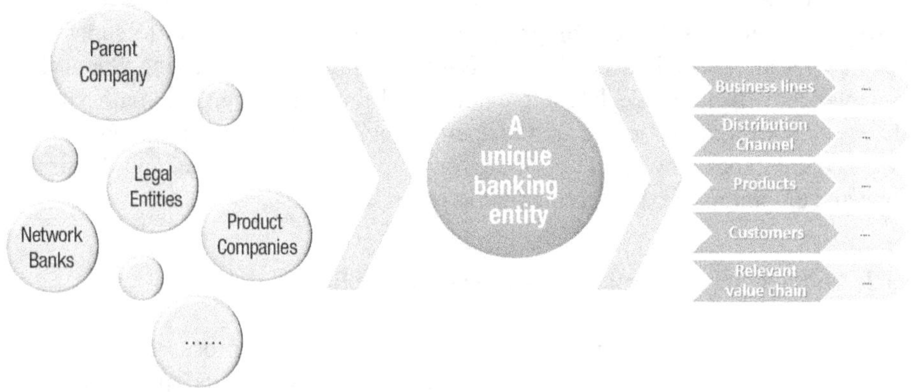

[Diagram: Multiple circles labeled "Parent Company", "Legal Entities", "Network Banks", "Product Companies" → "A unique banking entity" → arrows to "Business lines", "Distribution Channel", "Products", "Customers", "Relevant value chain"]

Source: Authors' elaboration.

trol model that goes beyond the traditional ongoing monitoring analysis and beyond the managed accounting scope. The quality of such a model clearly reflects the quality standards of its data governance and data quality systems and their ability to ensure a structured approach oriented towards good governance of information processing and holistic data management[16].

In fact, data governance does not represent a mere "IT project", but a real strategic asset through which to make the most of the entire information heritage. In addition to speed and timeliness of production, information should above all comply with implicit quality and certification requirements.

In order to design an effective data governance strategy[17], it is important to start from an accurate assessment in order to verify the maturity level of the company with respect to data management. It may be necessary to redesign the company's policies in order to define in detail responsibilities and ownership of data, roles and competences of the parties involved in the project, standards for data acquisition and validation, rules for access, use and storage.

In this regard, the priority of European supervision 2023–2025 also states that "Access to timely and accurate data and reports is a prerequisite for effective strategic steering, effective risk management and sound decision making, both in normal times and in periods of stress. Against this background, ECB Banking Supervision

---

[16] The vulnerabilities indicated by the European supervision 2023–2025 note deficiencies in risk data aggregation and reporting: "Banks should effectively address long-lasting deficiencies and have adequate and efficient risk data aggregation and reporting frameworks in place in order to support efficient steering by management bodies and to address supervisors' expectations, including in times of crisis."

[17] See Basel Committee, BCBS Circular 239 et seq.

has been paying close attention to supervised institutions' data quality, risk data aggregation capabilities and risk reporting practices. Material deficiencies in these areas have repeatedly been identified in annual SREP exercises, as banks' have been showing slow and insufficient progress in closing gaps with respect to supervisory expectations and compliance with the Basel Committee on Banking Supervision principles for effective risk data aggregation and risk reporting. The main vulnerabilities relate to weak oversight of management bodies, fragmented and non-harmonised IT landscapes, low capacity for aggregating data at group level and the limited scope and ambitions of banks' remediation plans."

4.5.3 Management control and cost allocation policies

Simplifying along the value chain and focusing on transparent processes and systems has never been more crucial. In fact, over the years, banks have adopted increasingly complex and complicated operating models and have grown rapidly by acquiring, without full integration, new products, business lines, processes and systems in order to meet the expectations of ever more demanding customers and onerous regulations.

This has led to the adoption of complex organisations and the launch of increasingly sophisticated products and channels that are often not supported by adequate IT for accurate monitoring purposes. However, in an environment where businesses are consolidated, regulation and capital requirements are increased and there are very limited opportunities for revenue leverage, banks are forced to "rethink" the adequacy of their cost structure in order to compete effectively.

Long-term sustainable cost reduction requires an analysis of one's own BM, appropriate governance and full integration with other business initiatives. Effective and efficient cost management requires a top-down approach. A key success factor is the involvement of the board in defining a clear cost strategy that is constantly and regularly monitored and reported through specific key performance indicators (KPIs) in order to intercept, monitor and correct any deviations from budget and RAF.

The focus on the analysis of organisational efficiency, as already mentioned in the previous steps, should be permanent and integrated within the company and should not be considered as a project aimed simply at responding to contingent market conditions.

In the light of these considerations, it goes without saying that at the basis of proper cost governance, it will be crucial to:

a. Establish clear ownership at senior management level, defining equally clear activities, roles and responsibilities in cost management within the organisation;
b. Rethink the cost mapping and cost allocation processes;
c. Communicate and explain the adopted cost strategies to the whole organisation;
d. Define robust KPIs for the main cost items (e.g. staff, IT and real estate) and monitor their trend;
e. Include scenario analyses in reports to help understand whether and how much of the costs should be cut, in the event of a downturn in profits, or strengthened, in the event of business support;

Figure 4.12 Dimension of analysis – Cost Allocation

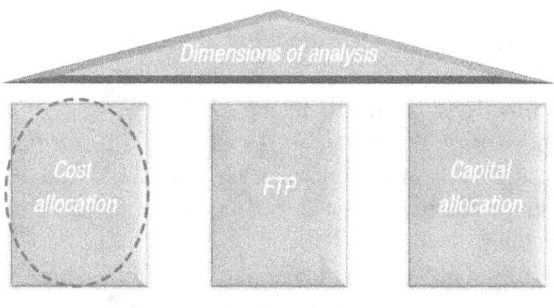

- **Cost structure mapping**
  (fixed, variable, mixed, ordinary, not ordinary, direct, indirect, figurative, marginal, incremental, etc...)
- **Cost driver definition**
  (transaction volume, FTEs, etc...)
- **Cost allocation to segment, sub-segment and corporate centre**
  (direct, indirect, proxies, distribution matrix based on operational parameters, etc...)
- **Cost center aligned to monitoring purpose**
  (Corporate Center, IT, maintance staff, accounting, etc...)

Source: Authors' elaboration.

f. Create incentives by including targets on expense management in the scorecards of the most relevant management in order to ensure proper accountability.

Along these lines, as indicated in **Figure 4.12**, in order to rethink the cost mapping and cost allocation mechanisms, it will be crucial to:

a. Understand one's cost structure (fixed, variable, etc.); define cost drivers for different cost categories and for different cost consumptions (e.g. by transaction volumes, number of employees, etc.);
b. Categorise costs and allocate them to business lines on the basis of cost drivers that reflect the true consumption of resources (businesses have to pay for the services they receive);
c. Design cost centres in line with monitoring objectives;
d. Identify cost drivers appropriate to the BM and reduce those that do not add value.

The corporate centre is a notional segment (a sort of transitional "car park") into which cost and revenue elements not allocated or allocable directly or indirectly to the other lines of business flow (taking into account system constraints).

The allocation of direct costs does not present any particular difficulty, since by nature they are directly attributable to the commercial segments. The problem arises with the allocation of indirect costs, and the nature of the "parking" from transitory could become definitive as the competent structures are not able to correctly allocate certain types of costs.

Within this framework, reporting should of course be timely and granular in order to intercept any opportunities in terms of productivity gains through the combination of business functions and restructuring of BMs.

Performance monitoring reports should be generated at various levels – business units, geographies, divisions and support areas – and should include scenario analysis in order to make productivity metric projections preparatory to certain analyses, such as peer group ones.

In order to capture economies of scale, banks need to simplify, consolidate and integrate core processes (e.g. opening of accounts), as well as eliminate discretionary projects that do not add adequate value, are not fully aligned with the group strategy or are not appropriately defined. The remaining projects should be prioritised and intermediaries should focus only on those with high added value.

When banks decide not to invest in new projects and reduce fixed costs, e.g. branches and full time equivalent (FTEs), they need to fully understand the implications and quantify first the long-term rather than short-term impacts. Banks often close branches under break even without assessing whether they actually destroy or create value from a management perspective. In this regard, the following chapter provides a few examples that help clarify the rationale behind closing or not closing an operating point.

Investments in new technology represent a typical business critical decision and therefore should be supported not only by the analysis of customer needs but above all by the possible returns on the investments required for the digital channel. In fact, digital innovation brings higher levels of profitability where processes are redesigned "ex-novo".

The rapid rate of obsolescence that characterises the introduction of new channels and technologies requires a significant re-engineering of the IT architecture to adequately support the change in the traditional banking operating model. However, modernising the IT system requires high rates of investment that need to be weighed against the opportunity. Low value-added transactions, such as cheque cashing, are typically migrated to direct channels and/or home banking/call centres, so that branches can focus on higher value-added transactions.

In view of all this, the processes of rationalising operating models therefore require a rigorous framework that hinges on a strategic review of the liability cycle and the supply chain, as well as on an activity of "extrapolation" of the maximum ROE from one's core businesses. This refers in particular to:

a. Reducing duplication in the cost structure;
b. Making efficient use of assets and renegotiating contracts with suppliers;
c. Divestment of non-core businesses, paying attention to "stranded costs", that is those that remain even after divestment (such as those of shared services or technology costs);

4   Analysing the business model in seven steps

d. Elimination of under-performing businesses or relaunch of the same by accelerating marginal growth through extraordinary transactions (acquisitions or agreements);
e. Rationalisation of the portfolio and customers.

4.5.4   From BMA to segment reporting

As part of the implementation of segment reporting, the following indicators can be used to analyse the profitability of the business units:

a. Asset liability (*loans, direct and indirect funding, funding gap, impaired loans*, etc.);
b. Cost income (*interests, commissions, gains/losses from negotiation activity, impairment loss/gain*, etc.)
c. Notional (*mark-up and mark-down determined through the FTP model, cost allocation, economic impacts from the capital allocation*, etc.);

These measures could be summarised on the basis of various dimensions: by product, by type of customer, by value chain, etc.

One performance metric which effectively measures the capacity to create value is the economic value added (EVA), which should also be analysed analytically through its many variants: customer EVA, product EVA, business unit EVA, geography EVA, etc. (**Figure 4.13**).

Figure 4.13   **From BMA to segment reporting**

INPUT

Balance Sheet
Loans, direct and indirect funding, funding gap, impaired loans...

Profit and Loss
Interests, commissions, gain/losses from negotiation activity, impairment loss/gain...

Figurative
Mark-up and mark-down determined through the FTP model, economic impacts from the capital allocation...

✓ EVA Customer
✓ EVA Product
✓ EVA Business Unit
✓ EVA Geography

OUTPUT
Per product, per customer type, per value chain...

Source: Authors' elaboration.

Figure 4.14   **How to implement a KPI system**

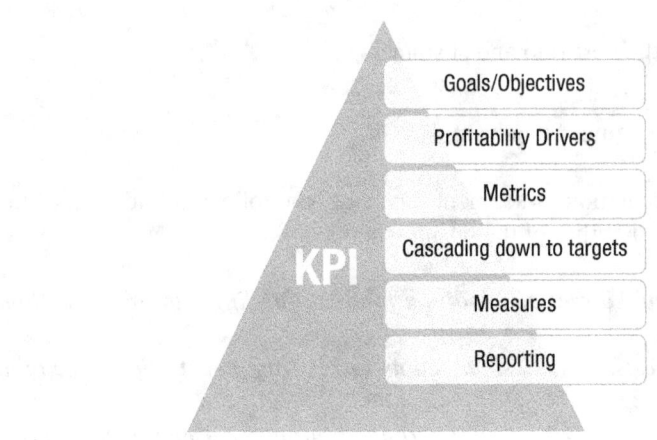

Source: Authors' elaboration.

The body with strategic supervisory functions and the top management, in principle, have at their disposal a wide range of KPIs and key risk indicators (KRIs) to better support the interpretative analysis of their segment reporting, but they must be consistent with their BM and with medium to long-term projects (e.g. those of digital transformation), methodologically robust, periodically measured at group level and subject to regular corporate reporting.

Even when they are qualitative in nature, such as customer-related projects[18], they should be easily "translatable" and traceable to the economic and financial benefits generated by the operations with the customers being analysed. Often, the competent structures carry out many analyses, but these are not shared with the board in the absence of a clear commitment or a precise stimulation from the latter. The list of KPIs and KRIs clearly needs to be reviewed periodically to assess its completeness and consistency with the current and prospective state of the BM and RAF and should be subject to a cascading process throughout the group's organisational structure and escalation process with dedicated remedial measures (**Figure 4.14**).

4.5.5 From the analysis of segment reporting to the review of the strategic planning process

The strategic planning process is undoubtedly an iterative process in which all the phases should be carried out with care and the moments of comparison, culminating for example in the analysis of segment reporting, have the purpose of examining the progress of the strategy and identifying prompt solutions to possible misalignments.

---

[18] For example, customer satisfaction and engagement, number of digital transactions, etc.

In fact, contrary to popular belief, the failure of a planning process is often more due to a lack of or poor monitoring of business execution than to the goodness or otherwise of the business strategy itself.

Correct execution is therefore crucial to the success of one's BM, and to operate effectively it is necessary to address this issue using a systemic approach, combining a cyclical process that aligns the organisation with the strategy and integrated management tools that converge to achieve the strategic objectives.

As a result of the performance reported in the segment reporting, the board can assess the soundness of business execution and, taking into account how each business or geographical sector contributes to the creation/destruction of value, it can also direct the ongoing strategic planning process.

To summarise then, on the basis of segment reporting, the board will not only have to approve the strategies, but above all supervise the implementation of the strategic objectives and the related risks. They will also have to verify the implementation and the effectiveness of the strategic choices as well as overcome, if existing, the weaknesses of the strategic process and replan the fine-tuning as in a Deming cycle (Figure 4.15).

4.6 Fifth step: Fund Transfer Pricing (FTP)

In recent years, as a result of the financial crisis and the ongoing requirements of the regulatory framework, FTP has become increasingly crucial for banks as they assess and refine their BMs in the face of increasingly challenging competitive environments.

This is because the FTP, before being one of the many regulatory requirements requested by the supervisors, is first and foremost a valuable strategic tool that requires close attention from top management, as well as regular review and/or updating by the owner functions and monitoring by the internal control functions so it does not distort its twofold function: firstly, as a tool to support the definition of strategic choices as well as to monitor the goodness of the same choices; secondly,

Figure 4.15 **Deming cycle**

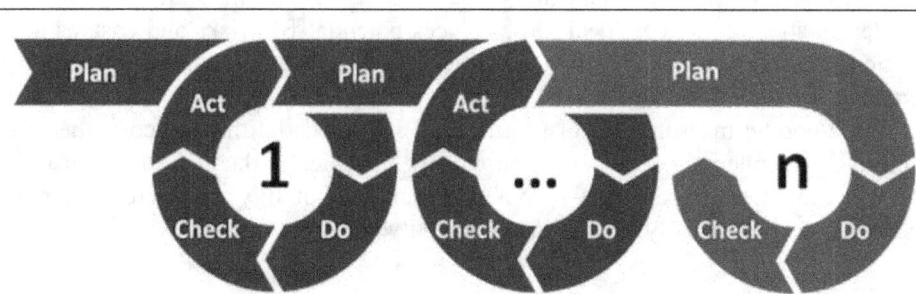

Source: Christoph Roser at AllAboutLean.com (CC BY-SA 4.0).

Figure 4.16   Dimension of analysis: FTP

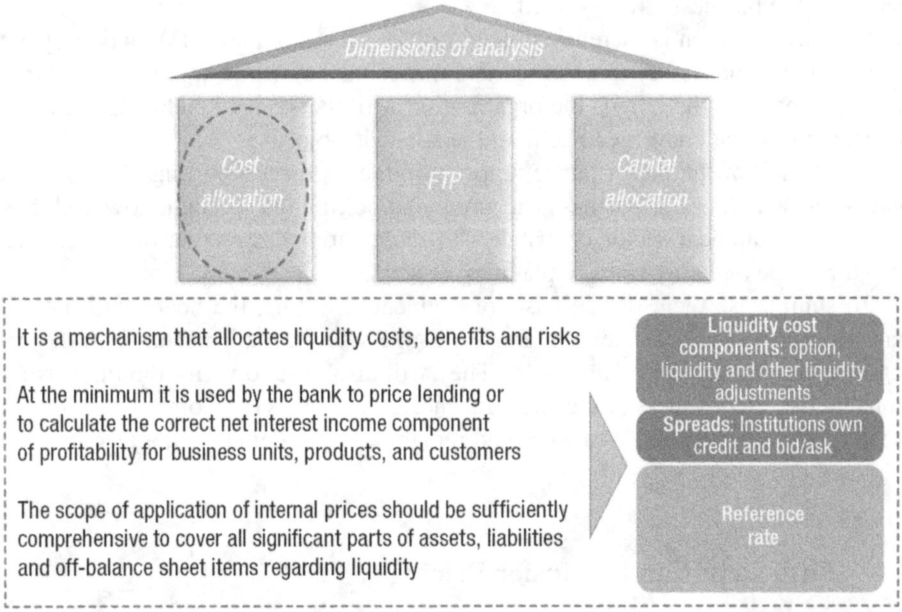

Dimensions of analysis

- Cost allocation
- FTP
- Capital allocation

It is a mechanism that allocates liquidity costs, benefits and risks

At the minimum it is used by the bank to price lending or to calculate the correct net interest income component of profitability for business units, products, and customers

The scope of application of internal prices should be sufficiently comprehensive to cover all significant parts of assets, liabilities and off-balance sheet items regarding liquidity

- Liquidity cost components: option, liquidity and other liquidity adjustments
- Spreads: Institutions own credit and bid/ask
- Reference rate

Source: Authors' elaboration on CEBS Guidelines on liquidity cost-benefit allocation.

as a tool to support liquidity risk management activities regarding the allocation of liquidity among all the business units in line with the RAF metrics (**Figure 4.16**).

Outside the typical components of the building block outlined in the European guidelines, in the definition of FTP a further "block" is most often added in practice, which expresses the strategic steering component of the balance sheet that could represent a cost increase or decrease for a certain product or business segment, depending on whether or not one wishes to discourage the trading of that product or the execution of a certain business.

In fact, FTP, as a strategic decision-making tool, allows accurate measurement and conveying profitability at business line, product and customer level, supports the implementation of strategic decisions, reduces potential BM risks and ensures adequate management of core business activities as well as correct alignment within the organisation of business execution.

For a correct measurement of profitability, it is essential that the costs, benefits and risks generated are clearly and consciously attributed to the originating business lines and that they appropriately take into account the liquidity and interest rate risks generated by the maturity transformation activity[19] (**Figure 4.17**).

---

[19] As is well known, in day-to-day business, banks make money by funding assets (long term loans) with liabilities (short-term deposits), a process commonly referred to as maturity transfor-

4   Analysing the business model in seven steps

Figure 4.17   **FTP implications**

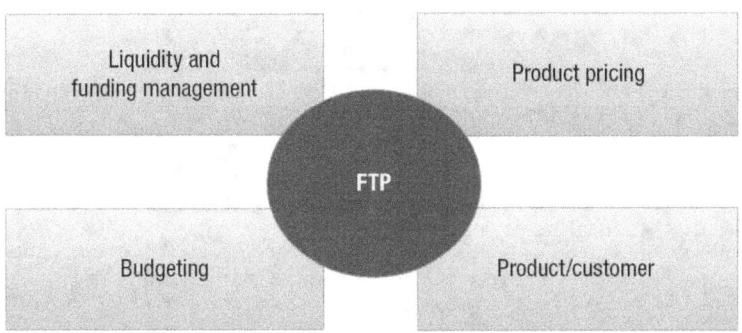

Source: Authors' elaboration.

If designed well, the incentive system can bring enormous benefits by encouraging behaviour that is in line with corporate culture and objectives. Banks that fail to properly "account" for costs, benefits and liquidity risk in pricing and/or to assess the performance of products and business lines, create profound distortions also in the remuneration system, as variables are attributed to performances that do not take into account the cost of capital and liquidity.

Clearly from a proportionality perspective, FTP should reflect the complexity of the intermediary[20]. Before investigating and analysing the best practices of governance, implementation and monitoring of the FTP system, let us try with a simple example to clarify the concept of FTP and its functionality.

The case proposed in **Figure 4.18** is a simplified hypothesis as it concerns the taking out of two deals of the same amount on the liabilities and assets sides.

Let us assume the case of a bank whose network provides a variable rate loan with a five-year maturity and repayment of the capital in full at maturity at a rate of 8% (customer interest rate).

As a result of this transaction, the bank guarantees the network a five-years (5Y) reference interest rate of 5% (given by a 5Y interest rate of 4.2% plus a 5Y funding

---

mation. As pointed out by the Basel Committee on Banking Supervision (BCBS Guidelines No 25, Principles for sound liquidity risk management and supervision, September 2008) this mechanism "makes banks inherently vulnerable to liquidity risk, both of an institution-specific nature and that which affects the market as a whole". Maturity transformation is not to be discouraged, what is important is to govern it with an appropriate FTP framework in order to not end up with a large amount of illiquid long-term assets, contingent commitments and shorter-dated volatile liabilities that significantly increase vulnerability to funding shortfalls. Liquidity is not free-good and should always be adequately priced.

[20] The financial literature has essentially identified four methodologies: net funding method (to be preferred in the case of highly complex and large banks), pooled funding method (to be preferred in the case of complex banks), matched maturity method and cost of funds method.

Figure 4.18   **An FTP example case**

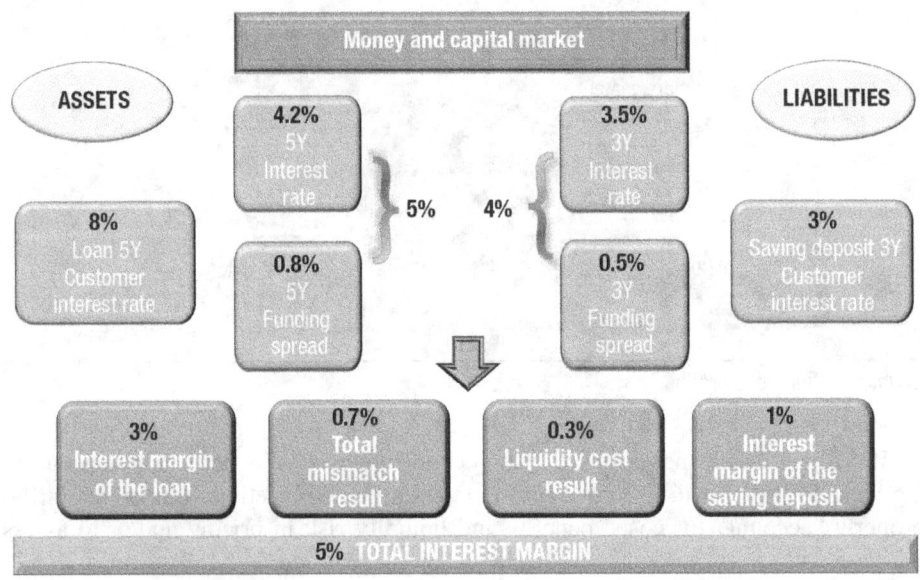

Source: Authors' elaboration.

spread of 0.8%). This will result in a markup of 3% (difference between customer interest rate of 8% and reference interest rate of 5%) and a mismatch result of 4.2% (difference between interest rate of 5% and 5Y funding spread of 0.8%).

Let us assume that the network, in order to finance the above customer loan, collects three-years (3Y) deposits at a customer interest rate of 3%.

Against this transaction, the bank guarantees the network a 4% reference interest rate (given by a 3Y interest rate of 3.5% and a 3Y funding spread of 0.5%). This will result in a markdown of 1% (difference between reference interest rate of 4% and customer interest rate of 3%) creating a mismatch result of -3.5% (difference between 3Y funding spread of 0.5% and 3Y interest rate of 4%).

The total mismatch result that the bank will have to manage will therefore be 0.7% (difference between the two mismatch results 4.2% – 3.5%) while the liquidity cost result will be 0.3% (difference between the two funding spreads, 0.8% – 0.5%).

After all this, the results of such operations are condensed into a total interest margin of 5%.

Based on this simple example, we will now attempt to draw up a list of key elements that should characterise and provide for an adequate and appreciable FTP system as prescribed by CEBS in relation to a stand-alone bank and intra-group transactions.

4 Analysing the business model in seven steps 79

> **Regulatory focus**
>
> CEBS, *GL on Liquidity Cost Benefit Allocation* – Guideline 2, points 7 and 8, require that given the importance of the FTP, the management body should expect that all relevant management levels use the information generated actively and properly. Moreover, the liquidity cost-benefit allocation mechanism should be controlled and monitored by an independent unit. In addition, the Guideline 3, point 14, requires that the liquidity allocation mechanism should generate prices that can be used at an appropriate level of granularity, reflecting the size and sophistication of the institution. Furthermore, the uncommitted line should be charged in a similar manner to the committed line (Guideline 4, point 17). In addition, Bank of Italy, *Circolare 285/13*, parte prima, tit. IV, cap. 4, sez. V, par. 3 requires that risk management function must contribute to development and must evaluate the FTP system.

Therefore, in light of the above, the FTP system should:

a. Hinge on a clear governance structure with a well-defined system of internal controls and clear systems of delegation;
b. Be applied to all internal transactions within a bank, including cash flows between the commercial division and treasury ("commercial FTP"), those between treasury and other business functions (such as "Finance" – "Financial FTP"), off-balance sheet activities and uncommitted lines, and subsidiaries;
c. Include in the calculation the different components affecting costs and risks generated by the transition (e.g. basis risk spread, prepayment adjustment, indirect liquidity costs, liquidity buffer, liquidity stress conditions and option switch spread);
d. Be appropriately granular, taking into account the products sold and the customers served;
e. For the calibration of sight items, ensure a consistent approach to the behavioural model implemented for ALM purposes;
f. Be regularly validated by the risk management function, which shall also assess any impact on liquidity risk and consistency with RAF metrics;
g. Be subject to regular reporting with warning signals on the main sources of risk within the bank and to data quality checks in order to verify the completeness and accuracy of the FTP at deal level[21,22].

Non-compliance with best practices could hinder a consistent allocation of liquidity and related direct/indirect costs and could generate distortion in incentives for individual business units.

---

[21] An early warning system will be all the more effective if the actions required to mitigate the reported risk are clearly defined.

[22] The more sophisticated the data quality and data aggregation process, the more robust and useful the reporting will be.

The lack of adequate and dedicated internal reporting of the FTP model could jeopardise the timely understanding of the consistency and effectiveness of the methodologies with respect to the group's profitability targets and market conditions, as well as the ability to incentivise and disincentivise certain behaviours at the business line level.

FTP is therefore a crucial element in identifying and calculating the drivers of value creation. Some subsidiaries may seem to create value but then, with the analysis of FTP, it becomes clear that they are destroying it. The examples in the following chapter help to clarify this concept.

More generally, the lack of a robust FTP could hinder a full and appropriate level of awareness on the part of the board of what are the profitability drivers at the basis of its own BM, also from a perspective viewpoint. This may undermine its ability to promptly take appropriate remedial action and to adequately address the strategic choices and the related strategic process.

Another business choice is product pricing, the construction of which, like FTP, is characterised by a building block approach.

In **Figure 4.19**, the grey block represents the "minimum hurdle rate", that is the minimum interest rate below which it is not prudent to go, as it is functional to cover all the components to the left of the minimum hurdle rate, most of which are related to FTP. The commissions to the right of the minimum hurdle rate, on the other hand, represent a sort of buffer, the size of which is normally determined by the commercial division and is functional to customer retention, cross-selling optimisation policies and maximisation of a sustainable margin.

The product pricing framework, like the FTP, will therefore also have to reflect the business strategy and the RAF and will have to hinge on a robust cost allocation process. The pricing policy should be well detailed and any exceptions adequate-

Figure 4.19 **Product pricing scheme**

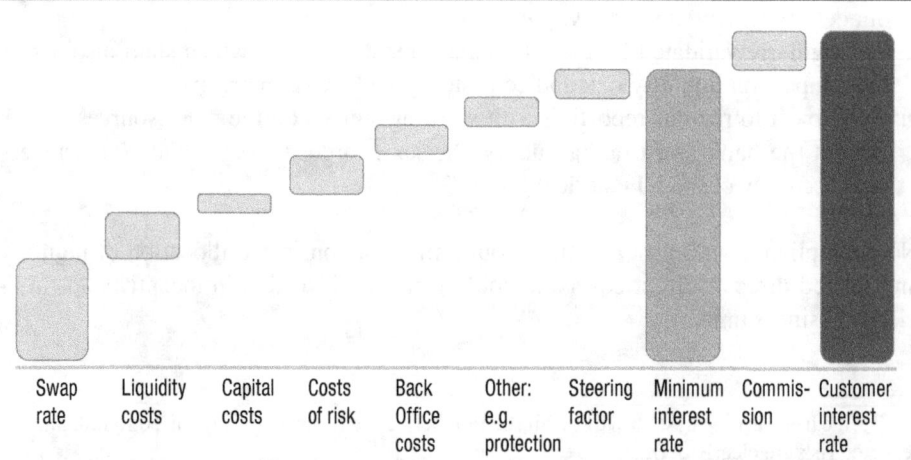

Source: Authors' elaboration on banking practice.

ly monitored. In particular, the roles and responsibilities, the pricing methodology, the monitoring, reporting and "feedback loop" process must be regulated. Countless players are involved in the pricing process: Senior Management, Risk Management, Finance, Treasury, Business, Legal/Compliance and IT.

4.7 Sixth step: Capital allocation

Capital allocation is a process that allows the bank to allocate internal capital to each business unit according to a risk/return logic. In particular, the absorbed capital is allocated to each business unit on the basis of the bank's decisions approved in the RAF on how to use the estimated capital surplus in terms of investment choices (**Figure 4.20**).

In this context, it is appropriate to provide for a formalised reporting and back-testing process that verifies *ex post* the efficiency of the capital allocated to the various business units with respect to the results achieved.

We will not dwell on capital allocation which, in the banking industry, is un-

Figure 4.20 **Consistency between capital allocation and RAF**

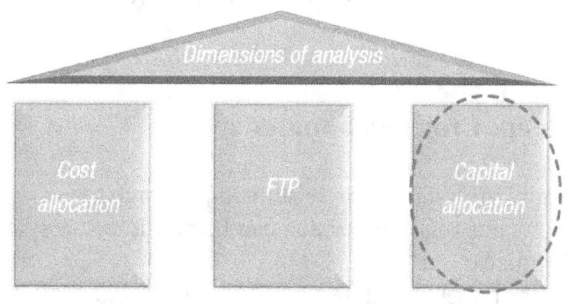

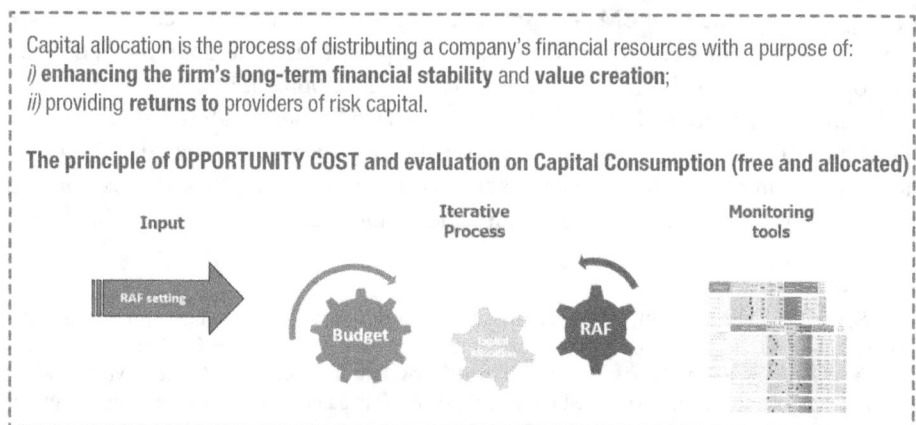

Source: Authors' elaboration on banking practices.

derstood as a process based on capital absorption determined by supervisory rules. However, we suggest implementing the process by comparing the value creation in relation to the capital allocated for each portfolio.

One of the key concepts of modern BMA is the calculation of profitability per customer[23], which is useful, for example, in a logic of profitability in credit line waivers. In the market, there are various ways of calculating the creation of value per customer. For reasons of synthesis, only three are highlighted:

a. *Remuneration of capital per individual credit operation*, it will be necessary to consider the type of counterparty, the guarantees, the amount of credit, the tax rate, the cost of equity calculated using the CAPM methodology, the duration of the credit line and the cost of credit risk (PD*LGD*EAD). The remuneration of capital is aimed at verifying the economical convenience of the individual credit line transaction;
b. *Customer portfolio profitability*, is determined on the basis of recurring margins (interest margin, management margin, banking services margin) and non-recurring margins (trading and underwriting margin) net of any payouts (e.g. network);
c. *Customer relationship profitability*, can be determined as an average between A and B, weighting the amount of the credit line (assuming maximum utilisation) with the customer's indirect deposits and comparing everything exclusively on indirect deposits.

4.8 Seventh step: Projection analysis

Wide-ranging planning systems and sustainability analyses of BMs should clearly hinge on solid projection analyses, which can be considered a synthesis of the entire business analysis process.

A prerequisite for projection analysis is the extrapolation and interpretation of the assumptions on which the BM is based. The probabilistic and multi-scenario analysis allows then to evaluate, with a certain level of probability, the degree of goodness and consistency of the ingredients in the business development forecasts.

Smaller banks often adopt a "business" approach to their analysis which involves "judgemental" adjustments to business projections, rather than a statistical approach based, for example, on Monte Carlo analysis, because of lack of expertise or adequate database. We will not discuss the calculation methodologies here, but it will

---

[23] Several methods for defining economic value to the customer have been proposed in the economic literature and in industry. For example, Economic Value to the Customer (EVC) is a value-based pricing methodology, developed in 1979 by John L. Forbis and Nitin T. Mehta, which outperforms the traditional cost-added methodology. EVC is calculated by adding tangible and intangible elements of value that a product or service provides to a customer. Therefore companies, including banks that have adapted the methodology, can use the approach to estimate the value that a customer derives from the purchase of a product or service.

4   Analysing the business model in seven steps   83

Figure 4.21   **Input drivers from internal analysis**

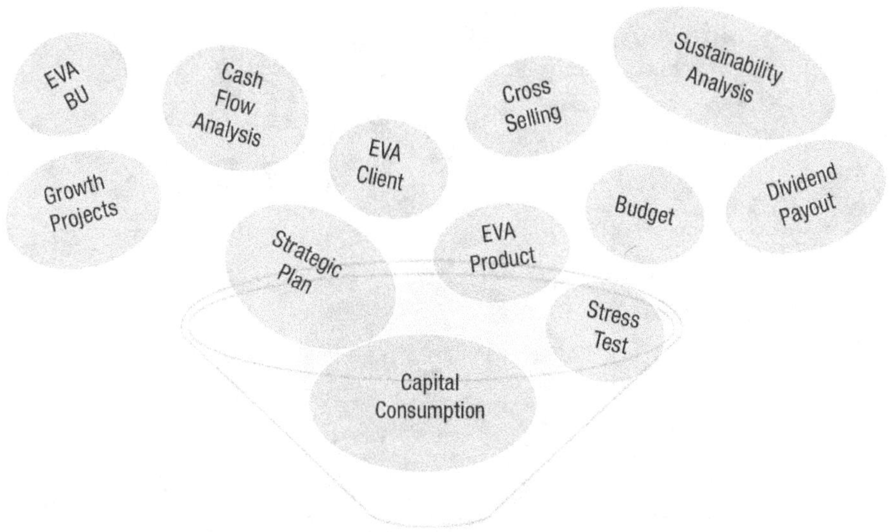

[Figure: ellipses labeled EVA BU, Cash Flow Analysis, Cross Selling, Sustainability Analysis, Growth Projects, EVA Client, Budget, Dividend Payout, Strategic Plan, EVA Product, Stress Test, Capital Consumption — arranged in a funnel shape]

Source: Authors' elaboration.

clearly be crucial that the models are intuitive, based on quality "input drivers" inspired by internal and third-party analyses (e.g. sector studies, rating agency data, surveys, etc.) and transparent about the rationale for any adjustments made on the basis of professional experience (**Figure 4.21**).

The analysis should therefore be aimed at verifying:

a. The reasonableness of the parameters used to estimate the macroeconomic variables and of all those used as future drivers of development (new regulatory, accounting and demographic developments, changes in the competitive landscape such as fintech, technological developments as well as macroeconomic environment and monetary policy decisions, e.g. interest rates);
b. The estimated effects of the assumed growth on the liquidity profile;
c. The impact of the forecast on the BM and on profitability, cost and risk drivers (e.g. on the effects of contribution margins on expected results);
d. The consistency with the business strategy and RAF;
e. The reasonableness of the forecasts (methods used, monitoring process, back-testing analysis);
f. The use of alternative scenarios and sensitivity analyses, including under stress assumptions and that they are sufficiently rigorous and strict[24];

---

[24] Unexpected events, black swans, are by definition unpredictable: there is no way of knowing in advance when they will happen but they have an enormous impact. According to philosopher

Figure 4.22 Projection analysis – framework

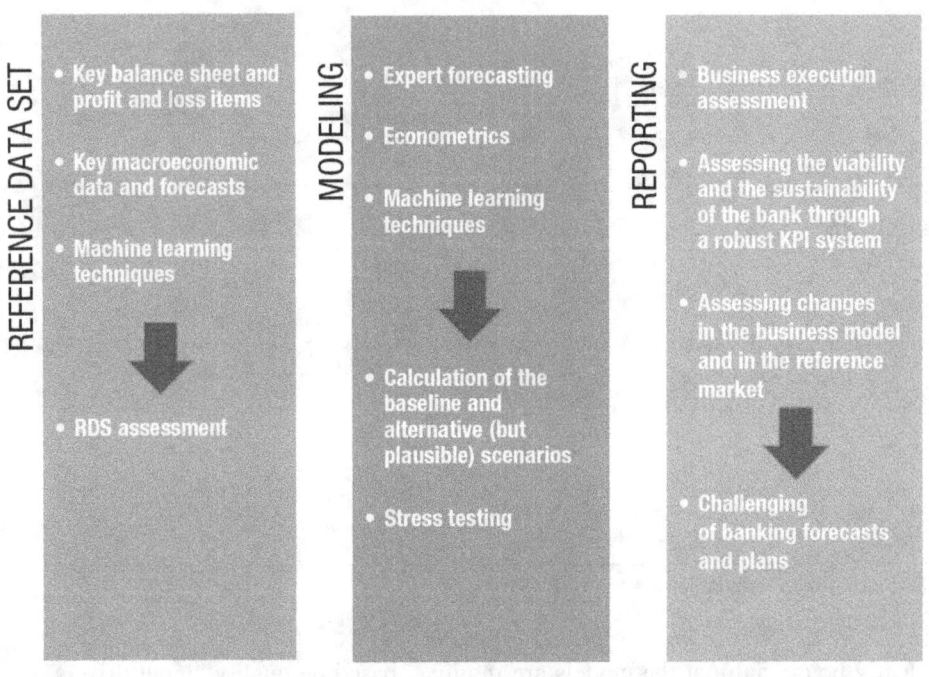

Source: Authors' elaboration on banking practice.

g. The estimation of projections at business segment levels, including in terms of RWA;
h. That the statistical models, when used, are subject to robust decision making and that the plausibility of the outputs in relation to one's BM, capital and funding plans and RAF are also challenged with the help of qualitative inputs.

To do this, the framework should be built on three fundamental pillars: data input, methodology and reporting (Figure 4.22).

The identification of the reference data set represents a crucial moment that could also be finalised using machine learning techniques. The choice of which forecasting methodology to favour will depend on the objectives of the exercise and the availability and characteristics of the reference data set. Once the baseline and alternative scenarios have been formulated and stress exercises have been conducted, it will be crucial that: i) the board discusses and/or challenges these scenarios in order to as-

---

and mathematician Nassim Nicholas Taleb, the risks and probability of future events should not be estimated, assuming that something will not happen because it never happened in the past ("The Black Swan", Taleb, 2009).

sess the degree to which they are good and the actual sustainability of the BM, both current and prospective; ii) future capital and funding needs are identified in a timely manner; iii) there is continuous monitoring of the "forecasts vs. actual" scenarios through appropriate KPIs and that appropriate remedial measures are identified; iv) the aforesaid analyses are promptly updated with the occurrence of events that have a significant impact on environmental factors (e.g. pandemics, wars, technological innovations, etc.) and take into account the results of periodic *ex post* analyses conducted on previous strategic decisions.

5 Case study

"We cannot solve our problems with the same thinking we used when we created them.
You have to rise above it to the next level"
A. Einstein

5.1 The toolkit

In the previous chapters, a seven-step tool was proposed to analyse the BM in the strategic process of banks. It was discussed inter alia how crucial it is for the board, once it has interpreted the macroeconomic framework (step 1), analysed and chosen its competitive positioning objectives (step 2), to define strategic plans aimed at achieving adequate profitability (step 3).

In this chapter we focus on certain aspects of the fourth and fifth steps, which represent new elements in the traditional BMA.

In the fourth step, as emphasised in the previous chapter, it is necessary to define and implement *ex ante* an adequate risk-adjusted segment reporting, to be analysed and exploited to make decisions consistent with these objectives.

The IT variable and digital innovations, such as AI, have created the pre-conditions for the availability of a vast amount of information. However, data is like the volumes of an encyclopaedia arranged in the studio's library: you can admire it from afar, or open it up, read it and learn from it to answer the questions and objectives set by the board.

After all, you find what you are looking for. A holistic analysis of the business situation can help identify the interdependencies created in the banking business and reduce the risk of vision tunnels, that is that sort of cognitive blinder or partial perspective that inevitably misses relevant aspects of the entire business process.

Building segment reporting, inspired by the most advanced industry principles, takes time and profound analytical skills. It is necessary to break down and recompose the entire banking business: the combination of resources, products and customer segments contribute, like the pieces of an enormous puzzle, to creating or destroying value in the various areas of activity. After all, to borrow from Gestalt therapy[1], "the whole is more than the sum of the parts", that is the representation of the bank's BM.

---

[1] Structuralist Gestalt theory is the contemporary psychological theory (also known as Gestalt, or form, psychology) developed in Germany in the second decade of the twentieth century by M.

In order to do this, it is necessary to leave the comfort zone created by the habit of established processes and procedures, to rethink management control, to reverse engineer the company's results and, according to a reframing principle[2], to try to reduce any cognitive biases and noises[3]. All of this is done by relativising what is happening inside and outside the company.

Therefore, segment reporting is the result of a more complex business intelligence activity aimed at measuring the health of a bank in terms of current and prospective business vitality. This activity should ensure a wider flow of information at different company levels of the results achieved, in order to act proactively with tactical action plans in the short term as well as broader strategic plans to ensure the sustainability of the company over time.

When carrying out a BMA it is therefore necessary to analyse a number of key elements that contribute to viability.

5.2 Business Case: Know your business

As already mentioned in the introduction, the book is substantially divided into two sections, one theoretical and the other applicative. The applicative part, which follows, deals with abstract and deliberately simple case studies, functional, however, to clarify the key concepts described in the theoretical section. These relate to the details of the proposed tool, focusing also on decisions that banks should take to achieve the strategic objective of overall value creation.

5.2.1 Segmentation and sub-segmentation process

It has already been said that in order for segment reporting to adequately support the strategic analysis of the BM and the identification and measurement of the driv-

---

Wertheimer, K. Koffka and W. Köhler in opposition to associationist psychology. According to this theory, perceptual phenomena cannot be explained on the basis of a juxtaposition or addition of single elementary units (sensations), but rather globally in their organisation into structures (Gestalten) according to well-defined laws.

[2] In the field of psychology, reframing is a process that involves changing the way a situation is perceived, and thus changing its meaning.

[3] The distinction between "bias" and "noise" is at the heart of the new work that Nobel prize-winner Daniel Kahneman recently published together with Cass Sunstein and Olivier Sibony ("Noise. A Flaw in Human Judgement". Harper Collins, 2021) aimed at explaining the essence of a new category of phenomena that continually risks misleading our decisions. Specifically, cognitive biases, understood as errors in judgement resulting from misinterpretations of the information we possess, are considered to be medium-sized, objective and measurable errors. Whereas cognitive biases are the result of contingencies and causalities of the moment, which differ from time to time, cognitive noises represent systematic deviations of our cognitive system that vary according to circumstances and individuals. The combination of "bias" and "noise", of course, can only further deteriorate the quality of strategic choices.

ers of value creation (or destruction), it is necessary that, prior to its construction, the bank adequately reflects on what its core business is, on which commercial segments it has focused, on the distribution channels used and on the categories of products marketed, as well as on the customer segment served. The next step will be to define the criteria for distributing the overall group activity along all the aforementioned variables.

A practical example will help to clarify this phase. Let us assume that the banking group "Target", the result of a progressive process of restructuring and concentration over time, wants to seize, like its competitors, new business opportunities in the light of the changed competitive environment.

Let us imagine that the banking group operates on the national territory and has a traditional vocation. Let us assume that the business strategy followed is to:

a. Create value by better focusing its business and entering new market segments;
b. Safeguard territorial roots, combining them, where possible, with a process of integration through aggregation;
c. Centralise coordination, planning and control and personnel management functions in the holding company;
d. Decentralise to the network banks (NB1, NB2, NB3) the core business, that is collecting financial resources from the customers and disbursing them as credit (hence B2C);
e. Use product companies (PC1, PC2) to provide services considered non-core, such as leasing and factoring, to the public (B2C) and also to support the core business carried out by the network banks (B2B);
f. Use a company under Swiss law to meet the varied needs of "Private" clients (LE1);
g. Outsource to a product factory under Luxembourg law (LE2) the "production" of financial products to be placed and distributed to customers (again, B2B);
h. Outsource to a group server provider the IT and real estate activities at group level (again B2B);
i. Maintain the brand of the network banks in their chosen territories, leaving decision-making autonomy for commercial and credit activities.

In this context, let us assume that, in the periodical monitoring of the commercial trend, the segment reporting in **Table 5.1** is presented to the board, prepared by its own management control and strategic planning structures on the basis of consolidated accounting procedures established in the past in the group even before the pursuit of the above-mentioned strategies.

What does the table suggest? What kind of information is represented? What information is missing?

The information in the table gives us a representation of the macro income and financial components of the different subsidiaries. What is shown is a subdivision of

Table 5.1 Segment reporting developed according to practices and customs

Segment Reporting (€/mln)	Network bank 1	Network bank 2	Network bank 3	Product Company 1	Product Company 2	Legal Entity 1	Legal Entity 2	Service Provider	Total
Net Performing Loans	950,000	1,800,000	935,000	13,537	12,687	16,776	-	-	3,728,000
Net Bad Loans	50,000	200,000	65,000	450	500	50	-	-	316,000
Direct and Indirect Funding	-1,211,730	-2,244,439	-1,118,000	-17,683	-16,907	-20,520	-100	-	-4,629,379
Capital Allocated	-90,000	-185,561	-85,000	-1,304	-1,280	-1,306	-80	-90	-364,621
Net Interest Income	55,000	110,000	53,600	1,350	1,250	1,700	-	-	222,900
Net Commisions	12,000	11,000	10,000	490	440	1,080	1,680	700	37,390
Trading and Other Income	35,000	49,000	27,000	25	33	995	930	-	112,983
Direct Operating Cost	-63,188	-97,420	-68,174	-549	-470	-1,202	-694	-252	-231,949
Indirect Operating Cost	-27,081	-64,947	-26,512	-468	-401	-478	-442	-168	-120,497
Result before taxes	11,731	7,633	-4,086	848	852	2,095	1,474	280	20,827
Adjustment	-8	-13	-5	-7	-9	-11	-8	-9	-70
Taxes	-3,871	-2,519	-	-280	-281	-691	-	-92	-7,735
Net Result	7,852	5,101	-4,091	561	562	1,393	1,466	179	13,022

Source: Authors' elaboration on banking practices.

the operating costs into direct and indirect, the capital allocated to each entity and a condensed version of the assets and liabilities of the balance sheet as well as the income and expenditure items of the profit and loss account, supplemented by some management information (direct and indirect costs).

From this representation, for example, we can see that the main subsidiaries contributing to the group's gross profit are NB1 (56%) and NB2 (37%), while NB3 is the only company making a loss, and a substantial one. The contribution of the other companies is modest, except for LE1 in Switzerland.

Of the network banks, NB1 is the best performing on average in terms of profitability, NPL ratio (5%) and CIR (88%). NB2 has higher levels of loans than NB1, but is inefficient in terms of NPL ratio (11%) and CIR (95%). The average CIR and NPL ratios recorded by the group companies stand at 68% and 8.5%, respectively.

This information becomes important when it shows the contribution rate of the individual subsidiaries to the net result. This information is certainly important, but it has a purely accounting vocation and is therefore substantially guided by the rationale of preparing consolidated financial statements. Less evident is the information useful to formulate hypotheses on which business segments create more value and which destroy it.

Hence the goal of building segment reporting based on a holistic approach that involves "breaking down and reassembling all the drivers of profitability". It is therefore necessary to abandon the concept of legal entities, brands and operating segments and to look at the entire group as if it were one huge corporate reality with its value chains to be identified and measured[4].

In order to do this, it is necessary to carry out a process of reverse engineering that leads us to break down the operating result as granularly as possible into several dimensions. In our case, those to be investigated could be related to the type of customers served (e.g. retail, corporate), the products offered (e.g. short term, medium-long term, wealth management, factoring and leasing), the distribution channels used (physical channel represented by branches and financial advisers or emerging channels such as online) and residual categories of cost and profit centres (e.g. ALM and corporate centre).

But we have not yet concluded, as most of the dimensions just listed can be categorised as business segments (Figure 5.1). What in mathematics we would call composite numbers, which unlike prime numbers, are multiples of other numbers. However, we are looking for granularity and a further effort at subdivision may be necessary until the trade-off of the operation makes the exercise uneconomic.

Trying therefore to further drill down through some "composite numbers" of the data present in the company, a breakdown of commercial segments and sub-segments to be represented as segment reporting could be that shown in Table 5.2, where the retail and corporate segments have been further subdivided into the customer categories served by the Target group.

---

[4] Such as those regulated by IFRS 8 e SFAS 131.

Figure 5.1 **Clustering of customers by turnover and assets**

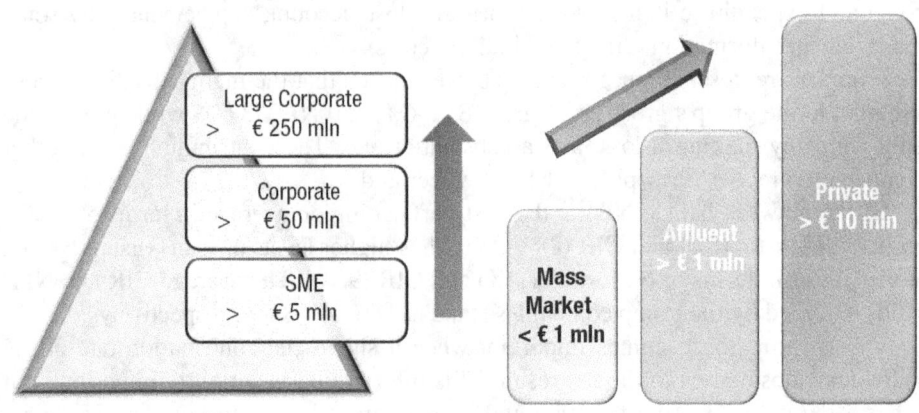

Source: Authors' elaboration on banking practices.

Let us assume that, based on the above assumption of customer management segmentation and taking into account the business units implemented, the bank prepares segment reporting as illustrated in **Table 5.2**.

This representation, contrary to the previous one, could lead the board to some reflections, such as, for example:

- a more accurate management of FTP;
- the opportunity to abandon or not possible residual categories of customers;
- to detect any potential sources of destruction of value and non-optimal use of the allocated capital.

From an income-accounting point of view, we can see from the **Table 5.2** that the mass market, corporate and corporate centre (CC) segments make a negative contribution to the group result (€20.8 million).

Moving instead to a value creation analysis dimension, our red flags unfortunately increase[5]. The segments that contribute most to the overall destruction of value recorded by the group (- €29.2 mln) rise to five: mass market, CC, large corporate, corporate and affluent. In the following paragraphs we will try to explore this issue in more detail.

Meanwhile, we know that, given the characteristics of the bank, there are several dimensions that could be investigated.

Therefore, in addition to customers and business units, a further dimension could

---

[5] In this analysis, assuming group ROE and COE levels of 5% and 12%, respectively, group EVA will be negative.

5 Case study

Table 5.2 Examples of commercial segments and sub-segments: customers and business units

Target Group	Private			Corporate			ALM	Corporate Centre	Gross Result
	Mass Market	Affluent	Private	SME	Corporate	Large Corporate			
Balance sheet amounts									
Financial assets	-	-	-	-	-	-	950,000	-	950,000
Net Performing Loans	1,192,960	260,960	186,400	708,320	1,043,840	335,520	-	-	3,728,000
Net Impaired Loans	107,440	3,160	6,320	88,480	101,120	9,480	-	-	316,000
Deposits	-1,607,000	-836,000	-734,075	-646,000	-195,000	-142,000	-	-	-4,160,075
Capital allocated	-108,330	-21,256	-15,670	-67,283	-95,642	-27,979	-85,500	57,039	-364,621
Funding gap	414,930	593,136	557,025	-83,517	-854,318	-175,021	-864,500	-57,039	-469,304
No. Clients	780	30	55	200	32	3	-	-	1,100
No. Branches	245	9	18	63	11	5	-	-	350
P&L amounts									
Net Interest Income	66,870	26,748	35,664	62,412	15,603	8,916	6,687	-	222,900
Net Commissions	5,609	7,104	12,348	9,721	3,365	2,617	1,496	-1,870	37,390
Trading and Other Income	10,168	2,260	3,389	9,039	6,779	7,909	73,439	-	112,983
Total Operating Revenue	82,647	36,112	51,401	78,172	25,747	19,442	81,622	-1,870	373,273
Cost of credit	-37,132	-12,641	-14,550	-24,749	-17,283	-3,008	-	-	-109,363
Operating Direct Cost	-52,830	-10,322	-13,617	-20,015	-15,818	-2,056	-7,928	-	-122,586
Operating Indirect Cost	-50,839	-8,820	-10,230	-20,714	-5,615	-2,410	-5,723	-16,147	-120,497
Profit before tax	-58,154	4,329	13,004	12,694	-12,969	11,968	67,971	-18,016	20,827
Fund transfer pricing	10	14	12	-6	-86	-8	64		
EVA	-71,135	-5,295	10,812	19,197	-10,855	-14,640	64,795	-22,038	-29,158

Source: Authors' elaboration on banking practices.

Table 5.3 **Examples of commercial segments and sub-segments: distribution channels**

Target Group	Branches	Financial Advisors	Online Channel
Balance sheet amounts			
Net Performing Loans	2,796,000	559,200	372,800
Net Impaired Loans	237,000	47,400	31,600
Deposits	-3,120,056	-624,011	-416,008
Capital allocated	-252,120	-50,424	-33,616
Funding gap	339,176	67,835	45,224
No. Clients	825	165	110
P&L amounts			
Net Interest Income	162,160	32,432	21,621
Net Commissions	28,323	5,665	3,776
Trading and Other Income	29,658	5,932	3,954
Total Operating Revenue	**220,140**	**44,028**	**29,352**
Cost of credit	-82,022	-16,404	-10,936
Operating Direct Cost	-85,994	-17,199	-11,466
Operating Indirect Cost	-73,971	-14,794	-9,863
Profit before tax	**-21,846**	**-4,369**	**-2,913**
Fund transfer pricing	-48	-10	-6
EVA	**-77,886**	**7,913**	**-1,942**

Source: Authors' elaboration on banking practices.

be the distribution channel. Let us suppose that the bank prepares a segment reporting as illustrated in **Table 5.3**.

From the analysis of the table, it can be seen that from the point of view of distribution channels, the BM is strongly characterised by the use of a traditional branch network, while the online and financial adviser channels are poorly developed.

A further example of a dimension that could be investigated is that of products.

Taking into account the characteristics of the BM outlined above, that is a bank with a commercial vocation, let us imagine that the relevant structures will prepare a business report as illustrated in **Table 5.4**.

To conclude this brief discussion, sometimes the board might also find it interesting to reflect on the advisability of using the Pareto analysis (or 80/20 Law), where from an optimisation perspective the bank could focus its steering on that 20% of the activities (but also products or customers) that would determine 80% of the results achieved by the group[6].

---

[6] The Pareto principle, called the "80/20 law" or the "Pareto effect", is a statistical-empirical result found in many complex systems with a cause-effect structure. The Pareto principle states that only 20% of an entire action can achieve 80% of the results. The remaining 20% therefore

Table 5.4   Examples of commercial segments and sub-segments: products

Target Group	Short Term	M/L Term	Mortgage	Wealth Management	Factoring	Leasing	Consumer Finance
			P&L amounts				
Net Interest Income	79,999	19,459	88,647	15,135	6,486	4,324	2,162
Net Commissions	13,973	3,399	15,483	2,643	1,133	755	378
Trading and Other Income	14,631	3,559	16,213	2,768	1,186	791	395
Yield	0	0	0	0	0	0	0
Cost of credit	-40,464	-9,843	-44,839	-7,655	-3,281	-2,187	-1,094
Operating Direct Cost	-42,423	-10,319	-47,010	-8,026	-3,440	-2,293	-1,147
Operating Indirect Cost	-36,492	-8,876	-40,437	-6,904	-2,959	-1,973	-986
Profit before tax	-10,777	-2,622	-11,942	-2,039	-874	-583	-291
Fund transfer pricing	-24	-6	-26	-4	-2	-1	-1
EVA	**-5,184**	**-24,916**	**-38,898**	**14,359**	**-3,582**	**-21,388**	**7,694**

Source: Authors' elaboration on banking practices.

5.2.2   Commercial segments and sub-segments: Performance analysis

Entering more deeply into the merits of the BMA, let us assume that during the last meeting the board asked the competent structures to carry out a sustainability analysis of the organisational model outlined in the post-restructuring phase described above.

There are only a few months left before the approval of the new strategic plan, and the directors hope that – given the resources available and the intrinsic complexity of the competitive environment in which the group operates – the relevant structures will draw up coherent, balanced strategic guidelines inspired by a gradual strengthening of its competitive advantage.

Let us imagine that the analysis of the contribution of the commercial segments

---

requires 80% of the time in most cases. This is why this principle is often referred to as the 80/20 law.

Figure 5.2 **Example of the contribution of commercial segments to the normalised group result**

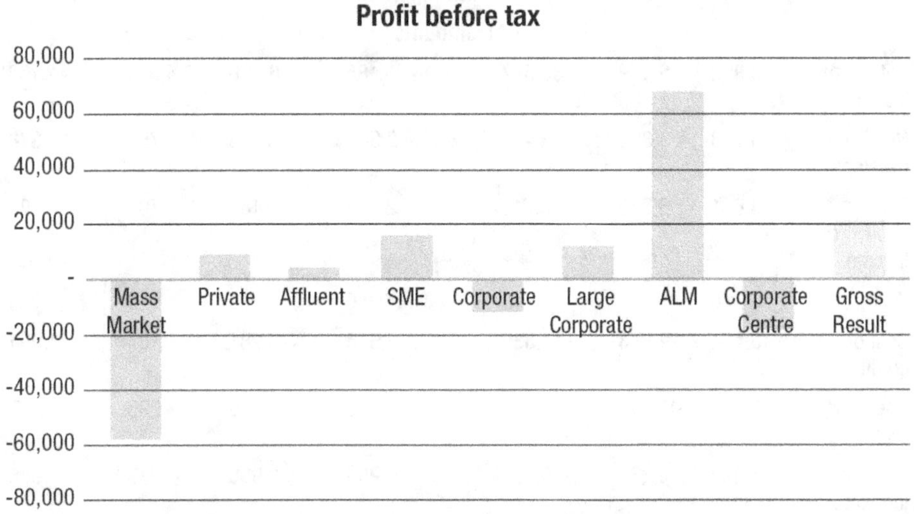

Profit before tax

[Bar chart showing values for: Mass Market (≈ -70,000), Private (small positive), Affluent (small positive), SME (≈ 15,000), Corporate (slightly negative), Large Corporate (≈ 10,000), ALM (≈ 65,000), Corporate Centre (small positive), Gross Result (small positive); y-axis from -80,000 to 80,000]

Source: Authors' elaboration.

and business units to the group's normalised result (just under €30 million after neutralising any one-off components) shows the graph in **Figure 5.2**.

From the point of view of profitability, what does the graph suggest?

The graph shows that the main positive components contributing to the group's normalised result are ALM (over €150 million) and wealth management (just under €100 million).

Let us assume that, from the analysis of the rationales underlying this overperformance, there is generally a fair exploitation of favourable and contingent market conditions and that, for example, more than 55% of the ALM's performance is attributable to the carry trade and that the funding cost is represented by liquidity injected by the ECB at virtually no cost[7].

Is this performance sustainable in the medium to long term?

In order to answer this question, we should first analyse possible developments in the macroeconomic scenario with specific reference to that of interest rates.

---

[7] Carry trade is a strategy based on buying financial instruments with a return higher than the cost of financing the investment. The investment is usually in low-risk instruments, such as government bonds.

Let us suppose, only as a hypothetical case given the current contingent post-Covid-19 environment, that the projections show a rise in interest rates characterised by a rapid trend, due to the abandonment of quantitative easing by the Central Bank.

The hypothesised change in the macroeconomic scenario therefore suggests repositioning the strategy by activating various profitability drivers, such as, for example, boosting traditional activities by revitalising the markup and markdown.

In this case, it would be necessary to neutralise the carry trade component, which, in the example shown, would exhaust its impetus in the short term and performance would deteriorate significantly in terms of the group's normalised result.

From the point of view of costs (and in this case of the CC) what does the graph suggest?

Analysing the various contributions, it emerges that the main negative component is represented by the performance recorded by the CC, that is by that notional segment into which, in this case, flow the cost elements not yet allocated and therefore waiting to be allocated to the respective business lines.

Given the values of the CC, can we consider these results robust and reliable?

Particularly negative CC performances represent clear overestimates of the results recorded by the remaining segments, with the risk of dangerous misinterpretations of the real levers of profitability.

We know that the allocation of direct costs does not present any particular difficulty since by their nature they are directly attributable to the commercial segments. The problem arises with the allocation of indirect costs and, as we have seen, the nature of the "parking" from transitory could become definitive as the competent structures are not able to correctly allocate certain types of costs.

Various methods for the allocation of indirect costs are proposed in the literature (full costing, cost centre based system, activity based costing, etc.). In contrast with the industrial sector, proxies are widely used in the banking sector[8], as the exact allocation of the complex system of indirect costs is undoubtedly extremely costly.

In abstract, the non-allocation of indirect costs in a range between 5% and 20% could be considered physiological, where the lower limit, if it gets increasingly close to 0, would represent the ideal situation. Clearly, this is a theoretical and indicative range that will have to be adapted to the banking reality and, if necessary, recalibrated, considering the trade-off relating to a non-total allocation of costs.

An example will help to clarify the concept. Let us imagine that management control decides to allocate the complex system of operating costs to the commercial segments on the basis of an ad hoc distribution matrix based on operational

---

[8] Statistical indicators aimed at describing the behaviour of a given phenomenon that cannot be observed directly.

Figure 5.3   **Example of the contribution of commercial segments to the group result**

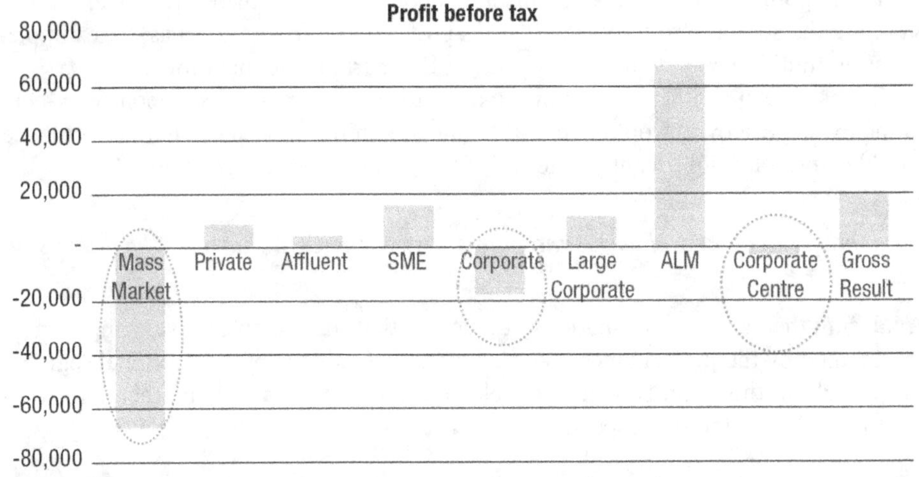

```
                       Profit before tax
80,000
60,000                                            ┌──┐
40,000                                            │  │
20,000                  ┌──┐                      │  │          ┌──┐
              ┌──┐┌──┐  │  │  ┌──┐   ┌──┐         │  │          │  │
  0   ╌╌╌╌╌╌╌╌┤  ├┤  ├╌╌┤  ├╌╌┤  ├╌╌╌┤  ├╌╌╌╌╌╌╌╌╌┤  ├╌╌╌╌╌╌╌╌╌╌┤  ├╌╌╌╌
       Mass   Private Affluent SME Corporate Large   ALM   Corporate Gross
-20,000 Market                           Corporate          Centre  Result
-40,000 │  │
-60,000 │  │
-80,000 └──┘
```

Source: Authors' elaboration.

parameters of consumption/absorption of resources and that the result is as follows (**Figure 5.3**).

An analysis of the graph shows that the already weak and often insufficient creation of value by core commercial segments – such as the mass market and corporate segments – has, in general, significantly worsened.

But the CC, as described above, also plays the central function in cash pooling, an activity based on a complex system of notional rates. As is well known, the FTP is primarily a steering tool[9], so the total remuneration could be influenced by the bank's choice to incentivise or disincentivise certain behaviours.

For example, in a scenario of a general excess of liquidity that cannot be used profitably within the group, the FTP could be set at a level where any generation of funding is penalised through a notional remuneration close to zero or even negative.

Similarly, in the event that it is desired to incentivise the level of lending to particular categories of consumers or the placement/distribution of particular types of products, the FTP will be set at levels such that this behaviour is rewarded through a higher notional remuneration than that paid to other types of customers and products.

Trying to sterilise the notional effects resulting from the steering activity through the FTP system, as well as the result generated by the CC, lets us imagine that the result is represented by the following graph (**Figure 5.4**).

---

[9] Il TIT è "il tasso di interesse che la funzione di ALM dovrebbe pagare/incassare sul mercato qualora volesse immunizzare ogni singola operazione d'impiego o investimento con un'operazione di uguale ammontare nominale ma di segno opposto".

5   Case study

Figure 5.4   **Example of the contribution of commercial segments to the group result**

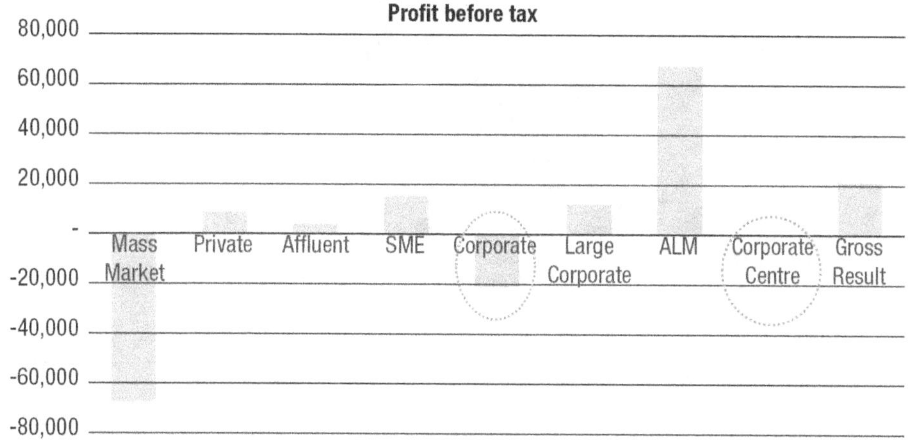

```
                          Profit before tax
 80,000
 60,000
 40,000
 20,000
      -   Mass    Private  Affluent  SME  Corporate  Large    ALM   Corporate  Gross
-20,000   Market                                     Corporate      Centre     Result
-40,000
-60,000
-80,000
```

Source: Authors' elaboration.

Compared with the previous results, we note a further deterioration in the performance of the corporate segment. This means that a notional remuneration has been attributed to this type of clientele in order to boost the level of related loans.

Can this steering operation be considered correct in principle? Or would it have been more profitable to support the SME and/or large corporate segments, which all in all perform well?

The answer is neither simple nor unambiguous and there are many underlying variables to be assessed. It is certainly necessary to ask whether the corporate segment is really a source of value destruction tout court as it would seem, or whether the choice is driven by certain strategic levers such as cross-selling.

At this point it is crucial to introduce the concept of cross-selling and customer EVA.

Let us imagine that there are three customers who generate different levels of customer EVA for the same loan (**Figure 5.5**).

Assuming that the bank can only invest €1,000, which of the three customers should the bank finance?

It goes without saying that, on the basis of the customer EVA generated, customer C (which, by analogy to the previous example, we assume to be the SME segment) is definitely to be preferred. If the bank had an additional €1,000 to invest, it could also finance customer B (which, by analogy to the previous example, we assume to be the large corporate segment). Customer A is undoubtedly to be discarded (which, by

Figure 5.5   Customer EVA levels - Loans hypothesis

HP 1	Loans
Customer A	1.000
EVA Customer A	- 10
Customer B	1.000
EVA Customer B	10
Customer C	1.000
EVA Customer C	11

Source: Authors' elaboration.

analogy with the previous example, we assume to be the corporate segment) since the bank would record a value destruction of ten.

Let us now assume that the three customers are provided with additional services and that the total EVA per customer is as shown in the last column in **Figure 5.6**.

Which of the three customers should the bank finance?

The previous answer is almost reversed. The customer to be favoured is customer A (corporate). If the bank then had further funds, it could finance customer B (large corporate) and then customer C (SME), in that order.

Figure 5.6   Levels of customer EVA - Wealth management hypothesis

HP 2	Loans	Services	Wealth Mgmt	EVA Customer
Customer A	1,000	100	1,500	
EVA Customer A	- 10	2	50	42
Customer B	1,000		150	
EVA Customer B	10		5	15
Customer C	1,000			
EVA Customer C	11			11

Source: Authors' elaboration.

5 Case study

Such simple examples highlight how crucial it is to always take a holistic approach, regardless of the phenomenon being investigated. Providing financing with negative EVA could be a sustainable practice only if the overall position of the client has positive EVA as a source of value creation.

5.2.3 Commercial network: Efficiency analysis

It is common to refer to the concept of business performance as the attitude and capacity of a company to create value, perhaps in a "Pareto optimality" logic.

It is also well known that while effectiveness indicates the ability to achieve the company's objectives, in this case value creation, efficiency, on the other hand, evaluates the ability to do so while optimising the available resources. These are clearly two distinct concepts but have become inseparable in the economic literature.

The solicitations of the board undoubtedly imply an analysis on several evaluation levels. If in some way a view has been conveyed on the capacity of the commercial segments and sub-segments to create value, on the other hand, it is not possible to identify any food for thought on the level of efficiency of certain strategic choices of an organisational nature.

Let us imagine, for example, that the board wants to include an objective of organisational efficiency in the strategic plan.

In general, one of the most immediate indicators used to measure the overall efficiency of a group, a bank or a branch is the cost/income ratio. The lower the value expressed by this indicator, the greater the management efficiency recorded.

Let us assume that we adopt a top-down approach and assess with increasing granularity the distribution of the level of efficiency within the group. Imagining that at group level the total CIR is 65%, we try to investigate the phenomenon adopting both a cross-sectional and a "silos" perspective.

In order to optimise the analysis, the starting point could be to investigate where, due to a combination of intrinsic factors, most of the group's operating costs are concentrated, namely the network banks and their branches.

Let us suppose that the overall analysis of the network banks shows the following representation (Table 5.5), where the average characteristics of the cost model adopt-

Table 5.5 **Efficiency levels of network banks**

	Loans	Deposits	Direct Cost/FTE	% Indirect Cost on total	Cost of credit on average	Cost Inome Ratio	Loan to Deposit Ratio on average
Network Bank 1	1,000	800	-100	30%	-0.68%	88%	125%
Network Bank 2	2,000	1,000	-80	40%	-1.10%	95%	200%
Network Bank 3	1,000	1,500	-95	28%	-0.90%	106%	67%

Source: Authors' elaboration.

ed are illustrated, while keeping an eye on the average loan to deposit ratio (LTD) levels recorded, in order to relativise the results.

How efficient are the network banks?

In terms of CIR, NB1 is the most efficient and outperforms NB3 by eighteen bps. NB3 is essentially a deposit-taking bank, while NB1, and even more so NB2, are essentially lending network banks.

However, there are operational differences in the core business between NB1 and NB2. NB2 is significantly less efficient and profitable than NB1, with an average cost of credit that is more than 40 bps higher. Finally, there is a higher absorption of direct costs in NB1 and indirect costs in NB2.

What objectives could the board assign to the three banks?

In light of this information, the board could:

a. Urge NB1 to increase lending, given its low cost of credit and CIR levels;
b. Invite NB2 to contain lending in order to reduce the high levels of credit costs;
c. Assign growth targets to NB3, given its low cost of credit levels.

In terms of average LTD, NB2 is an outlier that needs strong intervention by the board. NB1 is 25% "short" and could be financed by NB3.

More in general, trying to draw up a sort of "efficiency ranking", the first place could only be assigned to NB1, which has the lowest CIR and average cost of credit values, where cost of credit is the sum of the costs and charges that the bank incurs to carry out the financing operation.

The NB2 and NB3 network banks, on the other hand, record the lowest levels of indicators relating to the ratio of direct costs to FTE and of indirect costs to total costs, respectively. In the context of an internal peer analysis, NB1 could be chosen as a model to be followed in terms of CIR, to which the other network banks could try to align themselves in order to optimise the overall group CIR.

Two further considerations could be deduced from the analysis: i) the CIR reported by each network bank (including operating costs and cost of credit) is sensitive to the distribution of indirect costs allocated per network bank and to the LTD ratio; ii) the cost of credit is a differential factor.

Once the internal best performer has been identified, would the board be satisfied with the analysis conducted in terms of efficiency?

Analysing the distribution of the efficiency level at network bank level is only a first step. It is important information but partial. Network banks are made up of branches (in this case our prime numbers) and from the analysis just conducted we are not able to quantify and qualify the most efficient branches to be taken as a model and those that are to be made efficient and/or brought to break even.

5 Case study

The next step in the analysis will therefore be to assess the level of distribution of all branches in terms of CIR in an aggregate manner, regardless of whether they belong to individual network banks. The holistic view provides a powerful plus to the analysis, in order to direct the subsequent strategic action to the overall operational efficiency, rather than to the individual network bank. To that end, it would be useful to analyse the CIR per branch and divide it into quantiles in order to measure the degree of branch dispersion in the quantiles with the highest CIR. The higher the dispersion in these quantiles, the lower the efficiency.

Let us imagine that the analysis of the efficiency of individual branches represented by the following graph (**Figure 5.7**) shows a high percentage of CIR per branch (91%) with a wide dispersion along the peripheral network and that, in particular, most of the branches record a CIR above 70% with a strong component above 90%.

This condition will clearly have a negative impact on the average operating result recorded by the branches, as easily demonstrated by the **Figure 5.8**.

What kind of analysis could we conduct at this point?

Trying to carry out some simulations, such as aligning the performance of inefficient branches with those that proved to be more efficient in the analysis conducted, one could quantify the benefits that the group would be able to obtain and assess their feasibility and economic convenience.

For simplicity of analysis, let us assume that the branches maintain the same level of production so that the denominator of the CIR (income) remains constant (**Table 5.6**).

If the costs of all subsidiaries in the bucket >110% were aligned and brought back to break even (100%), the group would start to realise some limited efficiency gains (projection 1).

The savings would of course be much higher if the branches in the >110% and

Figure 5.7 **Distribution of CIR by branch in quantiles**

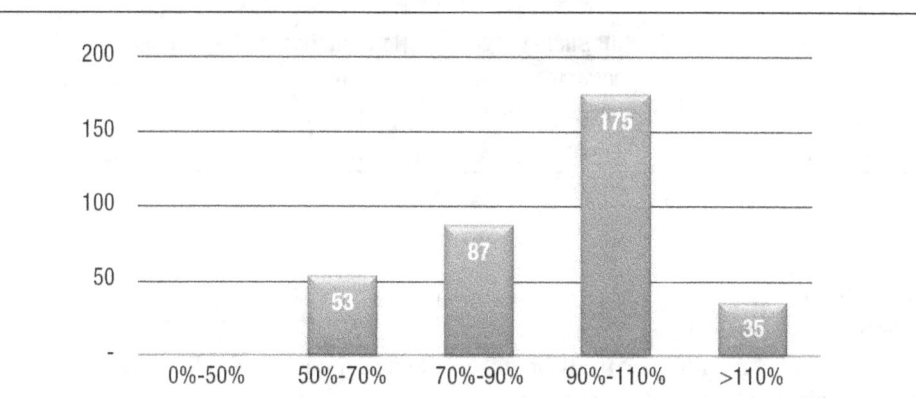

Source: Authors' elaboration.

Figure 5.8   **Average operating income per quantile**

CIR Bucket	No. Branches	% Branches	Average Result	Total Result
0%-50%	-	0%	-	-
50%-70%	53	15%	300,000	15,900,000
70%-90%	87	25%	150,000	13,050,000
90%-110%	175	50%	- 50,000	- 8,750,000
>110%	35	10%	-100,000	- 3,500,000
TOTAL	350	100%		16,700,000

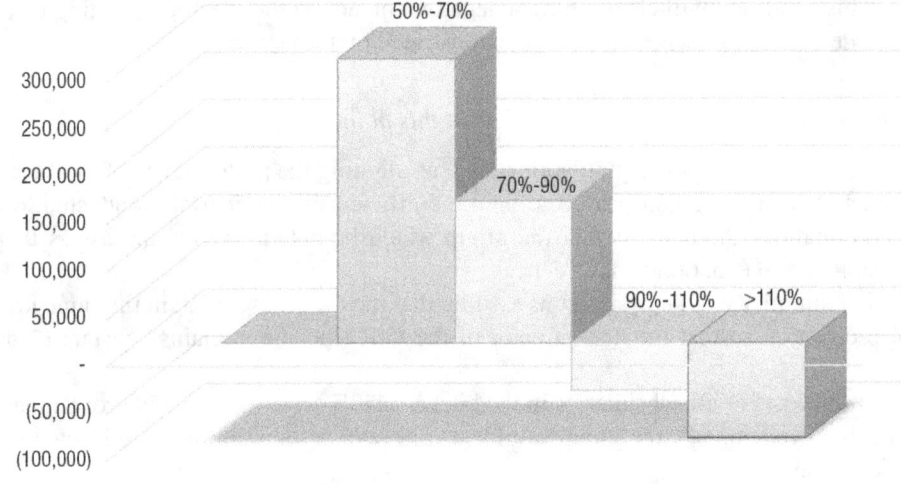

Source: Authors' elaboration.

Table 5.6   **Projection analysis**

	CIR Bucket	No Branches	Cumulated Savings
Projection 1	90%-110%	210	1,750,000
Projection 2	70%-90%	297	43,750,000
Projection 3	50%-70%	350	88,300,000

Source: Authors' elaboration.

90–110% buckets aligned their operational efficiency with those in the 70–90% buckets (projection 2).

It would be even higher if all branches adopted a cost model like the one in the best-performing branches (projection 3).

Against the backdrop of these simplified analyses of operational efficiency, mostly common to all banks, the deeper analysis of the results would involve a sort of back-testing to check whether the choices in terms of FTP, cost allocation and capital consumption are in line with the strategies outlined by the board in the business plans.

5.3 Business Case: Cost-cutting measures

5.3.1 Rationalisation of the organisational model

We have repeatedly emphasised the importance of a thorough understanding of one's own cost structure and the group's operating model, as a preparatory activity to the correct distribution and allocation of indirect costs, since these could "overturn" the result and lead to different scenarios (**Figure 5.9**).

This analysis will be even more crucial when the board mandates the competent structures to rationalise operating costs in order to improve the efficiency and profitability of the group. The changed competitive environment and the coexistence of particular regulatory and economic factors induce in fact to undertake strategic choices more and more oriented to the search for efficiency, and make the "banking risk" cyclically set in motion[10].

Concentration decisions, when not made in pathological situations, are inspired by principles aimed at better focusing the business, improving distribution efficiency, making the best use of technological variables and attacking new market segments in order to create value. A structured banking group, such as the "Target" group we supposed, while on the one hand guaranteeing high specialisation, proximity to the territory and the possibility of spin-off and subsequent sale of one of the companies in the group, on the other hand, could lead to lower profitability. Hence the widespread recourse to complex cost-cutting operations in banks' business plans.

Let us assume that the structures responsible for this area analyse the level of FTE allocation within the Target group (**Table 5.7**).

What data is recorded in the table?

An analysis of the distribution of personnel employed in the network banks shows that about 25% is dedicated to the provision of central services, typically administered by the parent company (2300 FTEs in the network banks and 2000 FTEs in the holding company). The percentage in itself does not assume any relevance since it is not possible to interpret that value until the degree of overlapping of central services provided by the network banks with those of the holding company is measured.

In this regard, in a BMA logic, one could see the possibility and/or the need to review the degree of "autonomy" of the network banks through, for example, the

---

[10] Risk is a strategy board game deriving from the 1957 French game "La conquête du Monde".

Figure 5.9 Distribution of direct and indirect costs

Operating cost DIRECT	Mass Market	Private	Affluent	SMEs	Corporate	Large Corporate	Total %
Staff	70%	69%	69%	75%	72%	55%	45%
Real Estate	15%	6%	12%	11%	6%	9%	25%
IT	10%	8%	13%	11%	10%	16%	20%
Other	5%	16%	7%	3%	12%	20%	10%
Total direct costs %	42%	15%	16%	18%	6%	3%	100%

Operating cost INDIRECT	Total indirect cost %
Group's service	40%
Central structure	50%
Amortization	6%
Other	4%
% direct costs on total	59%
% indirect costs on total	41%

	Mass Market	Private	Affluent	SMEs	Corporate	Large Corporate	Total %
Total operating costs	70%	8%	8%	9%	4%	1%	100%

Source: Authors' elaboration.

Table 5.7 Cost-cutting analysis and allocation of FTEs

Legal Entity	Total FTEs	o/w Branch	o/w Central services
Parent company	2,000		
Network Banks			
Network Bank 1	4,000	3,200	800
Network Bank 2	5,000	4,000	1,000
Network Bank 3	2,500	2,000	500
Total Network Banks	**11,500**	**9,200**	**2,300**
Product Company 1	500		
Product Company 2	450		
Legal Entity 1	200		
Legal Entity 2	300		
Service provider	1,700		
Total	**16,650**		

Source: Authors' elaboration.

centralisation of credit lines above a certain amount or simply through centralised information management.

The implementation of a central strategic intelligence function and a detailed central monitoring system could help to analyse potential synergies between the network banks and the parent company in terms of cost optimisation. Once the activities of the central services have been thoroughly screened, a further focus of our cost-cutting analysis could be on the branches.

Let us assume that the group's core business is carried out through an extensive network of physical branches (e.g. 350) that contribute to a high cost structure and that the situation outlined by the competent structures is as follows (Table 5.8).

Table 5.8 Breakdown of branches and FTEs

	No. Branches	FTEs per branches on average	Direct Cost/FTE	% Indirect Cost on Total	Cost of credit on average	Cost Income Ratio	Loan to Deposit Ratio on average
Network Bank 1	90	7	-100	30%	-0.68%	88%	125%
Network Bank 2	180	10	-80	40%	-1.10%	95%	200%
Network Bank 3	80	8	-95	28%	-0.90%	106%	67%

Source: Authors' elaboration.

What possible actions should be submitted to the board?

In situations where it is necessary to rationalise the organisational structure in a short period of time, the closure of some branches could be one of the options to be considered.

At first glance this might seem an effective option, but is it really?

Choosing how many and which branches to close and when to close them is a decision that needs to be carefully weighed. Closing a branch does not imply an automatic and simple cut in costs. On the contrary, closure activities are usually costly and could considerably lengthen the timeframe, proving to be non-functional to the strategic objective of efficiency.

It will be necessary to assess the existence of any penalties arising from the termination of contracts with suppliers[11]. It will also be necessary to assess the real risk that customers who are transferred to another company, whether external or internal to the group, may request withdrawal for just cause (pursuant to Article 58 of the Consolidated Law on Banking).

That is why it will be necessary to investigate the possible presence, in the branches selected for closure, of customers with high added value (i.e. those with a highly positive customer EVA) in order to evaluate possible retention strategies. It is not at all obvious that the customers of the closed branch will migrate to any of the group's operational branches or even to the online channel that the bank may have recently launched. The attempt to digitise the customer portfolio often clashes with customers with different needs and low digital literacy, especially in Italy. Finally, the impact in terms of reputation and operational risks should be thoroughly assessed.

The answer, therefore, as is always the case, is neither simple nor unambiguous and the risks of jeopardising value creation, collection, lending and cross-selling objectives are very high.

5.3.2 Optimisation of staff and their utilisation

Following restructuring processes, a very common analysis that should always be carried out is that of the distribution of human resources between staff, middle and senior management. Let us assume that the analysis carried out by the HR department shows the following distribution at group level (**Figure 5.10**).

---

[11] Think for example of lease contracts.

5 Case study

Figure 5.10   **Staff analysis at group level**

Source: Authors' elaboration.

What does the figure suggest?

From the analysis of the human resources function, a sort of inverted pyramid emerges, with the base of the pyramid populated by middle management, which represents the main cost item.

Such a scenario could be symptomatic, for example, of a high degree of decentralisation of corporate governance at subsidiaries. Short-sighted analyses driven by short-termism would lead to cost-driven cuts: "I do without those who cost me the most". Instead, the risk-adjusted performance of each manager will have to be assessed, and careful consideration will have to be given to whether the manager will take away the assets once he leaves the group.

It would therefore be interesting to carry out an internal peer analysis between the network banks and the parent company in order to analyse the distribution of human resources in the individual group companies. Let us therefore imagine that the following picture emerges from the analysis conducted by the human resources function (**Figure 5.11**).

What does the figure suggest?

A careful analysis of the distribution reveals a situation of high variability among the group companies. The group's best practice is undoubtedly network bank 3, where middle management accounts for approximately 35% of total FTEs. Therefore, if the board decides to align the performance levels of the best practice to the other group companies, the analysis could reveal interesting margins for manoeuvre in terms of efficiency and cost reduction, bearing in mind the caveats mentioned above.

Figure 5.11   **Staff analysis by group company**

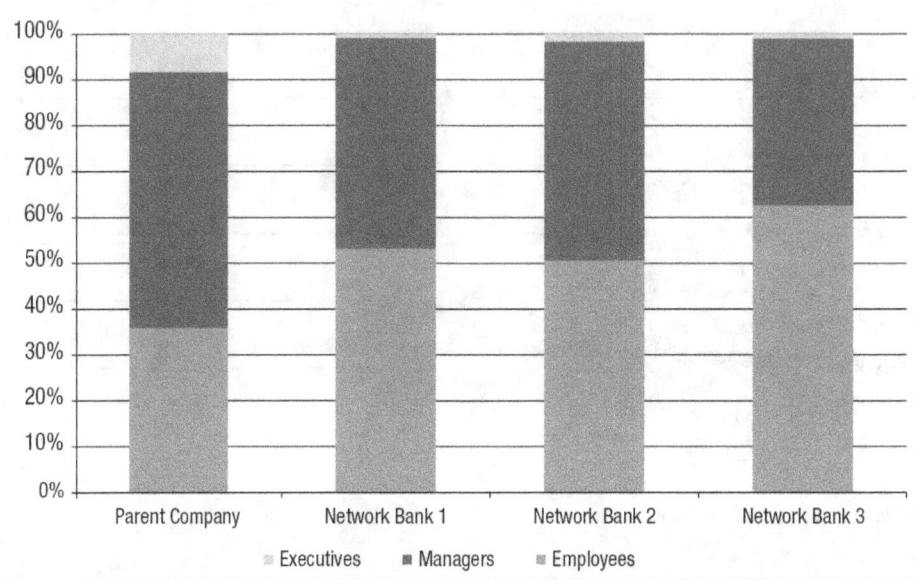

Source: Authors' elaboration.

In fact, the banking business is based on delicate commercial relations, so here too it is necessary to carry out in-depth analyses in order to not jeopardise the funding and lending objectives and the company's constraints in negotiating with the social partners.

5.3.3 Business Case: Deep dive pricing scheme

It has previously been discussed whether the low capacity to generate profitability may also be due to the lack of an appropriate pricing scheme.

In order to clarify the concept, a very simplified situation will be illustrated below (Table 5.9). Let us imagine that the Target group offers its customers (divided into three risk categories) two types of products (retail mortgages and business loans).

We know that, in order to cover at least the costs incurred by the bank in providing services, the price charged to customers may not be lower than the theoretical minimum price. The commercial spread, on the other hand, is the buffer on which the commercial function can act when setting the price to customers.

Does the pricing scheme adequately remunerate product and customer risk?

The trend of the commercial spread along the risk categories of the customer shows that it increases as the customer rating increases. The same correlation is shown be-

Table 5.9   Pricing scheme

Product	Customers rating	Minimun theorical price	Commercial Spread
Retail mortgages	low risk	1.05%	0.75%
	medium risk	2.19%	1.15%
	high risk	3.99%	1.99%
Corporate loans	low risk	2.02%	0.25%
	medium risk	3.89%	1.98%
	high risk	5.76%	3.37%

Source: Authors' elaboration.

tween minimum theoretical price and customer rating. In view of this, the bank network may have an incentive to finance those risk categories that have a higher spread, that is those that are riskier from an internal rating system perspective.

In order to avoid any bias, it is necessary to investigate a further correlation not represented in the above figure: that between RORAC (net income/RWA) and rating classes (**Figure 5.10**).

Again, does the pricing scheme adequately remunerate product and customer risk?

The answer can only be negative, since the RORAC decreases with the lowest rating classes. In this respect, an appropriate and timely update of the minimum theoretical price table will be necessary as it does not adequately cover the risks taken.

In this context, the network will certainly have to give preference, in its commercial activity, to those customer categories that present the highest, or at least positive, RORAC, even in the presence of lower commercial spreads.

Table 5.10   Pricing scheme and RORAC

Product	Customers rating	Minimun theorical price	Commercial Spread	RORAC
Retail mortgages	low risk	1.05%	0.75%	7%
	medium risk	2.19%	1.15%	1%
	high risk	3.99%	1.99%	-5%
Corporate loans	low risk	2.02%	0.25%	10%
	medium risk	3.89%	1.98%	-5%
	high risk	5.76%	3.37%	-15%

Source: Authors' elaboration.

What is our lesson learned?

Pricing policy needs a structured and robust methodological approach. Leaving too much autonomy to commercial management could result in pricing being defined on the basis of qualitative commercial benchmarking analyses. Therefore, it is crucial that the short-term oriented commercial view is supported and counterbalanced by the view of the risk management function, that is more intrinsically inclined towards risk culture and the search for methodological robustness.

Based on these considerations, the bank could evaluate possible strategic actions to improve competitiveness and its ability to create value through pricing that is able to remunerate all inputs in a context of limited cost rationalisation.

5.3.4 Segment Reporting: "An attempt"

In moving to the conclusion of this long story telling, here are some examples of templates to support the BMA.

The first is segment reporting that summarises the BM as a representation of the specific strategic choices concerning the overall bank. It can be built from different perspectives: products, commercial segments, customers and value chains. Here the example for commercial segments is proposed (Table 5.11).

Table 5.11   **Segment reporting by business segments**

€ million	Commercial Segment 1	...	Legacy Book	ALM	Corporate Center	Total Normalized Amount
Balance Sheet Amounts						
Financial Assets						
Net Performing Loans						
Net Impaired Loans						
Direct Funding						
Capital Allocated						
Funding Gap						
Nr Clients						
Number of Branches						
P&L amounts						
Net Interest Income						
Net Commissions						
Trading and Other Income						
Operating revenue						
Cost of Credit						
Operating Cost						

5 Case study

€ million	Commercial Segment 1	...	Legacy Book	ALM	Corporate Center	Total Normalized Amount
o.w:						
Staff Cost						
...						
Profit before taxes and adjustment						
Adjustment (if needed):						
o.w:						
Fund transfer pricing						
...						
KPIs: Profitability						
EVA						
RORAC						
Operating ROA						
...						
KPIs: Efficiency						
Cost to Income						
Cost of Credit to Income						
Total Cost to Income						
...						

Source: Authors' elaboration on banking practices.

From its reading, it will be possible to see how much a given activity costs in terms of funding and capital, how much value can be created, how rigid the structure is, which activities are supported, rightly or wrongly, by incentives, and so on.

This example of seemingly simple segment reporting is actually very complex in processing. Some banks are experiencing huge delays in their management control model.

One reason for this is that many banks prefer, or have preferred, to take on the role of "follower" rather than "front-runner" in the growing push for technological innovation in recent years. It is not uncommon for banks to embark on specific projects (e.g. the online channel) out of pure imitation of the competition, rather than as a result of an accurate and autonomous strategic choice that relies on realistic expectations of value creation, given the BM adopted.

Finally, below are two examples of analyses aimed at briefly illustrating the BM, understood as a representation of the specific strategic choices by virtue of which the combination of resources, products and customer segments contributes to creating value in the various areas of activity (**Table 5.12** and **5.13**).

Table 5.12   Segment reporting by activity type.

€ million	Capital allocated	Funding gap	Net result	Full cost allocation	Adjusted result
Core Business					
Other					
Legacy book					
ALM					
Corporate Centre					
Total Business Units					

Source: Authors' elaboration on banking practices.

Table 5.13   Segment reporting by customer type.

€ million	Capital allocated	Funding gap	Net result	Full cost allocation	Adjusted result
Mass Market					
…					
…					
Total Core Business					

Source: Authors' elaboration on banking practices.

5.4 Digitalisation Case: Better bank or distributed bank?

Let us imagine that the traditionally and commercially oriented Target banking group wants to digitise its process using new technologies and place it as one of the pillars on which to base its new strategic plan, in order to compete in a market with profoundly changed characteristics compared with the past[12].

For example, the board shows strong interest in embarking on a path of efficiency recovery accompanied by significant investments in digitalisation that affect both the management of customers and services provided and internal processes, and that it mandates the commercial, legal and IT functions to carry out a gap and peer analysis with respect to the possible solutions on the market represented in the box below.

---

[12] For the definitions of better bank and distributed bank, see Section 2.1 "The Banking Literature Approach. Overview" and the Basel Committee paper "Sound Practices Implications of fintech developments for banks and bank supervisors", February 2018.

5 Case study

Focus: Definition of main technologies

- Intelligent credit scoring: an automated system for evaluating customers' loan applications. It is based on automated systems involving the application of statistical methods or models to assess credit risk, the results of which are expressed in the form of summary judgements, numerical indicators or scores associated with the person concerned, aimed at providing a representation, in predictive or probabilistic terms, of his or her risk profile, reliability or punctuality of payments.
- Robo-advice: automated financial advice aimed at providing warnings or recommendations to clients to buy or sell financial instruments. The advisory service may also be provided to the consumer with the intervention of financial advisers. The service may be integrated with other, also non-automated, investment portfolio management services.
- Financial assets in virtual currencies: digital representation of value used as a medium of exchange for the purchase of goods and services or for investment purposes and transferred, stored and traded electronically.
- Digital payment services: providers of payment services based on the use of technology to facilitate digital payment transactions without the use of physical currency.
- Digital banking: banking financial intermediaries that offer banking services primarily through online channels.
- Cloud computing: technologies that enable widespread, easy and on-demand access to a shared, configurable set of data processing resources (e.g. networks, servers, storage, applications and services), provided and distributed rapidly and with minimal interaction with the service provider.
- Distributed Ledger Technology: technology in which all nodes in a system share a common database and contribute to its maintenance and updating in a non-centralised manner, using cryptography to authenticate transactions. Smart contracts are contracts written in computer language that can enter into execution and enforce their terms automatically and without human intervention, in the context of DLT technologies or for the execution of transactions involving virtual currencies.
- Artificial intelligence: computer technology capable of performing human-like functions. In particular, AI can formulate questions, test hypotheses and make decisions on the basis of a significant amount of data.
- Machine Learning: algorithms and learning processes for the realisation of applications whose performance automatically improves over time due to the processing of new data. There are various techniques for its realisation, depending on the use case (e.g. linear regression, classification, decision trees, neural networks, etc.). It excludes technological solutions used in the cases of Big Data and robot process automation (RPA).
- API: provision of banking services through the use of application programming interfaces that enable the development of applications and services that make use of data and functions offered by the technological infrastructure of a third-party financial institution.
- Biometric technologies: technologies for electronic identity authentication or digital identity authentication: electronic procedures and tools used, in compliance with the regulations in force, for the online identification and verification of the customer's personal details (e.g. via webcam) and for the assignment or validation of authentication credentials, capable of enabling the initial registration of the customer and the complete management of the contractual relationship exclusively through remote channels[13].

---

[13] For a more comprehensive overview of technologies see Basel Committee on Banking supervision: Implications of fintech developments for banks and bank supervisors, February 2018 and www.bancaditalia.it/pubblicazioni/indagine-fintech/index.html

Table 5.14 **Simulation proposed by the commercial, legal and IT functions of the Target group**

	Volumes per month	Cost per transaction	Margins per transaction
Improvement of marketed products	3,702,587	0.67	0.21
New digital products	5,674,193	0.51	0.79
Improvement of marketed services	1,375,419	0.55	0.35
New digital services	1,931,596	0.39	0.87

Source: Authors' elaboration on theoretical assumptions.

Let us suppose that the commercial, legal and IT functions, following the market survey conducted, develop a digital strategy aimed at supporting the generation of revenue by offering new products and services and improving existing ones.

Furthermore, let us imagine that the marketing of such products/services is hypothesised through a single integrated platform to be developed on the basis of one or more of the technologies most in use by competitors (e.g. data analytics, AI, digital signature, Open API, cloud computing, SDDC and BPM) and that the following simulation is proposed to the board, focusing on volumes and margins (Table 5.14)[14,15].

The latter in particular are generated by judgemental assumption of lower average costs in the acquisition of new customers and product subscription via digital channels by 36% compared with those incurred so far for customers and non-digital products. Thus, the goal of increased revenue would be achieved through an improved digital customer experience and optimised pricing resulting from increased efficiency and remote working.

First analysis step: the mandate. From a governance point of view, is the digitalisation project adequate?

The strategic commitment in the tone from the top analysis represents the first step in the project assessment.

Analysing the case at hand, it is quite evident that the involvement of the commercial and legal functions alone is undoubtedly a necessary condition, but nevertheless insufficient, since the proposed simulation is based solely on commercial assumptions that do not adequately take into account risk exposure (primarily cyber secu-

---

[14] In a software defined data centre (SDDC) "all elements of the infrastructure networking, storage, CPU and security are virtualised and delivered as a service." (Source: Rouse, Margaret. "Definition: Software Defined Datacenter". Retrieved 25 February 2014.)

[15] Business Process Modeling is a business discipline aimed at increasing the effectiveness of operations management through automation, control, integration, execution and optimisation of processes (source: wikipedia).

rity), the statistical significance of the drivers used, the digital literacy of customers and the impacts on existing processes, including IT.

While the aspects related to marketing and the benefits in terms of possible income returns are within the purview of the business functions, those related to risk exposure and mitigation, consistency with the RAF, organisational transversality with regard to the impacts on FTEs both from a quantitative (reallocation, incentives to leave) and qualitative (e.g. resources' aptitude for the use of new technological paradigms), as well as the mapping of technological, resource, process and corporate culture constraints, are not equally monitored.

Conversely, the mandate of a Central Intelligence Unit, or in its absence, of a dedicated interdisciplinary task force in which all the stakeholders involved participate, that is the main business and control functions (e.g. legal, commercial, IT, HR, risk management, compliance, internal audit, etc.), is necessary, especially in the embryonic phases of the digitalisation project in order to highlight with equal dignity both opportunities and threats.

It will also be necessary for the board to appoint a digital innovation manager and allocate them an appropriate budget for the execution of work at group level.

A prerequisite is to try to understand the level of appetite on the part of shareholders for such a technological transformation process. The expectation of significant investments on the digitalisation front and the concomitant need to revise choices made in the recent past could be a direct testimony to the short-lived nature of previous years or even the last industrial plan presented to the market.

Let us further hypothesise that some members of the Control and Risk Committee, during the challenging phase of a meeting in which the guidelines of the new strategic plan are presented by the functions entrusted by the board (commercial and legal), request and obtain from the board the establishment of an appropriate task force dedicated to the development of the digitalisation plan and articulated in the composition described above.

Let us imagine that the task force hypothesises, after a careful analysis of the objectives set by the board[16], the following eight scenarios characterised by increasing levels of complexity and technological sophistication ranging from digitalisation to automation of banking[17]:

1. Digitalisation of traditional services through apps and Internet banking (digital signatures and payments).
2. Opening of digital branches (assisted self-service channel through chatboxes/virtual assistants, 3D viewers and virtual interaction rooms).

---

[16] In this regard, the economic literature offers numerous methods to support robust decision-making (e.g. S.C.O.R.E. model, goal setting technique, etc.).

[17] By digitalisation we mean the introduction of devices and processes capable of transmitting and processing enormous masses of data at a speed hitherto unthinkable; by automation, we mean the availability of emerging technologies such as RPA, AI and ML capable of carrying out tasks of medium-high complexity, hitherto the prerogative of humans alone.

3. Automation and reorganisation of existing branches (e.g. use of RPA, BPM and digital workplace in the automation of back-office processes and streamlining of channel-banking with the integration of digitised processes).
4. Automation of traditional services (Credit score intelligence for credit disbursement, roboadvisor platforms for highly customised savings management, AI for automated payment collection and document management).
5. Offering new digital products (e.g. self-direct products, virtual currency financial business).
6. Establishment of a challenger bank (e.g. native cloud with services offered solely through apps, smartphones and biometric technologies without using branches[18]).
7. Presence in new digital markets (e.g. super-app[19], quantum computing, edge computing and 5G, programmable objects, blockchain, DLT, augmented reality, virtual reality, mixed reality and metaverse).

With reference to the operational modalities, we hypothesise that they will be defined as follows:

- for the implementation of the scenarios characterised by a higher technological sophistication (e.g. 6–7) it is planned to seek strategic agreements with leading and established IT and fintech companies, aimed at the creation of platforms and infrastructures
- for the implementation of scenarios characterised relatively by a more contained technological complexity (e.g. 1–5), a progressive strengthening of strategic IT skills is planned, through the internalisation of higher value-added professionalism and the creation of centres of excellence.

Let us imagine that the simulation presented to the board by the task force produces the following results (Table 5.15).

What does the table suggest? What kind of information is represented? What information is missing?

The analysis of the simulation shows that the involvement of the task force generally resulted in higher transaction costs and consequently lower returns for the same estimated monthly volumes.

Of course, this is a starting point, as the analysis will have to be enriched by risk-adjusted KPIs.

---

[18] In fact, challenger banks, which are particularly modest in size, generally rely (at least in part) on traditional institutions for certain activities such as the physical deposit of money.

[19] A super-app (also written as super app or superapp) is a mobile or web application capable of providing multiple services including the processing of payments and financial transactions, becoming an all-encompassing online commerce and communication platform that embraces many aspects of personal and business life (source: wikipedia).

5 Case study

Table 5.15 **Simulation proposed by the task force of the Target group**

	Strategic hypothesis	Estimated volume per month	Cost per transaction	Margin per transaction
Improvement of marketed products and services	Digitalisation of traditional products	3,702,587	0.79	0.15
	Digitalisation of traditional services	1,375,419	0.66	0.21
	Branch digitalisation	4,935,871	0.61	0.29
	Branch automation	3,965,234	0.57	0.36
	Automation of traditional products	7,256,945	0.55	0.41
	Automation of traditional services	5,674,193	0.51	0.52
New digital products and services	New digital products	7,856,214	0.69	0.64
	New digital services	2,956,874	0.55	0.72
	Challenger bank	9,645,782	0.47	0.89
	New digital markets	21,036,498	0.29	1.15

Source: Authors' elaboration on theoretical assumptions.

Let us therefore suppose that the task force to estimate the profitability and efficiency levels of each strategy uses, with the support of Risk Management, various risk-adjusted metrics (e.g. ROE, RORAC, ROA, CIR, EVA and the Payback Period expressed in years) and that the following "as is" vs. "to be" simulation is presented to the board (Table 5.16)[20,21].

From the perspective of profitability, costs and value creation, what does the table suggest?

Analysing the situation "as is", we see that the metrics were set equal for all product strategies ("improvement" and "new digital") as they capture the performance in terms of profitability, costs and value creation of the products currently marketed by the Target group. Similar equality was also applied for the strategies concerning services, branches/digital bank and markets served, whose starting point is the one "recorded" in the last available survey by the Risk Management function.

Starting from the costs in a "to be" perspective, it can be seen that the CIR per single strategy is higher when the relative payback is lower. The latter is in fact calculated as a function of the operating cash flow, which is also affected by non-cash

---

[20] The Payback Period (PBP) is used to calculate the time within which the capital invested in a project is recovered through the net cash flows generated by the project.

[21] For the sake of simplicity, Capital Expenditure (CAPEX), which represents the cash outflows for the realisation of investments in fixed assets of an operational nature, was not considered in the proposed simulation.

Table 5.16 Risk-adjusted KPI simulation proposed by the task force of the traditional banking group

	Strategic hypothesis	ROE % per year		ROA % per year		CIR % per year		EVA €/mln per year		Payback Period Y
As is		To be	As is	To be	As is	To be	As is	To be		
Improvement of marketed products and services	Digitalisation of traditional products	7%	10%	2%	3%	67%	65%	2,000	3,700	1
	Digitalisation of traditional services	9%	12%	3%	4%	64%	60%	5,000	7,200	1
	Branch digitalisation	11%	14%	4%	5%	67%	63%	17,000	29,000	3
	Branch automation	11%	17%	4%	6%	67%	60%	17,000	41,000	3
	Automation of traditional products	7%	19%	2%	6%	67%	59%	2,000	47,000	4
	Automation of traditional services	9%	23%	3%	8%	64%	57%	5,000	50,000	4
New digital products and services	New digital products	7%	25%	2%	8%	67%	62%	2,000	60,000	5
	New digital services	9%	29%	3%	10%	64%	59%	5,000	73,000	5
	Challenger bank	11%	33%	4%	11%	67%	55%	17,000	90,000	6
	New digital markets	10%	42%	3%	14%	65%	45%	23,000	1,000,000	10

Source: Authors' elaboration on theoretical assumptions.

expenses, including depreciation. For example, the digitalisation process of products for which a payback of one year has been estimated has a higher CIR (65%) because the share of depreciation and amortisation is predominant. Conversely, challenger banks or new digital markets, which have paybacks of more than five years, have significantly lower CIRs, below 56%.

It goes without saying that one of the success factors in a digitalisation-oriented strategy is the investment in specific skills and know-how, such as analytical and process mapping skills, technical skills, business knowledge and IT governance experience. The weight of structural costs must be weighed against the desired volumes and economies of scale. If, for example, significant costs are estimated for the implementation of financing platforms against low economies of scale, a rethink of the project will inevitably be required.

It has to be kept in mind that the digitalisation process is not a kind of "patching-up" of an already obsolete IT system; extending the lifecycle of sub-optimal legacy applications generates short-term savings compared with the introduction of new digital solutions, but also the underlying inefficiencies will inevitably be "masked" only in the short term. However, it should also be emphasised that "one size does not fit all" and advanced digitalisation strategies may not represent the same key to success for all operators; each will have to find the most appropriate interpretation. Moreover, the significant investments in HR and IT required by the projects, although very high during the transition phase to digitalisation and automation, represent an unavoidable opportunity to reduce IT costs in the medium to long term in view of a standardisation process that will require lower maintenance and asset mutualisation costs.

The reality in which the players operate challenges the certainties of the past. Banks therefore need to adopt a strategic and operational framework that is open to the new and to implement actions capable of flexibly facing an increasingly complex future. Hence the addition to the concept of resilience of "antifragility"[22], as it is desirable that systems and organisations are not only undamaged by external forms of disruption and stress, but even improved.

With reference to "to be" profitability, the results also suggest that, all other things being equal, there is a strong and positive correlation between the digitalisation of the banking business offering and profitability: the greater the intensity of digitalisation, the higher the bank's profitability, both in terms of ROA, ROE and value created (EVA). The higher profitability seems to be driven by the strong correlation between digitalisation and total fees, as well as by asset management activities. This result might indicate a better diversification of income due to digitalisation.

Furthermore, there is no evidence of any significant correlation between less advanced digitalisation projects and cost savings. In fact, the CIR registers values

---

[22] In 2012, philosopher and mathematician Nassim Nicholas Taleb formulated and described the "antifragility principle", which indicates the ability not only to benefit from shocks, but to thrive and grow under conditions of chaos and stress.

above 60% even after the automation of traditional services and the launch of new digital products. This means that the cost structure is still mainly influenced by lending, which relies more on traditional supply channels, such as branches, and depends on relationship-based interactions between the bank and its customers.

However, as highlighted by PBP, cost-saving policies induced by ICT investments may take time to become effective and generate significant impacts on profitability. Delayed execution of the digitalisation strategy or inappropriate investments could lead to a loss of customers and thus profitability.

What could be the risks associated with each strategy?

The previous analysis, however, cannot be considered concluded. While on the one hand, the investment driver would be driven by the profitability drivers, on the other hand, it must be kept in mind that each strategy will determine a more or less significant exposure to certain risks (strategic, reputational, operational, cyber, AML, compliance, third-party concentration, consumer protection, etc.) as described in **Figure 5.17**.

Let us therefore assume that the task force, with the support of the Risk Management function, presents the following estimate of risk exposures to the board, differentiating between operational, strategic and reputational.

Figure 5.17 **Risk exposure levels of each strategy estimated by the Risk Management function of the Target group**

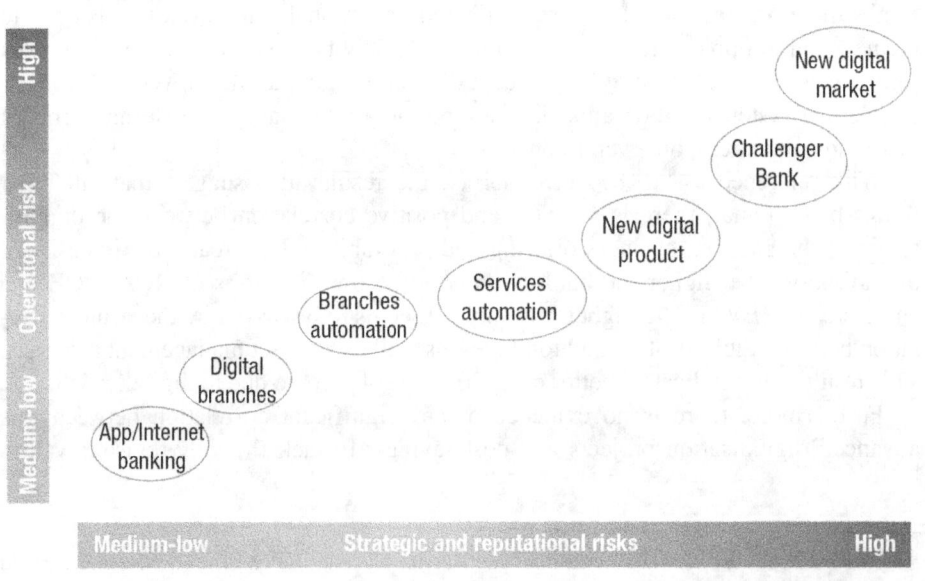

Source: Authors' elaboration on theoretical assumptions.

Strategies characterised by lower digitalisation impacts, being less disruptive, potentially expose less to operational, strategic and reputational risks than those characterised by higher technological sophistication. But for all of them, the execution phase is crucial.

The digitalisation of traditional services enables access to banking and investment services via apps and Internet banking. Information and dispositive functions require the creation of a digital identity and compliance with the regulatory requirements on, inter alia, security introduced by PSD2.

While customer behaviour is an enabling factor for digitalisation, it is often perceived as the main critical issue due to the remaining significant presence of less digitally-literate users. Indeed, customers who choose remote services inevitably need assistance in addition to frequency. Hence the strategy of establishing digital branches to support and strengthen the information and dispositive functions of digitised services.

While branch automation and restructuring is still characterised by a low level of complexity compared with other alternatives, the execution phase is very delicate. Branches have historically been created to support branch operations, and when their purpose is changed (e.g. consulting and product sales) it is necessary to ensure that the inevitable change of management platform is adequately integrated and that there is therefore synchronism between the process of staff reduction and/or displacement and that of full adoption of digital applications that could exacerbate the operational dysfunctionality of the physical network. There will need to be an assessment, for example, of whether call centres and back offices need to be strengthened in terms of FTEs against an expanded range of operations (e.g. F24s ordered online, remote management of cheques, all back-office operations in support of the network and the executive board).

If, for example, operations are doubled or tripled for the same FTEs, it will be necessary to understand whether the tools that resources have at their disposal are sufficient to guarantee the same quality of work without incurring greater exposure to operational risks.

Automation of traditional services allows greater distances to be covered with both customers and colleagues. However, branch closures and increased distances between debtor and creditor and between centre and periphery could negatively affect the availability of credit, especially for small businesses, whose credit relies more heavily on soft information and relationship lending, a sector that could theoretically remain more protected from competition by specialised fintech intermediaries and their online platforms.

With regard to the establishment of the digital bank, the project proposed by the task force takes the form of the transfer of target customers within the group. The choice of target customers is crucial. One could, for instance, target retail customers who do not have a portfolio to manage and therefore allow for mass rather than individual management or cater for all "digital" customers, but this could lead to varying degrees of inefficiency if certain services are not centralised. In fact, it will be necessary to deal not only with the simplest operations such as transactions, but also with sales, managing customer portfolios that were previously with agencies.

With the launch of new products and digital markets there is the possibility of satisfying those customers, not only private individuals, who are more self-directed[23]. Customising the offer and focusing it on the end customer for a better consumer experience is not easy to implement. Simple, high-potential solutions will have to be found that can be easily scaled up. Rapid scalability would ensure high added value capable of supporting further initiatives. But for scalability to be rapid, resources must be available in the organisation. Therefore, the focus should not only be on processing power and tailor-made algorithms, but above all on: (i) creating an efficient and consistent data collection with the algorithms to be used to ensure fast, easily updatable and sharable production models; (ii) building effective mechanisms to coordinate initiatives across the bank. In order to guarantee algorithms that are always "ready to use", it would therefore be necessary first of all to innovate the overall management of what is upstream of data processing, abandoning traditional approaches. The virtuous circle of digitalisation according to McKinsey is in fact represented by[24]: i) the presence of automated decisions and executions, solid KPIs that speed up the testing of new products; ii) the acquisition of business data that is linked to new models of machine learning, which, in turn, must interact with marketing technologies (MarTech) by feeding the resulting inputs into campaigns and then circulating the data again until the results are achieved.

What are the biggest obstacles that could undermine the success of each strategy?

Let us imagine that the task force, in responding to the board on what obstacles might be most likely to lead to failure of a digitalisation strategy, presented the following graph (Figure 5.18), from which several levels of constraints can be deduced. In particular, the task force estimates that the top obstacles are customer expectations, implications in terms of IT infrastructure, organisational set-up and FTEs.

What are the customer's expectations?

The analysis cannot disregard an assessment of the habits of one's target customers and their attitude to digitalisation. Attempting to move the greatest number of customers from physical branches to online platforms is not immediate, and at the national level the difference between north and centre–south from this point of view is significant: in the north the shift of customers to digital channels occurs more quickly because customer confidence in digital tools is higher, while it is slower in the centre–south due to deep-rooted cultural factors, including digital illiteracy and the use of cash.

---

[23] Namely customers oriented towards managing their financial interests in total autonomy through digital channels and remote interaction with their financial service provider, which is not always a bank (Deloitte).

[24] "Getting personal: How banks can win with consumers" by McKinsey and Company.

5   Case study

Figure 5.18   **The sixteen greatest constraints to the success of a digital strategy as estimated by the Target group task force**

Source: Authors' elaboration on theoretical assumptions.

What are the implications in terms of IT infrastructure?

Digitalisation, with due consideration for the proportionality principle, should not be driven by a single technological solution or partner, but by an effective and efficient combination of several technological solutions, which could include AI, machine learning, chatbots/conversational platforms and robot process automation (RPA)[25].

Therefore, it will be necessary to build a kind of toolbox of technologies that can flexibly support the necessary functional redesign phases of the new BM.

In order to guarantee flexibility of approach, it will be necessary to ensure an

---

[25] AI is the ability of a computer system to mimic human cognitive functions such as learning and problem-solving through the use of mathematics and logic. Machine Learning is an application of artificial intelligence. It is the process of using mathematical models of data to help a computer learn without direct instruction. This allows a system to continue to learn and improve autonomously, based on experience. Chatbots or conversational platforms are software that simulate and process human conversations (written or spoken), enabling users to interact with digital devices as if they were communicating with a real person. RPA is the automation of work processes using "intelligent" software (so-called "robots"), which can automatically perform the repetitive tasks of operators, imitating their behaviour and interacting with computer applications in the same way as the operator himself. (source: Microsoft, Oracle, Wikipedia)

adequate level of interoperability, that is the possibility of making different platforms communicate with the same language.

It will be crucial to adapt cyber security, infrastructural, application and data architectures and development methodologies. Algorithms should not be black boxes for banks but ensure adequate levels of auditability of the same.

It will also be necessary to establish IT competence centres for digital transformation, both in the technical divisions and in the control functions (primarily the internal audit function).

What possible repercussions are there for the organisational structure?

The previous analysis cannot be considered complete since the impacts on processes have not been highlighted. Given the characteristics of the Target group, it is inevitable that the processes with the highest impact are those of credit, payments, finance, IT systems management and security.

Furthermore, the main improvement impacts resulting from the digital transformation are undoubtedly to be found in the simplification/revision of existing processes and in the design/development of new processes, particularly for the commercial, back office and front office areas. The government area, which is difficult to automate, benefits less from digitalisation.

From a technology perspective, APIs have high organisational and strategic impacts, followed by Cloud and AI, which is relevant for certain business lines such as retail and control functions. As far as DLT is concerned, it is expected to be disruptive in the long term due to the current poor regulation and technical standards.

Therefore, before the actual implementation phase, it will be necessary to ensure that end-to-end processes are adequately tested in specific test environments and to assess the level of effort in terms of the number of steps and integrations required to adapt processes and the organisational system to the new BM.

The digitalisation process should not be understood as a mere copy/replication of manual processes, but they should be redesigned in order to improve the customer and employee experience.

Initiatives will have to be prioritised and post-production processes aimed at constantly monitoring the goodness of the design and implementation, as well as the degree of achievement of the set targets through specific KPIs, will be crucial.

Recently, the adoption of new organisational approaches based on the principles of design thinking has also spread in the banking[26], insurance and financial sector in

---

[26] Design thinking is a structured approach, supporting innovation and training processes, which envisages a series of phases (the number of which may vary according to the various models, such as those of the Standford School, Google, etc.) and different stages (Personas, Google, etc.) and various tools (Personas, Empathy map, Value proposition Canvas, etc.). One of the fundamental characteristics of this methodology is that of being customer/user centric. Starting from the customer/user, their needs, expectations, behaviour, experiences, etc. will enable the team and the company to align innovation with market demand.

order to foster innovation processes and activities and generate new business opportunities. Regardless of the organisational approach chosen, to support behaviour that promotes innovation, it is necessary to be able to manage a certain degree of error in order to encourage the generation of new ideas, competition, a positive attitude towards change and constructive confrontation.

Key to the successful implementation of each strategy is the constant and continuous involvement of all Level II and III control functions (compliance, AML, risk management and internal audit) in the implementation and execution phase.

And in terms of culture and quali-quantitative FTEs?

Let us assume that the recovery of efficiency took place during the previous business plan with the closure of 20% of branches and the reduction of 10% of staff over three years with instruments such as redundancy, early retirement and solidarity.

With the current industrial plan new redundancies are expected and one of the solutions used to contain the outflow could be to retrain resources with the new skills deemed necessary and re-internalise certain processes that had previously been delegated to external companies.

The predominant part of the new employment certainly has a more traditional banking profile for "light" digitalisation strategies, thus entering to perform tasks with contents very similar to those of the outgoing colleagues although in a completely different way, that is without that direct relational aspect that characterised traditional banking.

In the more "hard" digitalisation strategies, also due to the possible overlapping of personnel from the merger processes described in the first case study, new hires will certainly be reserved mainly for figures with radically new profiles for the banking context (IT engineers, designers, computer scientists and experts in marketing and organisational technologies).

In this context, investments of an intangible nature will assume great importance, and it will therefore be necessary to employ numerous technical and managerial figures dedicated to digital transformation.

Therefore, while further employment contractions can be expected in the current strategic plan, these will be accompanied by a qualitative change in the bank's employment with the gradual entry of radically new skills compared with traditional ones.

Of course, the reduction of personnel in the face of the introduction of technology that is not sufficiently tested before going live could invalidate the investments made as they do not reflect positively on the work of the operators. Various malfunctions could paradoxically lead to more operator intervention than was necessary before the changes were introduced, which should instead have reduced manual steps (by way of example, we have seen the digitalisation of cheques and digital signatures in the recent past).

It will be necessary for employees to be actively involved in the implementation of the change in order to facilitate its understanding and, consequently, its success.

What are the possible impacts on segment reporting?

The organisation of the management control system will have to be able to support the digitalisation process that could potentially have a disruptive impact on decision-making processes, organisational models and banking activities and processes.

Where more advanced digital solutions are adopted, it will be necessary for management control not to adopt an incremental approach, but rather a zero-based approach that aims not so much at predicting the future from the past, but observing, breaking down and examining the bank's present in detail.

Finally, it should be emphasised that the implementation of dynamic, flexible information systems adapted to the new requirements of management control can only take place in parallel with the adoption of technological innovation.

6 Conclusions

> "The real problem is not whether machines think but whether men do"
> B.F. Skinner

6.1 Red flags detected within the BMA

It has been argued in many quarters that the lessons learned from the 2008 crisis have been poorly adapted to the past pandemic context and the recipes used at the time have therefore not been replicated tout court[1]. In fact, although both events generated a deep liquidity crisis with consequent effects on the real economy, they differed in the nature of the triggering factors (speculative finance in 2008 and measures to contain the pandemic in 2020) which implied different responses from the European Authorities[2].

Given that in the pandemic context the financial industry, supported by an expansionary monetary policy, was stronger overall than in 2008 thanks to a higher level of capitalisation and improved loan quality, European supervision, using the flexibility margins of the prudential regulatory framework, loosened certain constraints to support the post-pandemic economic recovery.

Even in this new edition, which introduces further complex elements into the BMA, while taking into account the complex system of constraints that inexorably limit strategic possibilities, it is reiterated that the stability of revenue streams cannot be disregarded without conducting a BM assessment that follows a more industrial logic without losing the holistic vision of the interventions. These are all elements necessary to strengthen the sustainability analysis in the medium-long term of the adopted model.

---

[1] These include Italian and German banks, as well as Polish, Czech, Hungarian and Slovakian banks. "We have downgraded the outlook for six banking sectors to negative, as we expect a further deterioration in operating conditions, which will weaken banks' loan quality, profitability and access to funding, although the impact will vary from country to country", stressed Louise Welin, Vp-Senior credit officer at Moody's.

[2] Think of European Stability Mechanism (ESM), Support to mitigate Unemployment Risks in an Emergency (SURE program), European Investment Bank (EIB) and Recovery Fund measures. For Italy, see the Liquidity Decree No 23 of 8 April 2020 and the Relaunch Decree No 34 of 19 May 2020.

The European banking sector risk landscape is still characterised by a highly uncertain macro-financial outlook. Idiosyncratic shocks from the United States and Switzerland have also spread fear in the market[3,4]. The outlook in the macro-financial environment in the medium terms remains precarious not least due to four persistent themes:

1. A new monetary policy;
2. High geopolitical uncertainties;
3. Digitalisation that leads to the emergence of new challenges for banks;
4. Climate transition.

Therefore, a fundamental prerequisite that was already mentioned in the previous edition is the "restructuring" of planning and management control activities, which makes it possible to verify whether the hypotheses for profitability are sustainable in the medium and long term.

However, the following elements are still lacking:

a. Adequate consolidation of the accounting and management system;
b. Effective FTP mechanisms;
c. Management accounting models tailored to new businesses and, in particular for those linked to the IT variable, detailed analyses by channel and segment of operations;
d. Consolidated approaches that go beyond the logic of the individual legal entity;
e. Reporting that emphasises management data as well as accounting data;
f. Business case analyses based on the capital-liquidity-risk-return paradigm and what if/forecast and stress simulations.

In the previous edition, **Figure 6.1** provided examples of how some weaknesses in BM governance could be appropriately overcome by banks. Moreover, the business cases that make up the strategic plans could not disregard industrial analyses of the impacts that the initiatives themselves will have in terms of added value, in light of the three management dimensions reported in the book: correct allocation of costs, capital and liquidity in terms of FTP.

Such shortcomings were also found when analysing the design of the digital transformation undertaken by intermediaries.

In the previous edition we showcased (see box below) some abstract and deliberately simple red flags, which highlighted trade-offs to be managed by bank management.

---

[3] Early March 2023, US regional banks (Silvergate Bank, Signature Bank, Silicon Valley Bank) failed in relation to major weaknesses in ALM practices (high share of longer-term bonds) and a volatile deposit base. The US regional banks experienced massive deposit outflow, fueling a negative market sentiment on banks.

[4] When Credit Suisse was rescued through a merger with UBS, the full write-off of its AT1 bonds triggered wide-spread asset sell-off.

6 Conclusions

Figure 6.1   Potential red flags and possible remedial actions

- ✓ Strategic objectives **absent / unclear / untraceable**
- ✓ **Lack** of alignment between RAF and strategic plan
- ✓ **Standalone** HR, IT, outsourcing strategies not integrated with business strategy
- ✓ **Deficiencies** in people, culture, systems, channels and/or no mechanism to monitor performance
- ✓ **Overly optimistic** macroeconomic / interest rate outlook (selective sourcing, failure to back-test)
- ✓ **Lack** of 2nd line risk assessment of the strategy
- ✓ **No** mitigation plans for deviations.

Need...
- ✓ Strategic Intelligence **Unit**
- ✓ **Holistic** vision
- ✓ Strategy review **backtesting** process
- ✓ Integrated **CRO, CFO** and **research** functions
- ✓ measure performance in an **objective way** with a robust set of KPI and peer analyses

Source: Authors' elaboration on banking practices.

Examples of red flags in the previous edition

1. Following the achievement of the supervisors' expected ratio for holding NPLs, banks could proceed with proactive management of the positions or continue with asset disposal activities. Assuming that, for the proper management of anomalous loans, it is not possible to assign more than 200-300 positions to the bank's managers, we could have potential red flags where the business case does not consider the adequacy of the organisational set-up and does not properly allocate the related costs, the necessary liquidity and the allocated capital;
2. In the evaluation of exit strategies from quantitative easing – today more distant, due to the coronavirus – red flags could materialise where the view lacks a careful analysis of the roll over risk, such as, for example, the plan to replace ECB funding with covered bonds without evaluating the increase in cost deriving from the concentration of these strategies by intermediaries;
3. Lack of evaluation of the impacts deriving from the PSD2 directive, which facilitates the open banking and allows alternative operators to know investments and to make proposals, may constitute a red flag in wealth management development strategies;
4. Red flags could appear in the sustainability analyses of business cases relating to investment services, where the greater protection and transparency deriving from MIFID2 are not hinged in the sustainability analyses.

In the era of digital transformation, governance mechanisms show shortcomings in:

- the reporting of activities related to the processing, monitoring and review of products and services involved in digitalisation,
- inadequate involvement of the risk management function in the process of identifying and mitigating the risks taken,

- incompleteness in updating the relevant documentation and, more generally, the new task schedules relating to the "transformed" products,
- inadequate training of personnel assigned to the use of the new procedures in a framework of excessive complexity and articulation of IT processes and procedures, also as a result of previous corporate transactions with different original IT systems.

It is also reiterated in this edition that in the context of the strategic processes of the banking system, the challenges deriving from the constantly changing external context should not be faced with tools which, while facilitating the management of risks or the attainment of the stated objectives, cannot be considered accomplished BM analyses, since they are mostly capable of resolving the business case in "silos".

Some concrete examples can help to better clarify the concept of the need to develop a strategic approach in which risk and return profiles are analysed together.

Red Flag 1: Recent market tensions highlighting the importance of adequate IRRBB/liquidity and funding management in banks

Record high inflation rates and persistent inflationary pressures resulted in an unprecedented scale of monetary policy tightening in major advanced economies[5]. In the previous prolonged scenario of low/negative interest rates and weak credit growth, the margin of interest, the choices of maturity transformation and the management of the resulting liquidity risk have given impetus to "common responses" in the operations of commercial banks.

The traditional activity of credit "origination", financed largely with retail sight deposits, was flanked by a significant activity of investment in financial portfolios (especially domestic sovereign debt) financed mainly with wholesale interbank deposits and, above all, with the extraordinary liquidity made available in recent years by the monetary authorities.

The consequences of this phenomenon have been various, since the process of maturity transformation, the way in which interest rate and liquidity risks have been managed and mitigated and, ultimately, the very BM of banks had "structurally" changed.

The strategic process aimed at identifying the contribution to the exposure of the risks in question and to the company's overall profitability could not therefore disregard the analysis of the impact on the "maturity mismatch" and the consequent "duration gap" generated by the two business areas mentioned above (commercial/traditional and financial).

This requirement was more binding for those banks in which part of the funding of the commercial area was placed "at the service" of the financing of the financial portfolio.

---

[5] ECB increased its deposit rate and gradually reduced its asset purchase program holdings.

In addition, the "coexistence" and interrelationship of the two areas of operations mentioned above ended up having an impact on the duration gap, liquidity risk and profitability as a result of the company's decisions in terms of FTP, both in terms of pricing and the choice of the type of commercial funding (bonds and/or on demand) to be "figuratively" used to service the financing.

For example, having a bank that tends to under/overestimate the average duration of its demand deposits (due to some deficiency in the behavioural modelling adopted) assumes importance and produces different consequences depending on whether this "error" is "compensated" (or vice versa "aggravated") by an under/overestimate of the same (and different) sign for an asset item.

Furthermore, analysing whether and to what extent the duration gap and the transformation of the company's maturities are the result of the company's strategic business choices (commercial banking versus financial investment and wholesale funding) is fundamental to understand the extent to which the two areas of operation contribute to the creation/destruction of the company's risk-adjusted value and, ultimately, to its medium/long-term sustainability.

It is not the intention to argue that the technical analysis of individual analytical and modelling aspects of different instruments should be downsized in BM processes. Nor do we wish to suggest an approach whereby any modelling deficiencies for one or more instruments should be "accepted" to the extent that they may be "compensated for" by any problems of the opposite sign on other items/instruments.

Instead, what we want to emphasise is that, alongside the important attention to the analytical aspects of modelling and "idiosyncratic" calibration, an analysis should be developed to understand the joint effect in terms of risk/return deriving from the study of all the potential balance sheet instruments/items that contribute to the definition of the risk profiles in question.

The emphasis is therefore on the complexity of "gaining" an aggregate view alongside the idiosyncratic view of individual instruments/posts. The "holistic" approach that is invoked by the authors is based on the need, when carrying out a joint analysis, to manage the trade-off between the modelling and analysis complexity properly idiosyncratic compared with that which is compatible/admissible for an aggregate/integrated approach.

A current tightening path is leading to a re-assessment of financial asset prices and increasing debt servicing costs that may lead to further market corrections and/or increasing market liquidity and funding risks in financial markets.

Red Flag 2: The silos approach in the BMA

This being said, in the writer's opinion, a conceptually correct and exhaustively applied system is one in which the BMA, integrated into the daily risk management process, is able to holistically represent to its stakeholders the effects on the bank's profitability and, more generally, on the creation of value in the medium and long term.

This presupposes overcoming delays in the development of FTP models and in those of transfers of funds between different business units, as well as in the development of capital and cost allocation models.

It is also necessary to overcome the "mechanistic" confidence that the short-term effects of initiatives considered individually for the recovery of profitability, which perhaps benefit from certain contingent factors (perhaps what Porter calls barriers to entry), can always be re-proposed in a logic of sustainability in the medium and long term.

It is clear that the change of approach in the BMA in the strategic process of the banks requires a series of reflections by the management, which will have to seriously address issues hitherto considered not crucial, in order to overcome the sort of lemon problem of the initiatives implemented so far. For example, possible arbitrage between business units will have to be addressed, the needs of the commercial network will have to be mediated with the constraints of liquidity pricing models and the liquidity plan will have to be combined with capital allocation.

In this context, the policies will have to illustrate in detail the BM, the bank-client relationship, the sources of profitability, the methods of protection against risks and the information flows, going beyond those processes often written more to satisfy regulatory requirements rather than to support the correct implementation of the BM. In other words, the design of processes should also become business driven and not just regulatory compliance. The approach to risk also requires careful consideration, moving from an "accounting" approach to a more risk-based one.

In many cases risk is read only in terms of absorbed capital, margins being calculated as differences between nominal quantities, e.g. net interest income (NII). In the short term, the containment of absorbed capital, according to this approach, improves risk-adjusted performance (RAPM), where capital should keep the firm solvent in the most adverse scenarios.

However, risk should also be read as a potential loss, that is as a possible reduction in expected performance, and so margins should also be adjusted for expected losses.

Some evidence from the preparation of budgets and/or multi-year projections suggests that banks generally conduct rigorous stress tests to measure soundness and profitability even under different scenarios; however, there is a lack of assumptions for budget scenarios other than the baseline that take into account worst-case scenarios, which can be translated into sensitivity analyses of key variables. Current boosts to NII could be challenged by higher financing/operating costs and impairments. Profitability rose to record levels, thanks to higher rates and banks' intermediation margin. Despite banks' recent surge in profitability, structural weaknesses remain. Cost structures are still high and sticky, cost containment might prove challenging amidst high inflation and digital transformation remains a challenge. Banks should manage the envisaged short-term increase in costs without jeopardising the much-needed digital transformation.

Digital transformation is expected to foster the competitive position of banks and make them more resilient to completion stemming from non-banking financial institutions.

Figure 6.2 To sum-up...

- ✓ Sustainable business model(s) have to be supported by **strong Governance, Strategy and Risk Management & controls**
- ✓ **Segment reporting analysis** to embed decomposing P&L generation, identifying drivers and assessing impact of macroeconomic changes
- ✓ **Loan pricing** should cover all costs and risks to enable proper monitoring of profitability
- ✓ **Cost plans** & assumptions should be kept realistic

And in terms of forward looking also...

- ✓ MLT strategy and Projections should leverage **on realistic growth assumptions**
- ✓ Forward looking on KPIs is supported by **sensitivity/scenario analyses** over an appropriate horizon
- ✓ The sustainability of business models should rely on the **ability to generate the necessary capital** not just in baseline but also in severe but plausible adverse scenarios
- ✓ Adequate **reverse stress testing** to test key vulnerabilities of business model and risk profile
- ✓ **Results should be embedded** to shape business strategy & risk appetite

Source: Authors' elaboration on banking practices.

Red Flag 3: Deficiencies in risk data and reporting

In order to best communicate information in a clear and structured reporting model, the banks should:

a. Complete and revise the process of capital allocation across businesses;
b. Organise a robust collaboration model between the CFO and CRO and a strong integration of the related organisational mechanisms-processes-tools with coordinated and consistent methodologies to simulate ICAAP and ILAAP metrics simultaneously;
c. Decline the RAF from a consolidated level to a business unit level;
d. Manage the deficiencies in operational resilience framework, namely IT outsourcing and IT security/cyber risk.

It is crucial that the CFO and risk management areas interact on an ongoing basis with a view to quantifying the risk to be taken, according to shared methods that are clear to top management and solid from the point of view of the assumptions of the prospective scenarios, both under normal market conditions and under stress.

In **Figure 6.2** the ever-necessary ingredients that have to be considered in order to assess the robustness of a BMA are provided without any claim to exhaustiveness.

Red Flag 4: Shortcomings in governance in digital transformation

Several times in this book we have dwelt on the strategic process that should support the viability of BM implementations in the light of the new paradigms.

Within digital transformation in the context of the seven steps proposed in Chapter 4, the third step is the one that stands out, where it should be emphasised that in reality, strategic designs that are flawless on paper have found difficulties in the execution phase due to defects in the governance of processes.

Let us therefore try to understand the causes. First of all, in designing the activity subject of an automation process, it is necessary to be clear that digital transformation is a refinement path of the BM that does not contemplate shortcuts, guaranteeing greater efficiency and significant profitability effects only in the medium term.

As prerequisite to the implementation of the new processes, there is recognition of the state of play of the complex information systems, trying to identify the trade-offs of the new technologies in business as usual.

It has been observed that, in the implementation phase of new technologies, projects often follow "silos" development initiatives without foreseeing a possible holistic use of the new technologies. For example, in the case of the development of specific tools based on AI, tailored to the needs of the credit area, the business cases developed generally provide for studies and applications calibrated only for that segment of operations.

If the implemented processes guarantee the desired results, the failure to foresee a possible flexible use for several business segments from the beginning makes it difficult to redesign the approach for other business segments as well. It is also necessary to provide for investments that take due account of the fact that some costs are in fact difficult to reduce. In fact, it was noted in some initiatives that the projects in the *ex ante* allocation of budgets had underestimated the need for continuous IT support, assuming that after the test phase and the go-live of the initiatives, strict IT governance, whether in-house or outsourced, could be disregarded.

To think that the business can become computerised without human intervention in the IT field could be an implementation bias, where in the strategic design, against such savings, due consideration is not given to a prior mapping of the degree of IT knowledge of the team, which, as is known, is mostly not "digital native".

The circumstance, then, that banking personnel have been subject to frequent job changes as a result of corporate reorganisations, mergers and incorporations with consequent rapid changes in operating systems, some of which have stratified over time, makes the rapid learning of new policies and procedures based on the new IT paradigms all the stickier.

In short, digital transformation imposes, in the writer's opinion, organisational and governance mechanisms that in some ways can be traced back to the implementation of internal models for risk measurement, following with due parallelism the guidelines and standards published by the EBA and ECB. It is necessary, before the new BM is "put into production", to (Figure 6.3):

- Examine the business units, segments and channels being digitalised, especially in terms of relevant risk factors, and assess the adequacy of the model's scope;
- Verify the adequacy and adaptability of business processes associated with the new BM, including decision making, risk management, internal control and value creation processes, as well as document management;

Figure 6.3   **Digital Transformation concerns**

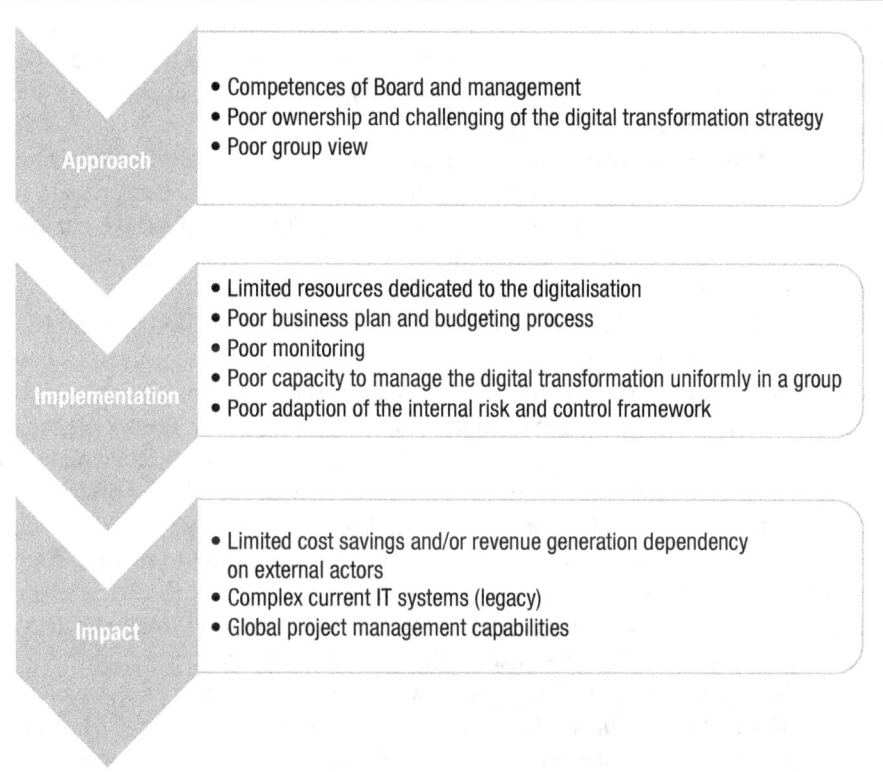

Source: Authors' elaboration on banking practices.

- Test technologies in a trial environment, verifying their proper functioning and ability to "predict" risks (by, inter alia, back-testing and "trialling" the model under various hypothetical and historical market conditions);
- Assess the capacity of the IT infrastructure, the input data and the data used to "build" the model;
- Subject the results of the model to critical analysis and continuously monitor, by means of appropriate KPIs and KRIs, the various release phases.

6.2   Open issues

The issues related to the viability and sustainability of the BMs still remain.

It is therefore becoming increasingly crucial that, starting from the series of questions suggested by the seven "moves" that characterise the tool proposed in the book, banks carry out a thorough assessment of the BM, including in terms of possible repositioning. It is therefore necessary to ask:

a. How have the macroeconomic scenarios underlying the BM been repositioned? In particular, in light of Moody's downgrading of the banks of six Old Continent countries, for example, how have the strategic and development plans been revised and corrected? Have the ROE targets been revised? In the post-pandemic framework, which is an exogenous variable, how should business areas and in particular lending activities be repositioned?
b. In light of the consolidation and aggregation process between intermediaries being viewed favourably by the supervisors, has careful thought been given to what the bank's positioning should be in the new competitive terrain? Have banks correctly repositioned their market share and business development objectives given the new peers and the expected post-pandemic environment?
c. In terms of strategies, have the long effects of the Covid-19 period been addressed and embedded in the various scenarios? Has any thought been given to how to deal with Unlikely to Pay scenarios, which are excluded from government guarantees? In the case of traditional banks, have the strategies for developing the digital variable in terms of robo-advisory and digital channels been accompanied by a revitalisation of the bank-customer relationship, with the idea of offering high added-value services in the form of personalised consultancy to a large number of small and medium-sized enterprises, which are struggling to recover from an unprecedented crisis?
d. How have the effects of the energy crisis and high inflation following Russia's invasion of Ukraine been assessed for the economies affected?
e. Has it been assessed how rising prices will affect the creditworthiness of many companies and households, likely triggering new problematic loans? Has it been assessed how the possible weakening of credit activity due to the economic slowdown, the increase in loan loss provisions and the rise in operating costs, as well as the repayment of the ECB's ultra-cheap TLTRO2 programme, could partly cancel out the benefits of the increase in loan yields as interest rates rise?
f. Have forecasts been made on the current and future impact of smart working? In particular, have scenarios been envisaged involving more decisive adherence to remote working and management of instrumental property?
g. Have the FTPs been reshaped to reflect the new ECB policies?
h. Has fine-tuning of the allocated capital been carried out, bearing in mind the forbearance effect on loans?
i. How were the risks of the new business paradigm introduced with the DLT and the different position in the value chain handled, based on the specific BM adopted?
j. Why the progress in bank's risk management and disclosures practices remains insufficient on the back of accelerating physical and transition risks[6]?

---

[6] Physical risks are likely to increase due to the rise of extreme weather events across geographies in terms of both frequency and severity. Delays in climate action are also expected to increase transition risks, as more drastic measures might be implemented.

Obviously, to a large extent these questions represent the challenges that the financial industry will have to face in a compelling way from now on. In the writer's opinion, the more flexible and rapid banks will be in adapting their BMs to fit this environment, the more they will be able to overcome these considerable challenges.

Acknowledgements

Many of those to whom we owe the idea for the new edition have intertwined our professional paths in the two years separating the publication of this book from the previous one.

They have been intense years, which have "forced" us to update the text in light of the new variables impacting on the BM, but also to confirm the validity of the "toolbox" proposed in the previous edition.

Thanks, therefore, to Professor Gimede Gigante of Bocconi University for his invaluable support in the publication of our project and for his participation in our initiative.

Thanks also to those who are always there.

To our colleagues and friends at the Bank of Italy and the ECB, the Paolo Baffi Library at the Bank of Italy and the London School of Economics and Political Science (LSE) Library, without whom we would never have been able to materialise the idea of a new edition.

Our final thanks go to all the students and professionals who followed us during our seminars with enthusiasm and confidence in search of their own Ariadne's thread.

Bibliography

ABBASI T., WEIGAND H., *The impact of digital financial services on firm's performance: a literature review*, Tilburg School of Economics and Management, The Netherlands 2017.

ADNER R., *The wide lens: a new strategy for innovation*, New York Portfolio Hardcover, New York 2012.

AFUAH, A., *Business models: A strategic management approach*, Irwin/McGraw-Hill, New York 2004.

AFUAH, A., & TUCCI, C. L. *Internet business models and strategies: Text and cases*, Irwin/McGraw-Hill, New York 2001.

AFUAH A., TUCCI C. L., VIRILLI F., *Modelli di e-business*, McGraw Hill Education, New York 2003.

AKAMAVI R.K., *A research agenda for investigation of product innovation in the financial services sector* in Journal of Services Marketing, Emerald Group Publishing, Bingley 2005, Vol. 19, No. 6.

ALTAVILLA C., BOCHMANN P., DE RYCK J., DUMITRU A-M., GRODZICKI M., KICK H., MELO FERNANDES C., MOSTHAF J., O'DONNELL C., PALLIGKINIS S., *Measuring the cost of equity of euro area banks*, ECB Occasional Paper Series, Frankfurt am main 2021, No. 254.

ALTUNBAS, Y., MANGANELLI S., MARQUES-IBANEZ D., *Bank risk during the financial crisis: do business models matter?*, ECB Working Paper Series, Frankfurt am main November 2011, No. 1394.

AMEL, D.F., RHOADES. S.A., *Strategic groups in banking* in The review of economics and statistics, MIT Press, Massachusetts 1988, No. 70.

AMIT, R., ZOTT. C., *Value creation in e-business* in Strategic Management Journal, Wiley, Hoboken 2001, No. 22.

AMIT R., ZOTT C., *Creating value through business model innovation* in MIT Sloan Management Review, MIT Press, Massachusetts 2012, Vol. 53.

ANDERSON C., *La coda lunga. Da un mercato di massa a una massa di mercati*, Codice Edizioni, Torino 2007.

ANSOFF H.I., *Corporate strategy: an analytic approach to business policy for growth and expansion*, McGraw Hill Inc., New York 1965.

ARDIZZI, G., GAMBINI, A., NOBILI, A., PIMPINI, E., ROCCO, G., *L'impatto della pandemia sull'uso degli strumenti di pagamento in Italia (The impact of the pandemic on the use of payment instruments in Italy)*, Bank of Italy Markets, Infrastructures, Payment Systems Papers, Rome 2021, No. 8.

ARNABOLDI F., CLAYES P., *Innovation and performance of European banks adopting Internet*, Centre for Banking Research University of London, London 2010, No. 4.

ARNAUDO D., DEL PRETE S., DEMMA C., MANILE M., ORAME A., PAGNINI M., ROSSI C.,

Rossi P., Soggia G., *The digital transformation in the Italian banking sector*, Banca d'Italia Questioni di Economia e Finanza, Occasional Papers, Rome 2022, No. 682.

Auer R., Haslhofer B., Kitzler S., Saggese P., Victor F., *The technology of decentralized finance (DeFi)*, BIS Working Papers, Bank for Internation al Settlements, Basel 2023, No. 1066.

Ayadi R., Bongini P., Casu B., Cucinelli D., *Banks' business model migrations in Europe: determinants and effects* in British Journal of Management, November 2020.

Ayadi R.E., *Banking business models definition, analytical framework and financial stability assessment*, Palgrave Macmillan Studies in Banking and Financial Institutions, London 2019.

Ayadi R.E., De Groen W.P., *Banking business models monitor 2014: Europe*, Joint Centre for European Policy Studies (CEPS) and International Observatory on Financial Service Cooperatives (IOFSC) publication, HEC Montréal, Montréal 2014.

Ayadi R.E., De Groen W.P., Sassi I., Mathlouthi W., Rey H., Aubry. O., *Banking business models monitor 2015: Europe*, Alphonse and Dorimène Desjardins International Institute for Cooperatives and International Research Center on Cooperative Finance (IRCCF), HEC Montréal, Montréal 2016.

Ayadi R.E., Ferri G., Pesic. V., *Regulatory arbitrage in EU banking: do business models matter?*, International Research Center on Cooperative Finance (IRCCF) Working Paper, HEC Montréal, Montréal July 2016.

Baden-Fuller C., Haefliger S., *Business models and technological innovation* in Long Range Planning, Elsevier, Amsterdam 2013, Vol. 46.

Baele L., De Jonghe O., Vander Vennet R., *Does the stock market value bank diversification?* in Journal of Banking & Finance, Elsevier, Amsterdam 2007, Vol. 31.

Bank for International Settlements, *Sound practices implications of fintech developments for banks and bank supervisors*, Basel Committee on Banking Supervision, Basel 2018.

Bank of England and FSA, *The bank of England, prudential regulation authority, the PRA's approach to banking supervision*, Bank of England, London October 2012.

Bank of Italy, *Indagine Fintech sul sistema bancario italiano 2021*, Banca d'Italia, Rome 2021.

Baravelli M., *Banche e crisi pandemica: quale impatto sui modelli di business* in Bancaria, Associazione Bancaria Italiana (ABI), Rome 2020, No. 6.

Barba Navaretti G., Calzolari G., G., Pozzolo, A.F., *FinTech and banks: friends or foes?*, European Economy – Banks, Regulation, and the Real Sector, Rome 2017.

Bátiz-Lazo B., Woldesenbet K., *The dynamics of product and process inovation in UK banking international,* International Journal of Financial Services Management, United Kingdom 2006, Vol. 1 No. 4.

Beccalli E., *Does IT investment improve bank performance? Evidence from Europe*, Journal of Banking and Finance, Elsevier 2007, Vol. 31 No. 7.

Beck T., Cecchetti S., Grothe M., Kemp M., Pelizzon L., Sánchez Serrano A., *Will video kill the radio star? – Digitalisation and the future of banking*, European System Risk Board Reports of the Advisory Scientific Committee, Frankfurt am main 2022, No. 12.

Bell J., Loane S., *'New-wave' global firms: Web 2.0 and SME internationalization* in Journal of Marketing Management, Taylor & Francis group, Milton Park 2010, Vol. 26 No. 3–4.

Berger A.N., Molyneux P., Wilson J.O.S., *The oxford handbook of banking*, Oxford University Press, Oxford, 2022.

BERNINI F., FERRETTI, P., ANGELINI A., *The digitalization-reputation link: a multiple case-study on Italian banking groups*, in Meditari Accountancy Research, Emerald Publishing Limited, Bingley 2022, Vol. 30 No. 4.

BONACCORSI DI PATTI E., FELICI R., SIGNORETTI F.M., *Euro area significant banks: main differences and recent performance* in Questioni di economia e finanza, occasional papers, Banca d'Italia, Rome 2016, No. 306.

BONACCORSI DI PATTI E., GOBBI G., MISTRULLI P.E., *The interaction between face-to-face and electronic delivery: the case of the Italian banking industry* in Banca impresa società, Il Mulino, Bologna 2003.

BRANDL B., HORNUF L., *Where did fintechs come from, and where do they go? The transformation of the financial industry in Germany after digitalization*, SSRN Working Paper, Elsevier, Amsterdam 2017.

BRANZOLI, N.O., SUPINO, I., *Fintech credit: a critical review of the empirical literature*, in Questioni di economia e finanza, occasional papers, Banca d'Italia, Rome 2020, No. 549.

BRIGHI P., VENTURELLI V., *How do income diversification, firm size and capital ratio affect performance? Evidence for bank holding companies* in Applied Financial Economics, Routledge, Oxfordshire 2014, No. 24.

BRIGHI P., VENTURELLI V., *How functional and geographic diversification affect bank profitability during the crisis* in Finance Research Letters, Elsevier, Amsterdam 2016, Vol. 16.

BROUSSEAU, E., & PENARD, T., *The economics of digital business models: a framework for analyzing the economics of platforms* in Review of Network Economics, De Gruyter, Berlin 2006, Vol. 6, No. 2.

BUCHAK G., MATVOS G., PISKORSKI T., SERU A., *Fintech, regulatory arbitrage, and the rise of shadow banks*, National Bureau of Economic Research Working Paper, Cambridge 2017, No. 23288.

CALOMIRIS C.W., NISSIM. D., *Crisis-related shifts in the market valuation of banking activities* in Journal of Financial Intermediation, Elsevier, Amsterdam 2014, Vol. 23.

CAMPA J.M., KEDIA S., *Explaining the diversification discount* in The Journal of Finance, Wiley-Blackwell for the American Finance Association (AFA), Hoboken 2002, Vol. 57.

CAMPBELL D., FREI F., *Cost structure, consumer profitability, and retention implications of self-service distribution channels: evidence from consumer behavior in an online banking channel* in Management Science, Institute for Operations Research and the Management Sciences, Hanover 2009, No. 56.

CARMIGNANI A., MANILE M., ORAME A., PAGNINI M., *Servizi bancari online e presenza delle banche sul territorio (Online banking services and branch networks)*, Bank of Italy Occasional Paper, Rome 2020, No. 543.

CASADESUS-MASANELL R., RICART J.E., *Competing through business models*, IESE Business School - University of Navarra Working Paper, Pamplona 2007, No. 713.

CASADESUS-MASANELL R., RICART J.E., *From strategy to business models and onto tactics* in Long Range Planning, Elsevier, Amsterdam 2010, Vol. 43.

CASOLARO L., GOBBI G., *Information technology and productivity changes in the banking industry*, Economic Notes by Banca Monte dei Paschi di Siena SpA, Siena 2007, Vol. 36.

CATTURI G., *Appunti di economia e governo aziendale*, Università degli studi di Siena, Siena 2005, No. 1, parte prima.

CHASTON I., *Independent financial advisors: open innovation and business performance* in The Service Industries Journal, Taylor & Francis group, Milton Park 2011, Vol. 33 No. 6.

CHEN L., DANBOLT J., HOLLAND J., *Rethinking bank business models: the role of intangibles* in Accounting, Auditing & Accountability Journal, Emerald Group Publishing, Bingley 2014, Vol. 27.

CHESBROUGH H.W., *Open innovation: the new imperative for creating and profiting from technology*, Harvard Business School Press, Cambridge 2003.

CHESBROUGH H.W., *Open business models: how to thrive in the new innovation landscape*, Harvard Business School Press, Cambridge 2006.

CHESBROUGH H.W., *Business model innovation: opportunities and barriers* in Long Range Planning, Elsevier, Amsterdam 2010, Vol. 43.

CHESBROUGH H.W., *Open services innovation: rethinking your business to grow and compete in a new era*, Jossey-Bass, San Francisco 2011.

CHESBROUGH H., ROSENBLOOM R.S., *The role of the business model in capturing value from innovation from Xerox corporation's technology spin-off companies* in Industrial and Corporate Chang», Oxford University Press, Oxford 2002, Vol. 11.

CHESINI G., GIARETTA E., *Innovazione, redditività e stabilità in banca nell'era della rivoluzione digitale* in Bancaria, Associazione Bancaria Italiana, Rome 2019, Vol. 6.

CHRISTENSEN C., *The innovator's dilemma*, Harvard Business School Press, Cambridge 1997.

CHRISTENSEN C., RAYNOR M., *The innovator's solution*, Harvard Business School Press, Cambridge 2003.

CICIRETTI R., HASAN I., ZAZZARA C., *Do internet activities add value? Evidence from the traditional banks* in Journal of Financial Services Research, Springer, Berlin 2009, No. 35.

CLOHESSY T., ACTON T., MORGAN L., *The impact of cloud-based digital transformation on ICT service providers' strategies*, Bled eConference, Bled, Slovenia 2017.

COTUGNO M., STEFANELLI V., *Geographical and product diversification during instability financial period. Good or bad for banks?* in International research journal of finance and economics, Eurojournals, London 2012, Vol. 85.

DANDAPANI K., LAWRENCE E.R., RODRIGUEZ J. *(2018), Determinants of transactional internet banking* in Journal of Financial Services Research, Springer, Berlin 2018, No. 54.

DASILVA C.M., TRKMAN P., *Business model: What it is and what it is not* in Long Range Planning, Elsevier, Amsterdam 2014, Vol. 47.

DE JONGHE O., DIEPSTRATEN M., SCHEPENS G., *Banks' size, scope and systemic risk: what role for conflicts of interest?* in Journal of Banking & Finance, Elsevier, Amsterdam 2015, Vol. 61.

DE MEO E., DE NICOLA A., LUSIGNANI G., ZICCHINO L., *European banks in the XXI century: are their business models sustainable?* in The Italian banks: which will be the "new normal"? Industrial, institutional and behavioral economics, Edibank, Rome 2016.

DELL M., *The early entrepreneurial years in starting a business*, Harvard Business School Press, Cambridge 2008.

DEMIL B., LECOCQ X., *Business model evolution; in search of dynamic consistency* in Long Range Planning, Elsevier, Amsterdam 2010, Vol. 43.

DEMIRGÜÇ-KUNT A., HUIZINGA H., *Bank activity and funding strategies: the impact on risk and returns* in Journal of Financial Economics, Elsevier, Amsterdam 2010, 98.

DEMSETZ R.S., STRAHAN P.E., *Diversification, size, and risk at bank holding companies* in Journal of Money Credit and Banking, Wiley, Hoboken 1997, No. 29.

DEYOUNG R., LANG W.W., NOLLE D.L., *How the Internet affects output and performance at community banks* in Journal of Banking & Finance, Elsevier, Amsterdam 2007, Vol. 31.

DEYOUNG R., RICE T., *Noninterest income and financial performance at US commercial banks* in Financial Review, Wiley, Hoboken 2004, No. 39.

DEYOUNG R., ROLAND K.P., *Product mix and earnings volatility at commercial banks: evidence from a degree of total leverage model.* in Journal of Financial Intermediation, Elsevier, Amsterdam 2001, Vol. 10.

DEYOUNG R., TORNA G., *Nontraditional banking activities and bank failures during the financial crisis* in Journal of Financial Intermediation, Elsevier, Amsterdam 2013, Vol. 22.

DIAMOND D.W., *Financial intermediation and delegated monitoring* in Review of Economic Studies, Oxford University Press, Oxford 1984, Vol. 51.

DIAMOND D.W., *Monitoring and reputation: the choice between bank loans and directly placed debt* in Journal of Political Economy, University of Chicago Press, Chicago 1991, Vol. 99.

DIRECTIVES (UE) 2013/36, 2014/59, 2019/878, 2019/879, 2022/2555, 2022/2557 of the European Parliament and of the Council, Official Journal of the European Union, Bruxelles 2013, 2014, 2019 and 2022.

DUBOSSON-TORBAY, M., OSTERWALDER, A., & PIGNEUR, Y., *E-business model design, classification, and measurements* in Thunderbird International Business Review, Wiley, Hoboken 2002, Vol. 44 No.1.

EBA, *Guideline on common procedures and methodologies for the supervisory*, La Défense 2014.

ECB BANKING SUPERVISION, *SSM SREP methodology booklet, level playing field-High standards of supervision-Sound risk assessment*, Frankfurt am main 2015.

ECB BANKING SUPERVISION, *Recent trends in euro area banks' business models and implication for banking sector stability* in Financial Stability Review, Frankfurt am main May 2016.

ECB BANKING SUPERVISION, *Guide on climate-related and environmental risks Supervisory expectations relating to risk management and disclosure*, Frankfurt am main November 2020.

ECB BANKING SUPERVISION, *Report on good practices for climate stress testing*, Frankfurt am main December 2022.

ECB BANKING SUPERVISION, *Annual report on supervisory activities 2023*, Frankfurt am main March 2023.

ECB BANKING SUPERVISION, *SSM priorities 2023–2025*, Frankfurt am main January 2023.

EIOPA, *Joint committee report on risks and vulnerabilities in the EU financial system*, Frankfurt am Main 2021, JC 2021 45.

EIOPA *Supervisory statement on management of non-affirmative cyber exposures*, Frankfurt am Main 2022, EIOPA-BoS-22-414.

EIOPA *Supervisory statement on exclusions in insurance products related to risks arising from systemic events*, Frankfurt am Main 2022, EIOPA-22/419.

ELSAS R., HACKETHAL A., HOLZHÄUSER M., *The anatomy of bank diversification* in Journal of Banking & Finance, Elsevier, Amsterdam 2010, Vol. 34.

EUCHNER J., GANGULY A., *Business model innovation in practice* in Research-Technology Management, Innovation research interchange, Virginia 2014, Vol. 57.

FASNACHT D., *Open innovation in the financial services: growing through openness, flexibility, and customer integration*, Springer-Verlag, Berlin 2009.

FISHER M., *Fintech business models: applied canvas method and analysis of venture capital rounds paperback*, De Gruyter, Berlin 2021.

FOMBRUN C.J., GARDBERG NO.A., BARNETT M.L., *Opportunity platforms and safety nets: corporate citizenship and reputational risk* in Business and Society Review, Wiley-Blackwell, Hoboken 2000, Vol. 105 No. 1.

FORCADELL F.J., ARACIL E., ÚBEDA F., *The impact of corporate sustainability and digitalization on international banks' performance* in Global Policy, Wiley-Blackwell, Hoboken 2020, Vol. 11 No. S1.

FRIEDMAN, J.P. AND LANGLINAIS, T.C., *Best intentions: a business model for the eEconomy*, Andersen Consulting, Chicago, 2000.

FSA, *The turner review. A regulatory response to the global banking crisis*, London March 2009.

FSB *Achieving greater convergence in cyber incident reporting*, Basel 2023.

G7 Fundamental elements for third-party cyber risk management in the financial sector, Krün 2022.

G7 Fundamental elements of ransomware resilience for the financial sector, Krün 2022.

GALARDO M., GARRÌ I., MISTRULLI P.E., REVELLI D., *The geography of banking: evidence from branch closings* in Economic Notes Review of Banking, Finance and Monetary Economics, John Wiley & Sons, Hoboken 2021, Vol. 50 No. 1.

GALLO J.G., APILADO V.P., KOLARI J.W., *Commercial bank mutual fund activities: implications for bank risk and profitability* in Journal of Banking & Finance, Elsevier, Amsterdam 1996, Vol. 20.

GEORGE, G., & BOCK, A. *The business model in practice and its implications for entrepreneurship research.* Working Paper, Imperial College, London 2009.

GEORGE G., BOCK A.J. *The business model in practice and its implications for entrepreneurship research* in Entrepreneurship Theory and Practice, Baylor University, Waco 2011, No. 35.

GERTNER R., SCHARFSTEIN D., STEIN J., *Internal vs. external capital markets* in Quarterly Journal of Economics, Oxford Academic, Oxford 1994, No. 109.

GHAZIANI A., VENTRESCA M.J., *Keywords and Cultural Change: Frame Analysis of Business Model Public Talk, 1975–2000* in Sociological Forum, Wiley for Eastern Sociological Society, Hoboken 2005, Vol. 20 No. 4.

GIROTRA K., NETESSINE S., *The risk-driven business model: four questions that will define your company*, Harvard Business Review Press, Boston 2014.

GOBBI L., *Buy now pay later, caratteristiche del mercato e prospettive di sviluppo*, Banca d'Italia Occasional paper, Banca d'Italia, Rome 2022, No. 270.

GODDARD J., MCKILLOP D., WILSON O.J., *The diversification and financial performance of US credit unions* in Journal of Banking & Finance, Elsevier, Amsterdam 2008, No. 32.

GRAHAM J.R., LEMMON M.L., WOLF J.G., *Does corporate diversification destroy value?* in The Journal of Finance, Wiley-Blackwell for the American Finance Association (AFA), Hoboken 2002, 57.

GUALANDRI E., *Vigilanza unica: traguardi raggiunti e cantieri aperti* in Bancaria, Associazione Bancaria Italiana (ABI), Rome 2016.

HERNANDO I., NIETO M.J., *Is the Internet delivery channel changing banks' performance? The case of Spanish banks*, Journal of Banking & Finance, Elsevier, Amsterdam 2007, Vol. 31.

HERRING R.J., SANTOMERO A.M., *The corporate structure of financial conglomerates* in Journal of Financial Services Research, Springer, Berlin 1990, No. 4.

KAPLAN R.S., NORTON D.P., *Execution premium: applicare la strategia per il vantaggio competitivo*, Etas Libri, Milan 2009.

KEARNS D., NADLER D., *Prophets in the dark: how Xerox reinvented itself and beat back the Japanese*, Harper Business, New York 1992.

KLANG D., WALLNÖFER M., HACKLIN F., *The business model paradox: a systematic re-*

view and exploration of antecedents in International Journal of Management Reviews, Wiley-Blackwell for the British Academy of Management, London 2014, Vol. 16.

KLEIN P.G., SAIDENBERG M.R., *Diversification, organization and efficiency: evidence from bank holding companies,* Center for Financial Institutions Working Papers, Wharton School Center for Financial Institutions, University of Pennsylvania 1997.

KÖHLER M., *Does non-interest income make banks more risky? Retail-versus investment-oriented banks* in Review of Financial Economics, Wiley in collaboration with the University of New Orleans 2014, No. 23.

KÖHLER M., *Which banks are more risky? The impact of business models on bank stability* in Journal of Financial Stability, Elsevier, Amsterdam 2015, Vol. 16.

LAEVEN L., LEVINE R., *Is there a diversification discount in financial conglomerates?* in Journal of Financial Economics, Elsevier, Amsterdam 2007, 85.

LAUTENSCHLAGER S., *European banking supervision business model analysis*, CEO/CFO/CRO-Roundtable Madrid, 7 July 2016.

LEASK G., *Is there still value in strategic group research?* Aston business school research papers, Aston University, Birmingham 2004, No. RP0404.

LEPETIT L., NYS E., ROUS P., TARAZI A., *Bank income structure and risk: an empirical analysis of European banks* in Journal of Banking & Finance, Elsevier, Amsterdam 2008, No. 32.

LINDER J., CANTRELL S., *Changing business model: surveying the landscape,* working paper from the Accenture Institute for Strategic Change, 2000.

LUCAS A., SCHAUMBURG J., SCWAAB B., *Bank business models at zero interest rates*, ECB working paper series No. 2084, European Central bank, Frankfurt am main 2017.

MAGRETTA J., *Why business models matter,* Harvard Business Review Press, Boston 2002, Vol. 80 No. 5.

MARTOVOY A., DOS SANTOS J., *Co-creation and co-profiting in financial Services* in International Journal of Entrepreneurship and Innovation Management, Inderscience Publishers, Ginevre 2012, Vol. 16 No. 1-2.

MARTOVOY A., MENTION A-L., TORKKELI M., *Role of the inbound open innovation in banking services,* Innovation for Financial Services, Conference Paper, Luxembourg 2012.

MAZZÙ S., *Strategie, innovazione, modelli di business e diverse forme di intermediazione finanziaria,* Giuffré, Milan 2020.

MERCIECA S., SCHAECK K., WOLFE S., *Small European banks: benefits from diversification?* in Journal of Banking & Finance, Elsevier, Amsterdam 2007, Vol. 31.

MERGAERTS F., VANDER VENNET R., *Business models and bank performance: a long-term perspective* in Journal of Financial Stability, Elsevier, Amsterdam 2016, Vol. 22.

MERLI G., GELOSA E., FREGONESE M., *Surpetere, la competizione creativa, efficace e sostenibile*, Edizioni Angelo Guerini e Associati, Milan 2010.

MILES R.E, MILES G., SNOW C., *Collaborative entrepreneurship: how communities of networked firms use continuous innovation to create economic wealth*, Stanford University Press, Palo Alto 2005.

MOLONEY NO., *Supervision in the wake of the financial crisis: achieving effective 'Law in Action'- a challenge for the EU.* In Wymeersch E., Hopt K.J., Ferrarini G., (eds.) Financial Regulation and Supervision: a Post-Crisis Analysis, Oxford University Press, Oxford 2012.

MORRIS M., SCHINDEHUTTE M., ALLEN J., *The entrepreneur's business model: toward a unified perspective* in Journal of Business Research, Elsevier, Amsterdam 2005, Vol. 58.

MOTTURA P., *Banche; strategie, organizzazione e concentrazioni*, Egea, Milan 2011.

NIEMAND T., RIGTERING J., KALLMUENZER A., KRAUS S., MAALAOUI A., *Digitalization in the financial industry: a contingency approach of entrepreneurial orientation and strategic vision on digitalization* in European Management Journal, Elsevier, Amsterdam 2020, Vol. 39 No. 3.
OLIVEIRA P., VON HIPPEL E., *Users as service innovators: The case of banking services* in Research Policy, Elsevier, Amsterdam 2011, Vol. 40 No. 6.
OSTERWALDER A., *The business model ontology – a proposition in a design science approach*, Université de Lausanne 2004.
OSTERWALDER A., PIGNEUR Y., *Business model generation: a handbook for visionaries, game charges and challengers*, John Wiley, Hoboken 2010.
OSTERWALDER A., PIGNEUR Y., *Business model generation*, John Wiley, Hoboken 2012.
OSTERWALDER A., PIGNEUR Y., TUCCI C., *Clarifying business models: origins, present and future of the concept* in Communication of the association for information systems, 2005, Vol. 15.
PALEPU K., HEALY P.M., BERNARD V., PEEK E., *Business analysis & valuation*, Cengage Learning EMEA, Andover 2019.
PASSMORE S.W., *Strategic groups and the profitability of banking*, Research Paper Federal Reserve Bank of New York 1985, No. 8501.
PATIL P., DWIVEDI Y., RANA NO., *Digital payments adoption: an analysis of literature*, 16th Conference on e-Business, e-Services and e-Society (I3E), Delhi 2018.
PAVIE X., HSU E., RODLE H.J.T., TAPIA R.O., *How to define and analyze business model innovation in service*. ESSEC Working Paper Business School, Cergy 2013, No. 1323.
PENROSE E., *The theory of the growth of the firm*, Oxford University Press, Oxford 1959.
PHILIPPON T., *The fintech opportunity*, NBER Working Paper, National Bureau of Economic Research, Cambridge 2016, No. 22476.
PORTER M.E., *What is strategy?* Harvard Business Review Press, Boston 1996.
PRAHALAD C.K., BETTIS R.A. *The dominant logic: a new linkage between diversity and performance* in Strategic Management Journal, Wiley, Hoboken 1986, Vol. 7.
RAJAN R., SERVAES H., ZINGALES L., *The cost of diversity: the diversification discount and inefficient investment* in The Journal of Finance, Wiley-Blackwell for the American Finance Association (AFA), Hoboken 2000, No. 55.
RAJAN R.G. *Insiders and outsiders: the choice between informed and arm's length debt* in The Journal of Finance, Wiley-Blackwell for the American Finance Association (AFA), Hoboken 1992, No. 4.
REGULATIONS (UE) 2013/575, 2019/876, 2022/2554 of the European Parliament and of the Council, Official Journal of the European Union, Bruxelles, 2013, 2019, 2022.
ROENGPITYA R., TARASHEV NO.A., TSATSARONIS K., *Bank business models* in BIS Quarterly Review, BIS, Basel December 2014.
ROSSI S.P., SCHWAIGER M.S., WINKLER G., *How loan portfolio diversification affects risk, efficiency and capitalization: a managerial behavior model for Austrian banks* in Journal of Banking & Finance, Elsevier, Amsterdam 2009, Vol. 33.
SCHALTEGGER S., LUDEKE-FREUND F., HANSEN E.G., *Business cases for sustainability and the role of business model innovation: developing a conceptual framework* in International Journal of Innovation and Sustainable Development, Inderscience Enterprise, Ginevra 2012, Vol. 6.
SCHUEFFEL P.E., VADANA I-I., *Open innovation in the financial services sector – A global literature review* in Journal of Innovation Management, Faculdade de Engenharia da Universidade do Porto, Porto 2015, Vol. 3 No.1.

SEDDON P., LEWIS G. *Strategy and business models: what's the difference?*, 7th Pacific and Asia Conference on Information Systems 2003.

SEELOS, C., & MAIR, J., *Profitable business models and market creation in the context of deep poverty: a strategic view* in Academy of Management Perspectives, Academy of Management, New York 2007, Vol. 21.

SHAFER S.M., SMITH H.J., LINDER J.C., *The power of business models* in Business Horizons, Elsevier, Amsterdam 2005, Vol. 48.

SHORT J.C., KETCHEN D.J., PALMER T.B., HULT. G.T., *Firm, strategic group and industry influences on performance* in Strategic Management Journal, Wiley, Hoboken 2007, No. 28.

SIBANDA W., NDIWENI E., BOULKEROUA M., ECHCHABI A., NDLOVU T., *Digital technology disruption on bank business models* in International Journal Business Performance Management, Inderscience Publishers, Ginevre 2020, Vol. 21 No. 1-2.

STANDARD ISO/IEC 27001:2022 *Information security, cybersecurity and privacy protection - Information security management systems – Requirements*, Geneva 2022.

STEIN J.C., *Internal capital markets and the competition for corporate resources* in The Journal of Finance, Wiley-Blackwell for the American Finance Association (AFA), Hoboken 1997, No. 52.

STEIN J.C., *Information production and capital allocation: Decentralized versus hierarchical firms* in The Journal of Finance, Wiley-Blackwell for the American Finance Association (AFA), Hoboken 2002, No. 57.

STEWART, D. W., & ZHAO, Q., *Internet marketing, business models and public policy* in Journal of Public Policy and Marketing, American Marketing Association, Chicago 2000, Vol. 19.

STIROH K.J., *Diversification in banking: is non-interest income the answer?* in Journal of Money, Credit, and Banking, Blackwell Publishing, Oxford 2004, Vol. 36.

STIROH K.J., *A portfolio view of banking with interest and noninterest activities* in Journal of Money, Credit, and Banking, Blackwell Publishing, Oxford 2006, Vol. 38.

STIROH K.J., *Volatility accounting: a production perspective on increased economic stability* in Journal of the European Economic Association, Wiley for British Science Association 2009, No. 7.

STIROH K., RUMBLE. A., *The dark side of diversification: The case of US financial holding companies* in Journal of Banking & Finance, Elsevier, Amsterdam 2006, Vol. 30.

STUBBS W., COCKLIN C., *Conceptualizing a sustainability business model* in Organization & Environment, SAGE, New York 2008, Vol. 21.

STULZ R., *Managerial discretion and optimal financial policies* in Journal of Financial Economics, Elsevier, Amsterdam 1990, Vol. 26.

THAKOR A.V., *Fintech and banking: what do we know?* in Journal of Financial Intermediation, Elsevier, Amsterdam 2020, Vol. 41.

TEECE D.J., *Towards an economic theory of the multiproduct firm* in Journal of Economic Behavior & Organization, Elsevier, Amsterdam 1982, Vol. 3.

TEECE D.J., *Profiting from technological innovation: implications for integration, collaboration, licensing and public policy* in Research Policy, Elsevier, Amsterdam 1986, Vol. 15.

TEECE D.J., *Business models, business strategy and innovation* in Long Range Planning, Elsevier, Amsterdam 2010, Vol. 43.

TEECE D.J., PISANO G., *How to capture value from innovation: shaping intellectual property and industry architecture* in California Management Review, SAGE New York 2007, Vol. 50.

TEECE D.J., PISANO G., SHUEN A., *Dynamic capabilities and strategic management* in Strategic Management Journal, Wiley, Hoboken 2007, No. 18.

TIMMERS P., *Business models for electronic markets* in International Journal of Electric Markets, Springer, Berlin 1998, Vol.8.

TURBAN D.B., REENING D.W., *Corporate social performance and organizational attractiveness to prospective employees"* in Academy of Management Journal, Academy of Management, New York 1997, Vol. 40 No. 3.

TUSHMAN M.L., O'REILLY C.A., *Ambidextrous organizations: managing evolutionary and revolutionary change* in California Management Review, SAGE, New York 1996, Vol. 38.

VALLASCAS F., CRESPI F., HAGENDORFF J., *Income diversification and bank performance during the financial crisis* in Banking & Insurance eJournal, 2012.

VAN OORDT M., ZHOU C., *Systemic risk and bank business models*, De Nederlandishe Bank Working Paper, Amsterdam 2014, No. 442.

VIAL G., *Understanding digital transformation: a review and a research agenda* in The Journal of Strategic Information Systems, Elsevier, Amsterdam 2019, Vol. 28 No. 2.

WEBER A., *Bank consolidation, efficiency and profitability in Italy*, International Monetary Fund, Washington 2017.

WEILL P., VITALE M., *Place to space: migrating to e-business models*, Harvard Business Review Press, Boston 2001.

WILLIAMS B., *The impact of non-interest income on bank risk in Australia* in Journal of Banking & Finance, Elsevier, Amsterdam 2016, Vol. 73.

WILLIAMSON O.E., *Organizational innovation: the transaction-cost approach* in American Journal of Sociology, The University of Chicago Press, Chicago 1981, Vol. 87.

WIRTZ B.W., PISTOIA A., ULLRICH S., GÖTTEL V., *Business models: origin, development and future research perspectives* in Long Range Planning, Elsevier, Amsterdam 2016, Vol. 49.

WIRTZ B.W., *Business model management: design instrument-success factor*, Gabler, Wiesbaden 2011.

XUE M., HITT L.M., CHEN P.Y., *Determinants and outcomes of internet banking adoption* in Management Science, Institute for Operations Research and the Management Sciences, Hanover 2011, No. 57.

ZHOU, D., KAUTONEN, M., DAI, W., ZHANG, H., *Exploring how digitalization influences incumbents in financial services: the role of entrepreneurial orientation, firm assets, and organizational legitimacy* in Technological Forecasting and Social Change, Elsevier, Amsterdam 2021, Vol. 173.

ZOTT C., AMIT R., MASSA L., *The business model: recent developments and future research* in Journal of Management, SAGE 2011, Vol. 37.

Web references

www.abicloud.it
www.abilab.it
www.annuariabionline.it
www.areastudimediobanca.com
www.atoz.ebsco.com
www.bancaditalia.it
www.bankingsupervision.europa.eu
www.bis.org
www.centralbanking.com
www.clusit.it
www.compass.it
www.darwinbooks.it
www.eba.europa.eu
www.ecb.europa.eu
www.eif.org
www.eiopa.europa.eu
www.elibrary.imf.org
www.eur-lex.europa.eu
www.gartner.com
www.gazzettaufficiale.it
www.gsi-alliance.com
www.ifm.com
www.mckinsey.com
www.oecdilibrary.org
www.risk.net
www.snl.com
www.som.polimi.it
www.treccani.it
www.weforum.org
www.wikipedia.com

www.ingramcontent.com/pod-product-compliance
Lightning Source LLC
Chambersburg PA
CBHW082329220526
45470CB00008B/2449